realism in watermedia

Sister Jolanta

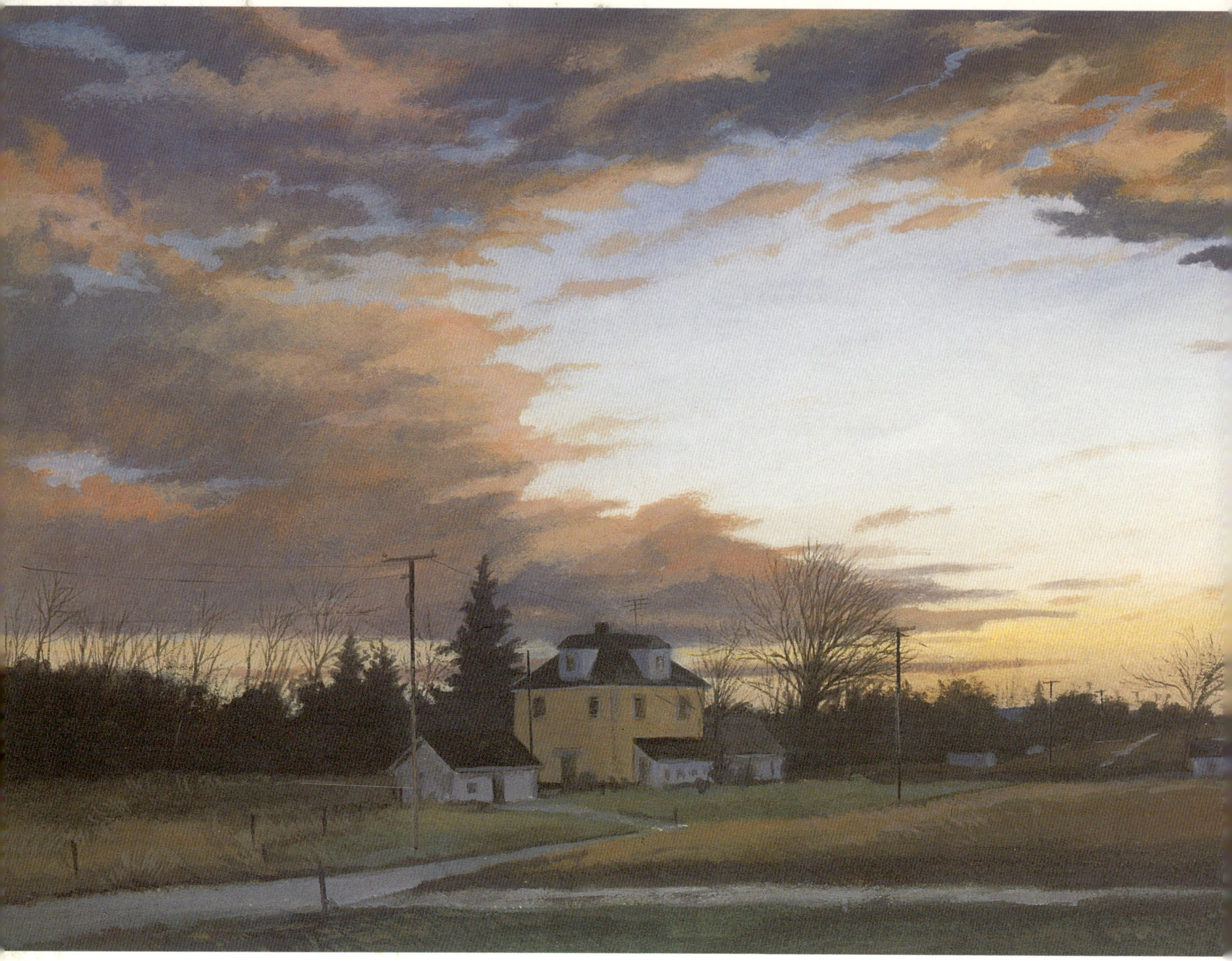

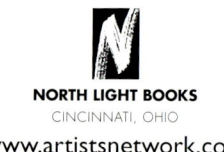

NORTH LIGHT BOOKS
CINCINNATI, OHIO
www.artistsnetwork.com

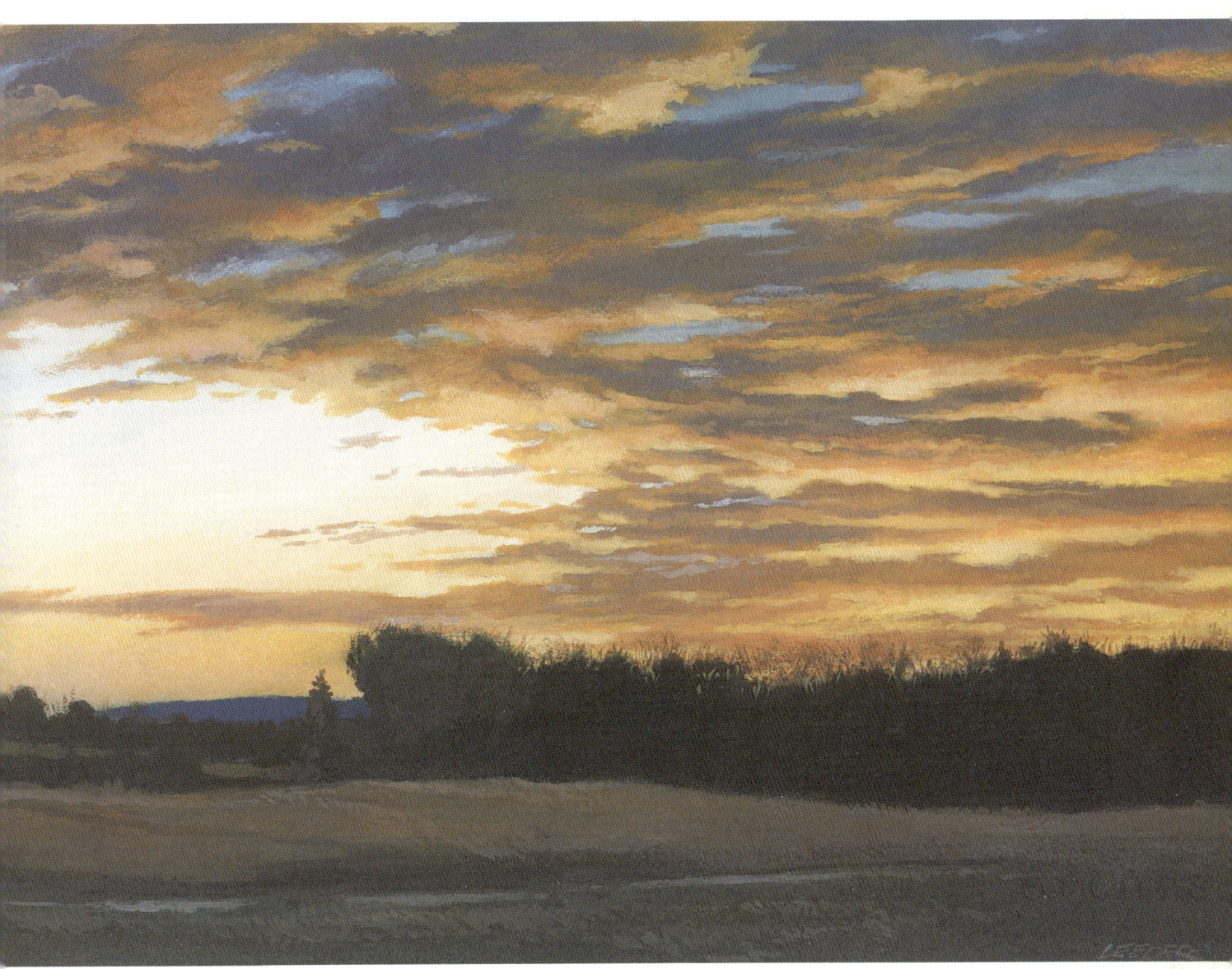

realism in watermedia

18 painting techniques for achieving realistic results

CHRISTOPHER LEEPER

ABOUT THE AUTHOR

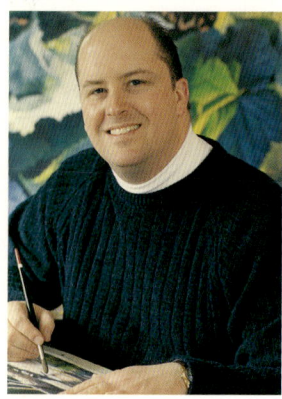

Photo by Tony Mancino

Christopher Leeper divides his time between fine art, illustration and teaching. His illustration credits include the children's books *River Otter at Autumn Lane*, *Ema Rhino's Risky Rescue*, *Norman the Lion* and *Jeshi the Gorilla*, all published by Soundprints for the Smithsonian Institution. His paintings have been reproduced in several books including *Art From the Parks: 74 Artists Celebrate America's National Parks* (North Light Books, 2000), *How Did You Paint That? 100 Ways to Paint Landscapes* (International Artist, 2004) and *The Best of Landscape Painting* and *The Best of Acrylic Painting* (Rockport Publishing). His work has also been featured in *The Artist's Magazine*. His paintings have been chosen twice for the Arts for the Parks Top 100 annual exhibition. He is also a two-time winner of the Pennsylvania Trout/Salmon stamp competition.

A graduate of Youngstown State University in Youngstown, Ohio, he is currently a member of the adjunct faculty in the Department of Art at his alma mater. In addition, he is a signature member and office holder in the Ohio Watercolor Society. Christopher, his wife, Kathy, and their son, Jack, live in Canfield, Ohio.

Metric Conversion Chart

To convert	to	multiply by
Inches	Centimeters	2.54
Centimeters	Inches	0.4
Feet	Centimeters	30.5
Centimeters	Feet	0.03
Yards	Meters	0.9
Meters	Yards	1.1
Sq. Inches	Sq. Centimeters	6.45
Sq. Centimeters	Sq. Inches	0.16
Sq. Feet	Sq. Meters	0.09
Sq. Meters	Sq. Feet	10.8
Sq. Yards	Sq. Meters	0.8
Sq. Meters	Sq. Yards	1.2
Pounds	Kilograms	0.45
Kilograms	Pounds	2.2
Ounces	Grams	28.3
Grams	Ounces	0.035

ART ON PAGES 2-3:

Christmas Day Sunset » Mixed media on 140-lb. (300gsm) cold-pressed paper » 10" x 29" (25cm x 74cm)

ART ON PAGES 6-7:

Detail of **Early Morning Whitetails** » Mixed media on 140-lb. (300gsm) cold-pressed paper » 22" x 30" (56cm x 76cm)

Detail of **Sleeping Betty** » Watercolor on 140-lb. (300gsm) cold-pressed paper » 11" x 16" (28cm x 41cm)

Detail of **Kenny** » Watercolor on 140-lb. (300gsm) cold-pressed paper » 22" x 15" (56cm x 38cm)

Detail of **Vacation Tomatoes** » Gouache on 140-lb. (300gsm) hot-pressed paper » 10" x 15" (25cm x 38cm)

ART ON PAGES 8-9:

River Otter » Acrylic and gouache on 140-lb. (300gsm) cold-pressed paper » 8" x 12" (20cm x 30cm)

Drawing Room Props » Watercolor on 140-lb. (300gsm) hot-pressed paper » 15" x 22" (38cm x 56cm)

September Flowers » Watercolor on 140-lb. (300gsm) cold-pressed paper » 22" x 22" (56cm x 56cm)

Onions and Garlic » Watercolor on 140-lb. (300gsm) cold-pressed paper » 20" x 24" (51cm x 61cm)

Realism in Watermedia: 18 Painting Techniques for Achieving Realistic Results. Copyright © 2005 by Christopher Leeper. Manufactured in China. All rights reserved. No part of this book may be reproduced in any form or by any electronic or mechanical means including information storage and retrieval systems without permission in writing from the publisher, except by a reviewer who may quote brief passages in a review. Published by North Light Books, an imprint of F+W Publications, Inc., 4700 East Galbraith Road, Cincinnati, Ohio, 45236. (800) 289-0963. First edition.

Other fine North Light Books are available from your local bookstore, art supply store or direct from the publisher.

09 08 07 06 05   5 4 3 2 1

Library of Congress Cataloging-in-Publication Data
Leeper, Christopher J.
 Realism in watermedia : 18 painting techniques for achieving realistic results / Christopher Leeper.
   p. cm.
 Includes index.
 ISBN 1-58180-508-X
 1. Painting—Technique. I. Title.

ND1473.L44 2005
751.42—dc22   2004057562

Adobe and Adobe Photoshop are either registered trademarks or trademarks of Adobe Systems Incorporated in the United States and/or other countries.

Editor: Stefanie Laufersweiler
Production editor: Amy Jeynes
Designer: Wendy Dunning
Production artist: Joni DeLuca
Production coordinator: Mark Griffin

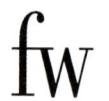

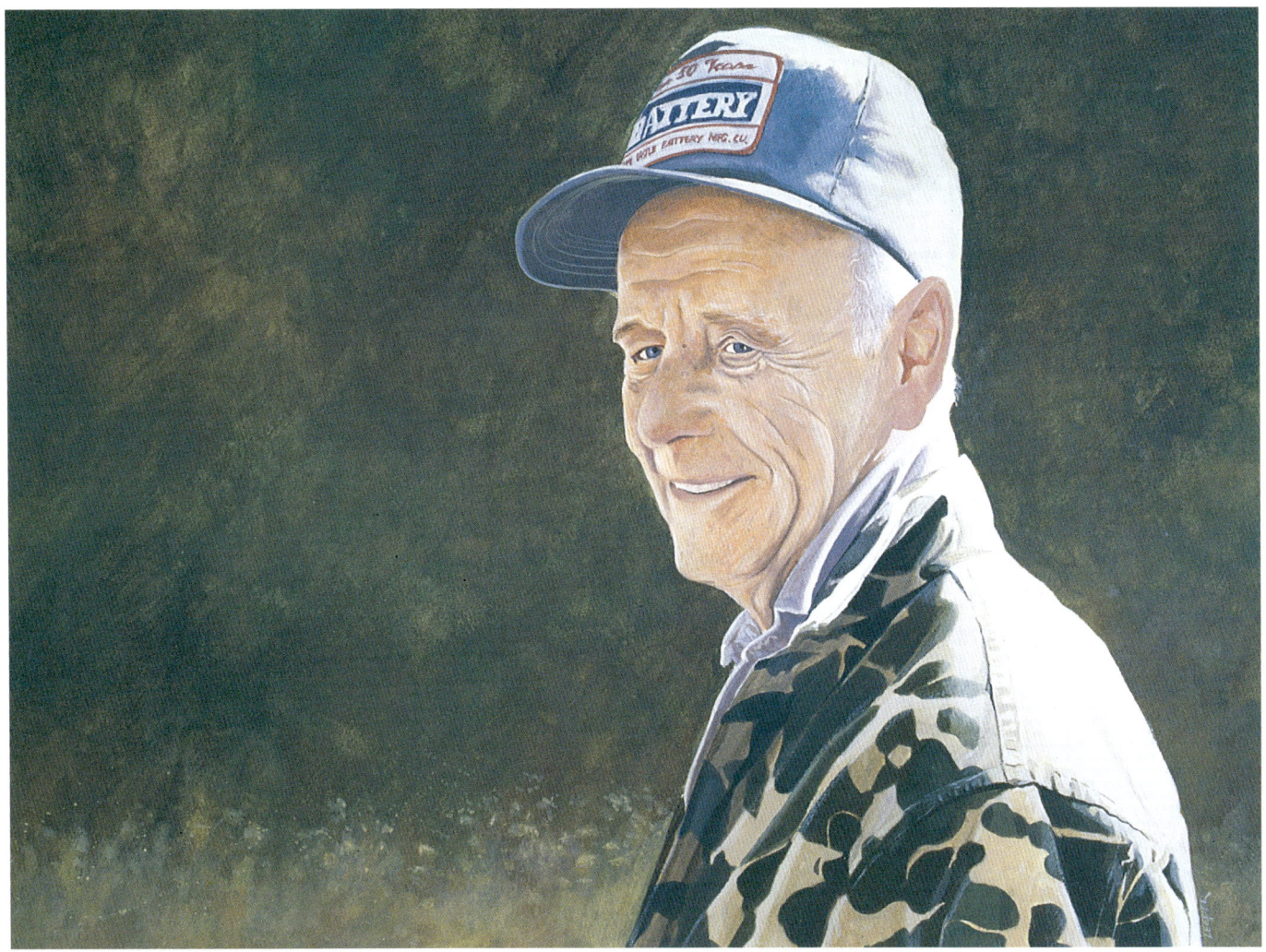

Bub (Donald Leeper) » Watercolor on 140-lb. (300gsm) cold-pressed paper » 15" x 22" (38cm x 56cm)

ACKNOWLEDGMENTS

I would like to thank and acknowledge the people who made this book happen: my wife, Kathy, for her unwavering support of my art and this project; Tony Mancino, for his photographic expertise and instruction as well as the generous contribution of his time; friends, family and patrons, who let me borrow and photograph paintings; and my editor, Stefanie Laufersweiler, for her good nature, patience and vision, which made what seemed like an overwhelming project manageable and thoroughly enjoyable.

DEDICATION

To Mom and Dad

table of contents

INTRODUCTION » 8

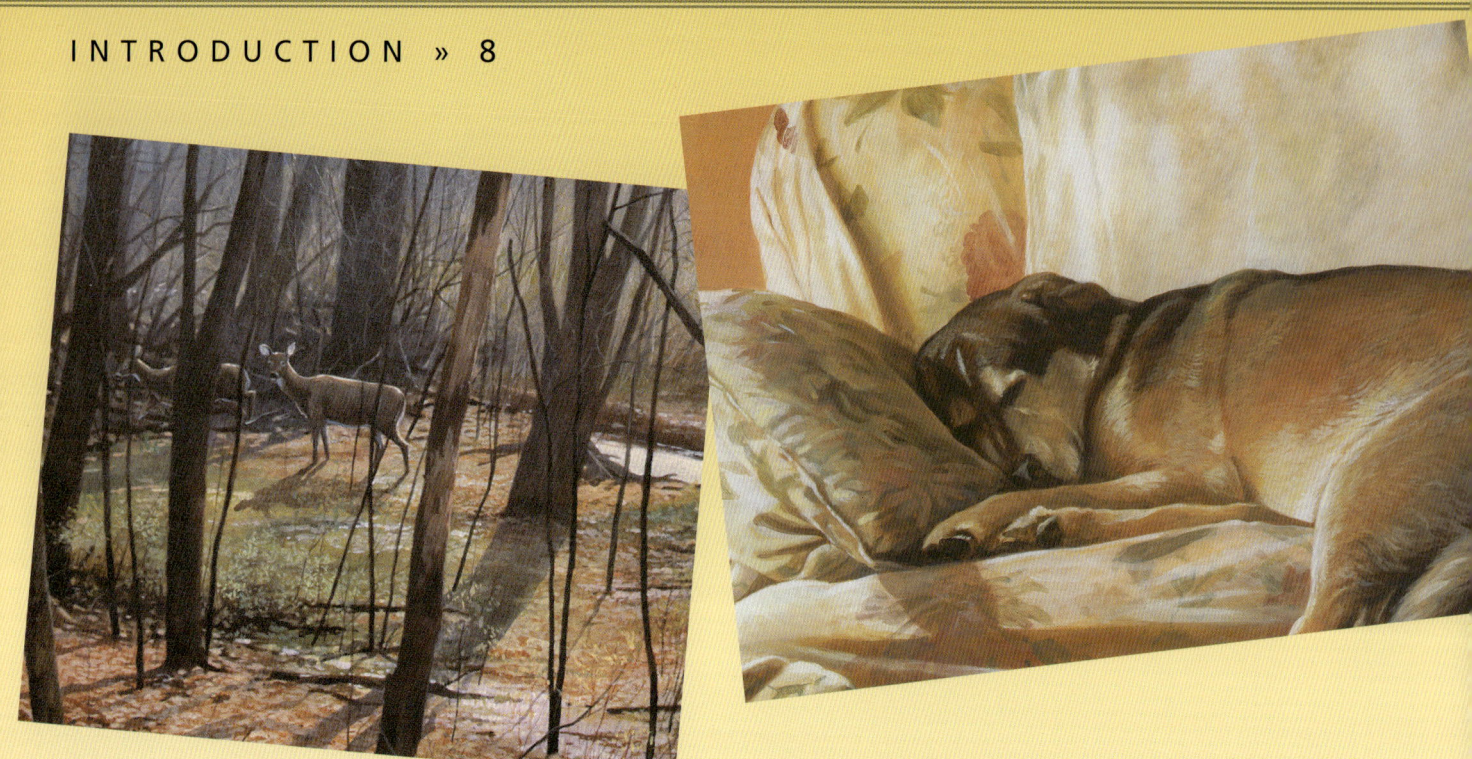

1» basic materials 10

Certain types of paper, paints, brushes and palettes can suit your painting goals better than others. Find out what materials—including watercolors, acrylics, gouache, colored pencils and pastels—you need to be a multimedia painter.

2» plan values for impact 20

Of all the art elements that make up a representational painting, value could be considered the most important. Without interesting value relationships, the most wonderful colors and techniques are wasted. Composing with value lets you build your painting upon a solid foundation. One mini-demonstration.

3» painting from life 30

The best way to understand your subject is to paint it live. However, the wealth of visual information can be overwhelming. Successful paintings from life demand that we simplify the scene, edit the details and use techniques that let us record as much information as possible as quickly as possible. Three mini-demonstrations.

4» painting from photographs 44

The advancement of new photographic technology gives artists powerful tools in understanding and interpreting subjects. The key is incorporating these tools into your painting process so that they support but do not overwhelm your painting goals.

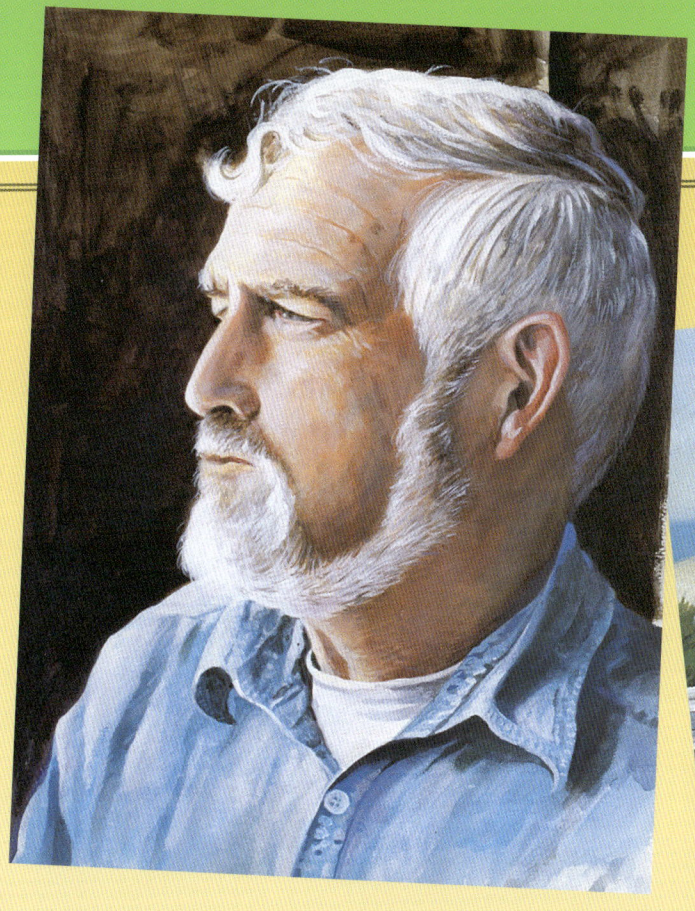
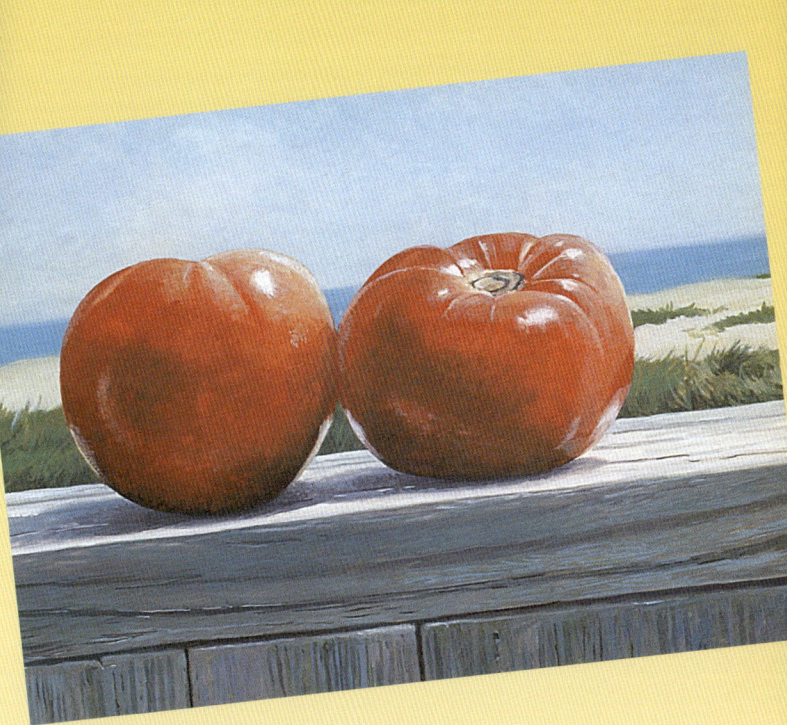

5» watermedia techniques 60

From opaque to transparent and everything in between, watermedia techniques are as varied as the artists who use them. Learn how to get the most out of your watercolors and acrylics and how to combine mediums for the best results. Five mini-demonstrations.

7» step-by-step demonstrations 102

Three complete demonstrations explore the use of watercolor, acrylic and mixed media for stunning results. Paint a sun-drenched vegetable still life, a napping figure under an elaborate quilt, and a fog-filled harbor scene.

6» mixed media techniques 92

Explore the potential of adding gouache accents and dry media, including pastels and colored pencils, to your watermedia paintings. Use these tools to add final color notes or to rescue a tired, lifeless painting. One mini-demonstration.

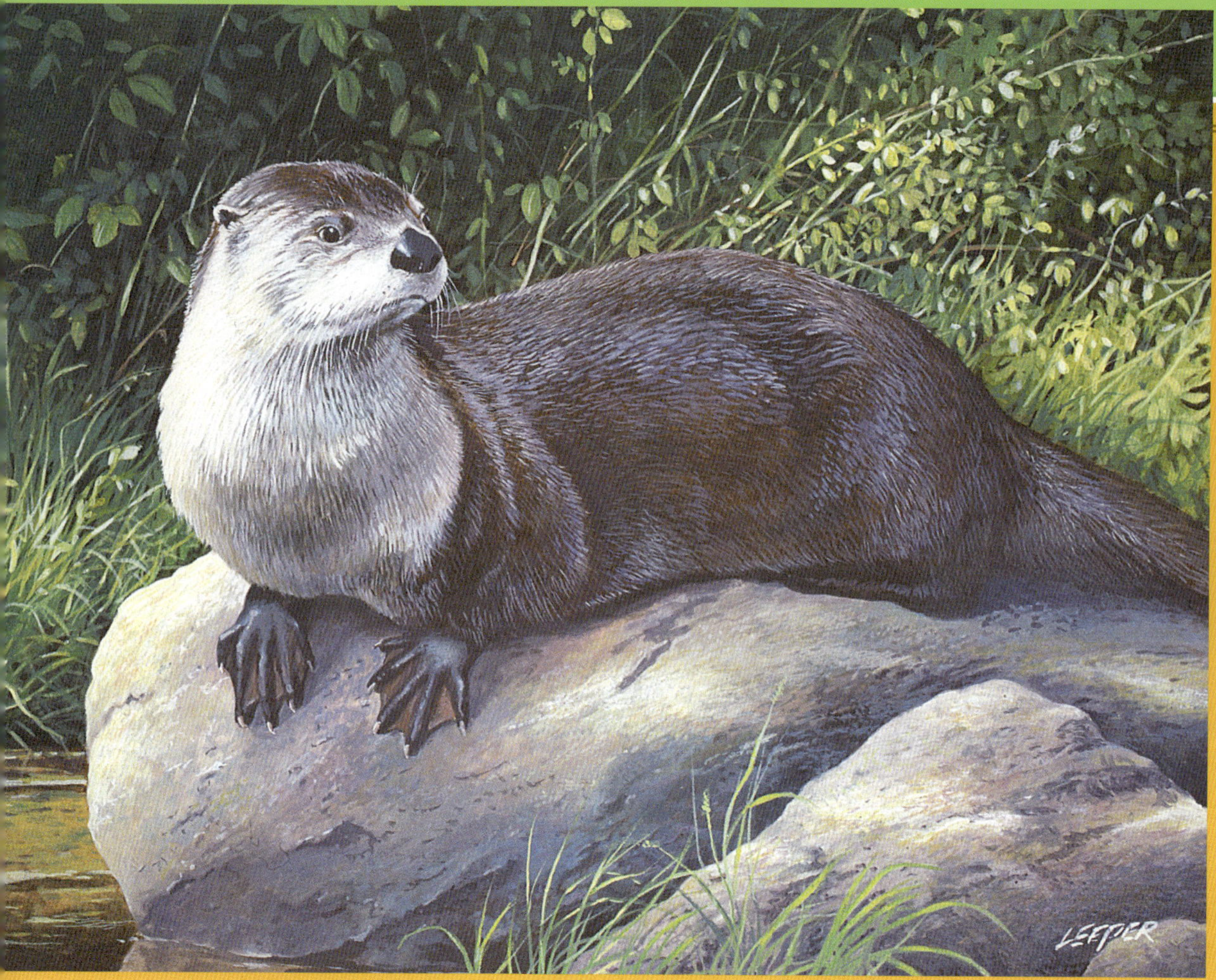

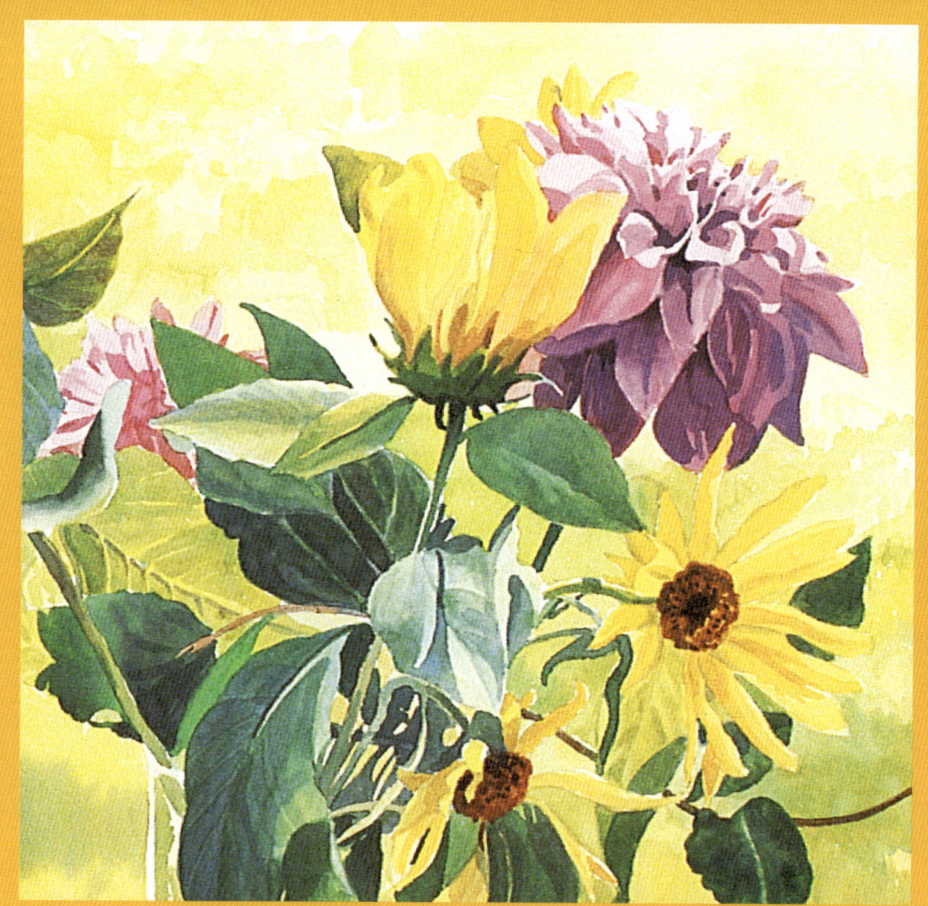
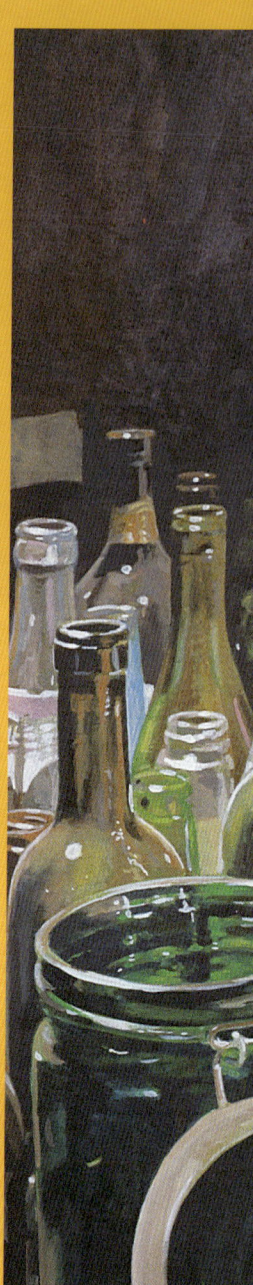
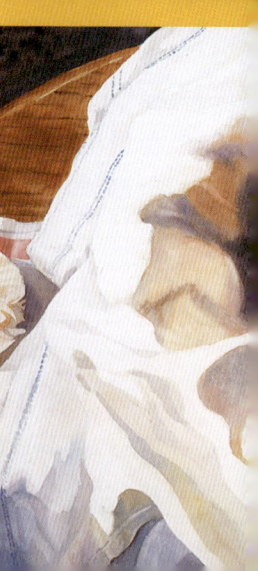

introduction

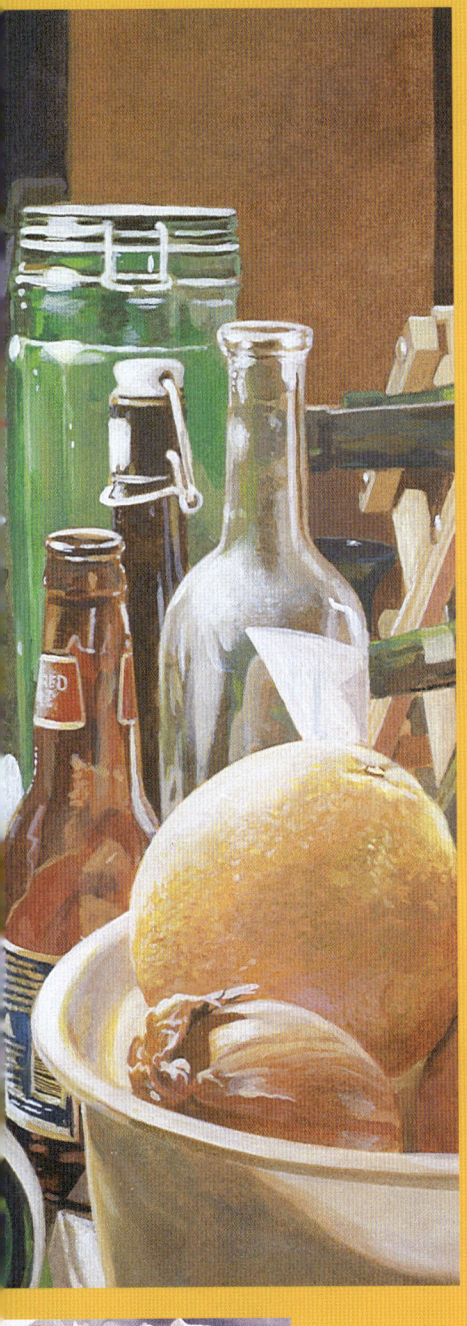

I painted in transparent watercolor exclusively for several years. One painting, however, changed my thinking. I had finished a full-sheet watercolor landscape and was frustrated with the results. Besides being disappointed with my painting, I was also troubled by having just ruined an expensive sheet of paper. Deciding I had nothing to lose, I squeezed out some acrylics and began reworking the painting. To my surprise, when I added acrylic to a mediocre watercolor, it became a dynamic mixed-media painting.

Since that day several years ago, I have painted hundreds of watermedia paintings. I now reach for whatever combination of media I think best suits my subject or painting intentions.

Each type of watermedia has its own special properties, and when the watermedia are mixed with each other and with dry media, the possibilities are endless. This book explores these possibilities as applied to realistic painting. Hopefully you will be inspired to try the techniques that are discussed and apply them in your own paintings.

In the end, the best teacher is experience. Try to paint as much as you can, and have fun! Remember, it's the journey, not the destination, that makes life so interesting.

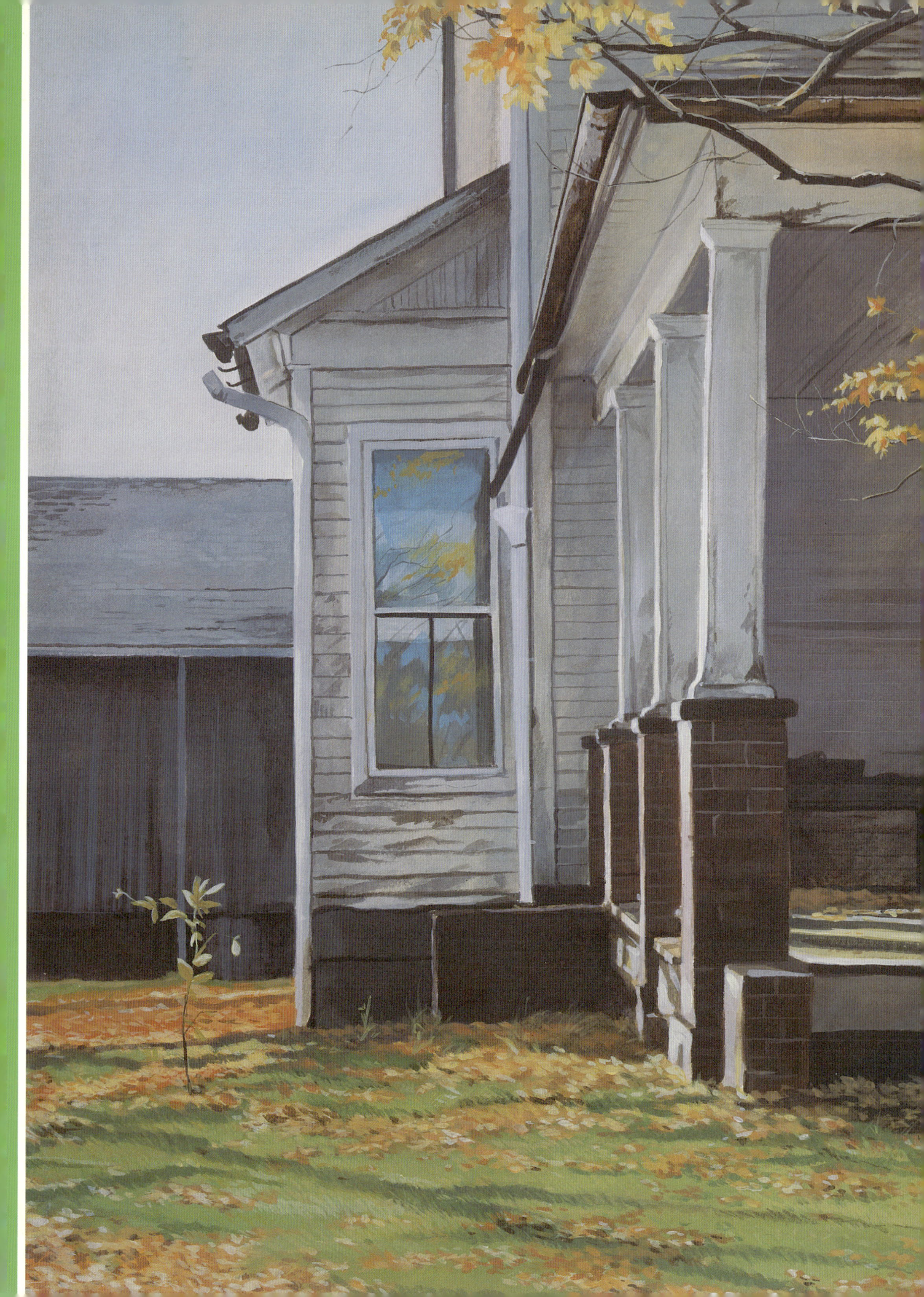

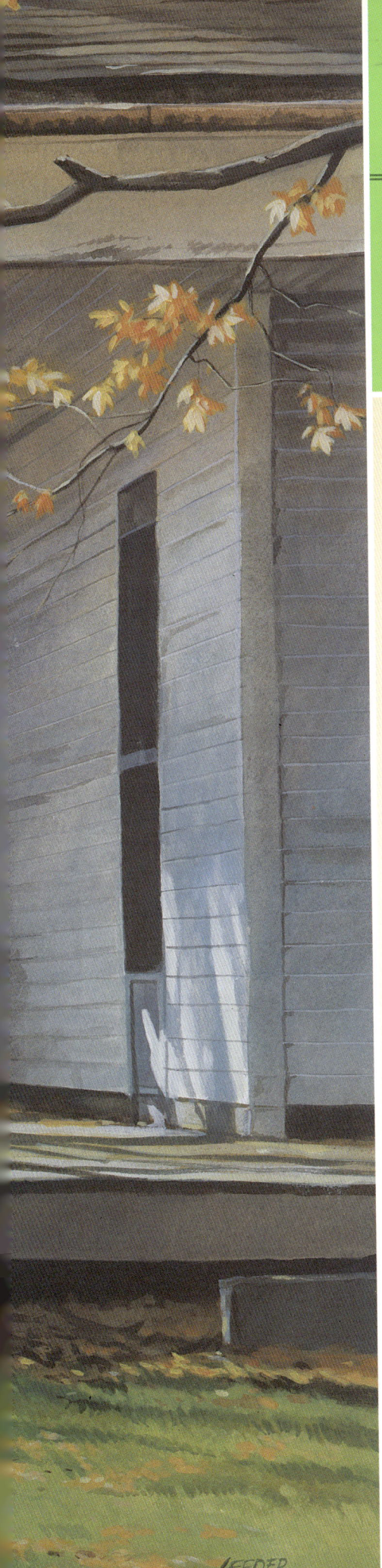

1»
basic materials

Artists today have a wealth of materials to choose from. In fact, new watermedia products, especially papers, come out each year. Experiment with as many different materials as you can afford to purchase. You may find that certain types of paper, paints, brushes and palettes suit your painting goals better than others. This chapter covers the basic materials that I find useful, although I consider any materials list in this book a work in progress. I'm always on the lookout for an exciting new paper, brush or color to try.

Forgotten » Acrylic on 140-lb. (300gsm) cold-pressed paper » 22" x 22" (56cm x 56cm)

Watermedia

Any artist should use high-quality paint, regardless of the medium. The better paints have less filler or binder and more pigment. They are more expensive than student-grade colors, but a benefit is that you can use less paint and still get intense, brilliant color.

My color choices have been formed through many years of trial and error. However, the principle of color temperature can help you choose your colors.

A color's temperature can be warm, cool or neutral depending on its relative position on the color wheel. Let's examine the blues, for example. Cobalt Blue is a relatively neutral blue. Ultramarine Blue is a slightly reddish blue and thus is considered warm. Phthalo Blue tends toward green and is considered cool. These three colors would represent the blue family effectively on your palette.

Having a variety of color temperatures in each primary color family gives you the most versatility in color mixing. I round out my palette with a few greens, violets and earth tones.

Watercolors

There are many fine paint brands available. I use Schmincke, Winsor & Newton and Daniel Smith colors. My palette for the demonstrations in this book includes:

- Alizarin Crimson
- Aureolin
- Burnt Sienna
- Burnt Umber
- Cadmium Orange Light
- Cadmium Red
- Cerulean Blue
- Cobalt Blue
- Emerald Green
- Green Gold
- New Gamboge
- Phthalo Blue
- Quinacridone Gold
- Quinacridone Red
- Quinacridone Violet
- Rose Madder Genuine
- Sepia
- Ultramarine Blue
- Winsor Red
- Winsor Violet (Dioxazine)
- Winsor Yellow
- Yellow Ochre

Gouache

I typically use gouache as a detail medium rather than as the sole medium in a painting. Usually, I use Titanium White combined with my existing watercolor palette for many of my mixes. The brand I use is Winsor & Newton Designers Gouache. The colors I use for the demonstrations in the book are:

- Alizarin Crimson
- Azo Yellow
- Burnt Sienna
- Burnt Umber
- Cadmium Orange
- Cadmium Red
- Cadmium Yellow
- Cerulean Blue
- Cobalt Blue
- Gold Ochre
- Ivory Black
- Permanent Green Light
- Phthalo Blue
- Quinacridone Red
- Titanium White
- Ultramarine Blue
- Yellow Ochre

creating rich earth tones

Although earth tone colors are an important part of any watercolor palette, they can adversely affect your color mixtures. Earth tone colors are made up of all three primary colors. When you add them to other colors the result can be a gray, lifeless mixture.

If you want a brown or tan color try finding that color first by using your primary palette. A good primary palette to work from is Cobalt Blue, Rose Madder Genuine and Aureolin. I mostly use Burnt Umber and Burnt Sienna mixed with staining colors like Phthalo Blue or Alizarin Crimson to create rich darks.

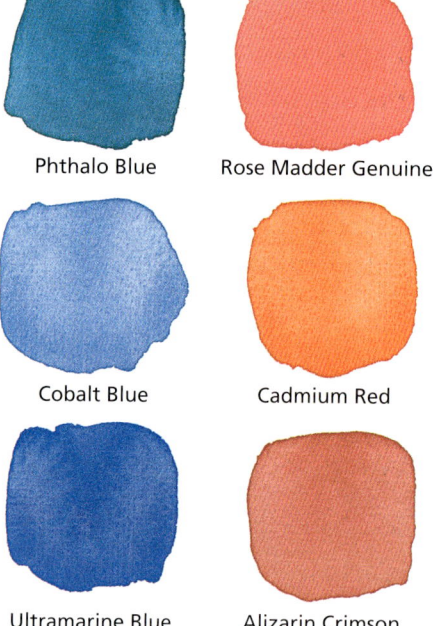

Phthalo Blue · Rose Madder Genuine · Aureolin
Cobalt Blue · Cadmium Red · New Gamboge
Ultramarine Blue · Alizarin Crimson

Workhorse Watercolors
These colors are the ones that I turn to most often in my watercolor mixtures.

Acrylics

I try to have a mix of warm and cool primary colors similar to my watercolor palette. Since acrylic colors will eventually dry out, I put out a warm and cool primary palette first and add other colors as I need them. I prefer Liquitex High Viscosity Artist Colors, but try different brands to see what you like. Here is my basic acrylic palette for the demonstrations in the book:

- ACRA Crimson
- Alizarin Crimson
- Brilliant Blue
- Burnt Sienna
- Burnt Umber
- Cadmium Orange
- Cadmium Yellow Medium
- Dioxazine Purple
- Hooker's Green Deep
- Indo Orange Red
- Naphthol Crimson
- Naphthol Red Light
- Permanent Green Light
- Phthalo Blue
- Phthalo Green
- Titanium White
- Ultramarine Blue (Green Shade)
- Vivid Lime Green
- Yellow Light Hansa
- Yellow Medium Azo
- Yellow Ochre
- Yellow Orange Azo

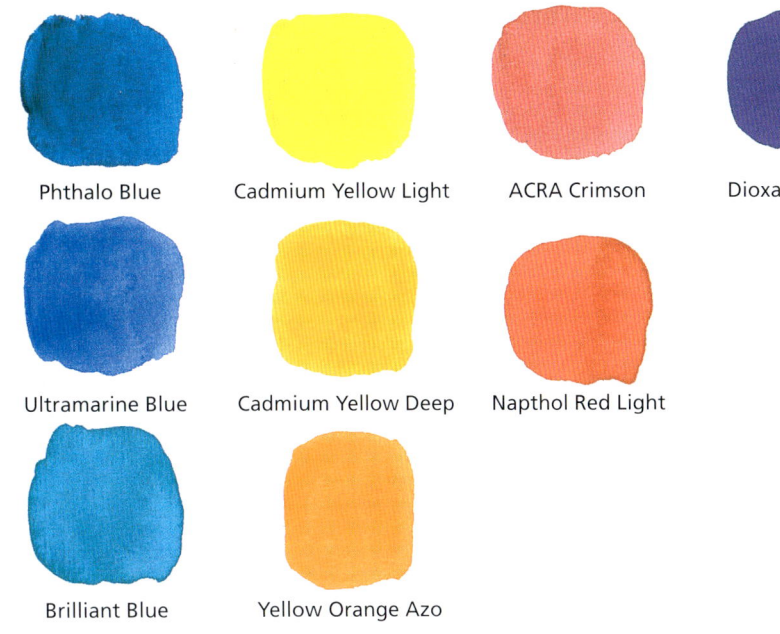

Workhorse Acrylics

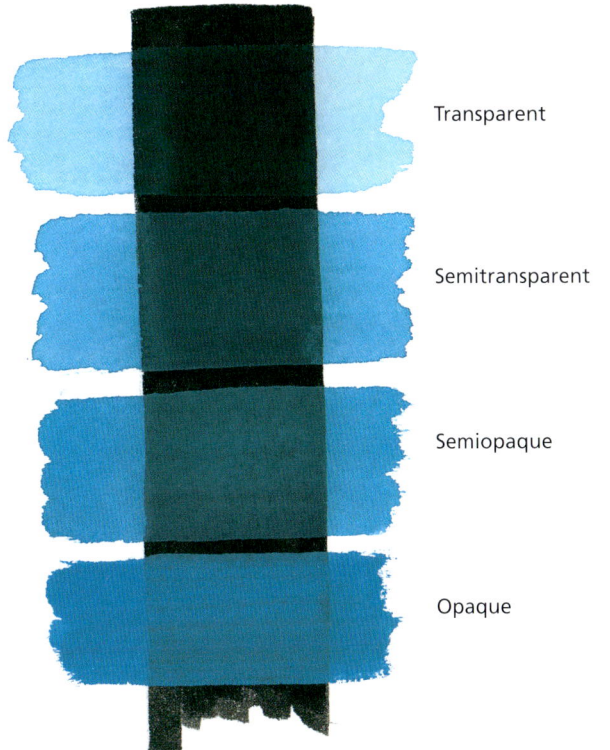

Opacity Chart

Throughout this book are many references to the degree of transparency or opacity of acrylic color and watercolor mixtures. This chart illustrates this terminology.

Dry media

Sometimes I like to accent my paintings with light-value colored pencils or pastels. Darker pencils or pastels do not produce a clear color note and can "muddy" a color area. I use a variety of light-value primary color shades. I also like to accent with violets and lavenders and a variety of greens.

Colored Pencils
For subtle color accents I like to use Berol Prismacolor watercolor pencils. Used like a regular colored pencil, they don't make as distinctive a mark and can be useful in accenting shadow areas. The pencil colors I use for the demonstrations in this book are:

- Blue Slate
- Burnt Ochre
- Orange
- Parma Violet
- Sand
- Spanish Orange
- White

Pastels
I prefer Nupastels hard pastels and Rembrandt soft pastels. If you are adding distinct accents or need a subtle glaze of color, hard pastels work best. Use soft pastels when covering larger portions of your painting and when you want a broad, loose accent of color.

Usually, pastels are added as accents, so a small set of 45 pastels should cover most of your color needs. If you want to develop a painting more extensively using pastels, you may want to invest in a larger set.

Although pastel accents are shown in several examples throughout this book, you do not have to purchase any pastels to follow along with the demonstrations.

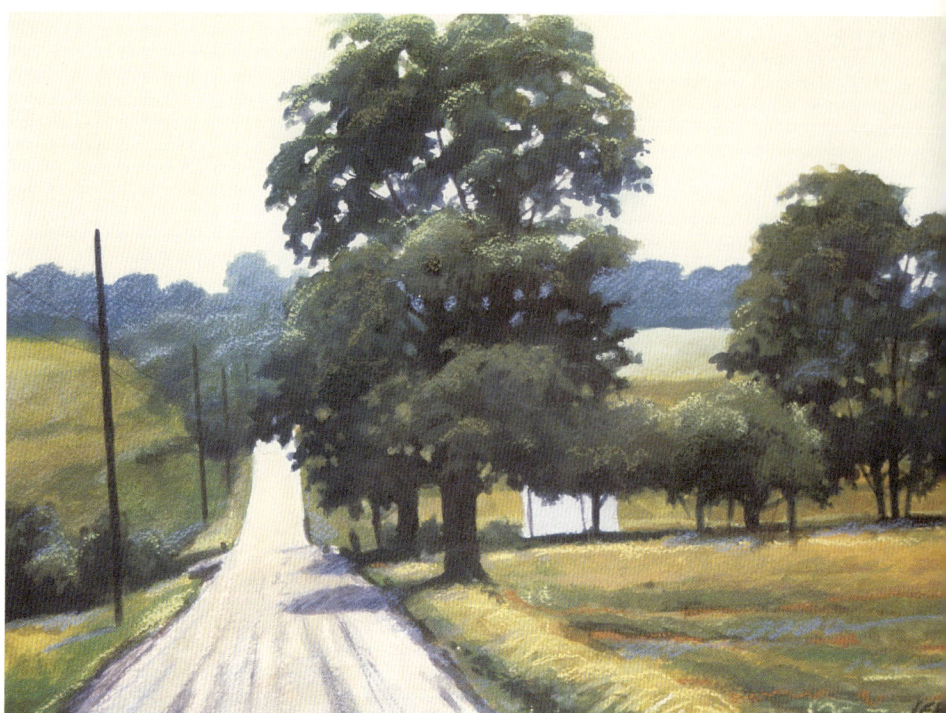

Spruce Up a Watermedia Painting With Dry Media
This painting started out as a watercolor and acrylic demo. A few weeks later I looked at it and decided it needed something else. Using pastels and colored pencils, I lightly accented almost every form. This not only gave it some color but introduced interesting visual textures.

Summer Heat » Mixed media on 140-lb. (300gsm) cold-pressed paper » 11" x 15" (28cm x 38cm)

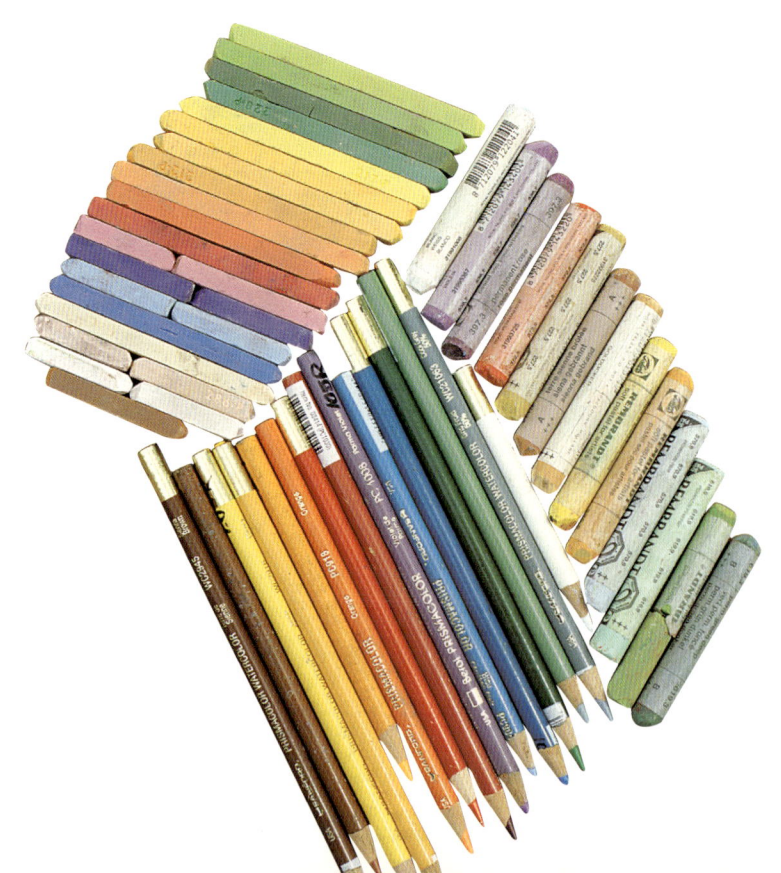

Brushes and palettes

Brushes and palettes are very personal choices, so be sure to shop around. Here are the ones that I use.

Palettes
My palette of choice for watercolors and gouache is the John Pike palette. I find it essential to have a separate area for colors and a large area for mixing. The Pike palette gives me both. I use one palette for transparent watercolor and another for my watercolor-and-gouache paintings.

Since acrylics dry so quickly it is important to use a palette that will keep them fresh. There are brand-name acrylic palettes that work well, but I prefer a simple plastic food-storage container. When I am done painting, I sprinkle some water over the paint, then seal and press down on the lid. When stored this way, the paint stays moist for several days.

Brushes
An incredible variety of soft-hair brushes is available to the water-media artist. I prefer the synthetic Taklon and the sable and Taklon blend since they are affordable and perform well. But I do splurge on smaller brushes. I prefer kolinsky sable rounds for no. 2 and smaller because of their durability, superior color loading and fine point.

I keep my watercolor brushes separate from my acrylic brushes. Acrylic paint is notoriously hard on brushes and eventually will ruin them. Also, I am sometimes rather rough with my application of color. Because of this I often use "retired" watercolor brushes as scumble brushes, and I tend to buy less-expensive Taklon brushes that I can beat up without feeling too guilty. I use similar styles and sizes for both mediums. I do, however, use some long-handled brushes that are made specifically for acrylics. Their hairs are somewhat stiffer than those in traditional watercolor brushes, and they work better for applying opaque color.

Generally, you will work from large to small and your brush use will reflect this. I like 1-inch (25mm) and 2-inch (51mm) flats for painting large washes such as skies. Smaller flats work well when you need a chiseled edge, as when painting man-made structures. The large rounds, 10, 12 and 16, hold a lot of color yet still come to a fine point. They can be used to cover large areas as well as to paint finer, linear elements. Obviously, the smaller rounds create smaller washes and are used for more detailed sections of your painting. Riggers are great for fine lines and for rendering tree branches and grasses.

The brushes you will need to complete the demos in this book are:
- Nos. 16, 12, 10, 8, 6, 4, 2, 1 and 00 synthetic rounds
- Nos. 2 and 1 kolinsky sable rounds
- 2-inch (51mm), 1-inch (25mm), ¾-inch (19mm), ½-inch (13mm) and ¼-inch (6mm) synthetic flats
- Sable rigger
- Stiff bristle brush (for lifting color)

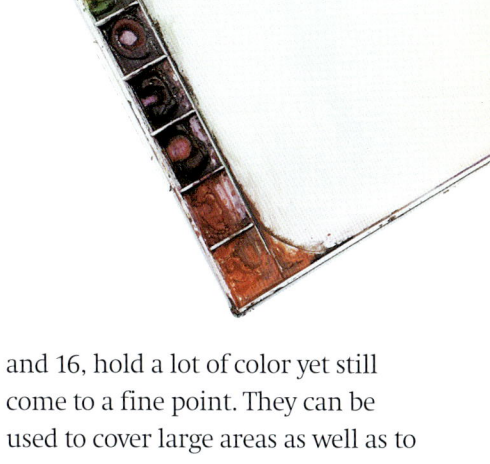

save those old brushes
I keep several old brushes around for my acrylic paintings. These brushes work well for scumbling color and blocking in large passages. You can be very aggressive without worrying about damaging the brush.

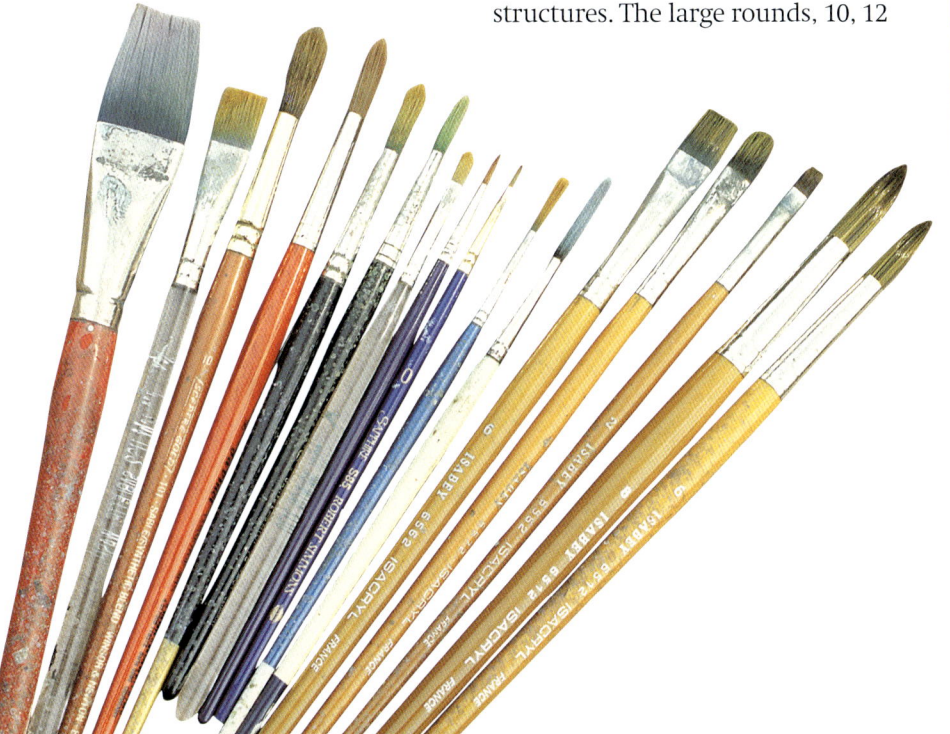

Painting surfaces

The best watermedia paper is 100-percent rag and heavy enough to take multiple washes and a modest amount of abuse. These papers can seem expensive, but there is no substitute for good-quality paper. Cheaper papers do not react well to multiple washes and do not take color as well. I prefer using 140-lb. (300gsm) paper, but I occasionally will use a 300-lb. (640gsm) sheet for larger works (over 22" × 30" [56cm × 76cm]).

Watercolor paper can be one of three surfaces: hot-pressed, cold-pressed and rough. Hot-pressed paper is very smooth. It is the least forgiving surface for transparent watercolor. Because of the smooth surface, washes dry fairly quickly and leave the artist with less time to manipulate the wash. Cold-pressed paper has a medium-textured surface and is the most popular. Rough paper is just what its name implies—very textured.

Within these three surface categories, each brand has its own qualities. I use Arches and Fabriano hot-pressed papers. I use several different brands of cold-pressed sheets. Arches cold-pressed paper is a great sheet and the one I suggest for anyone learning watercolor. It allows ample working time, it is durable, it is versatile for a number of techniques and it is readily available at most art stores. However, I have found that Arches cold-pressed requires more effort when lifting color. Papers such as Fabriano, Lanaquarelle and Waterford release color a bit easier. Other good-quality cold-pressed sheets I occasionally use are Winsor & Newton and Strathmore. I do not use rough paper often, but occasionally I pull it out for plein air painting. All of these sheets work well with watermedia or mixed

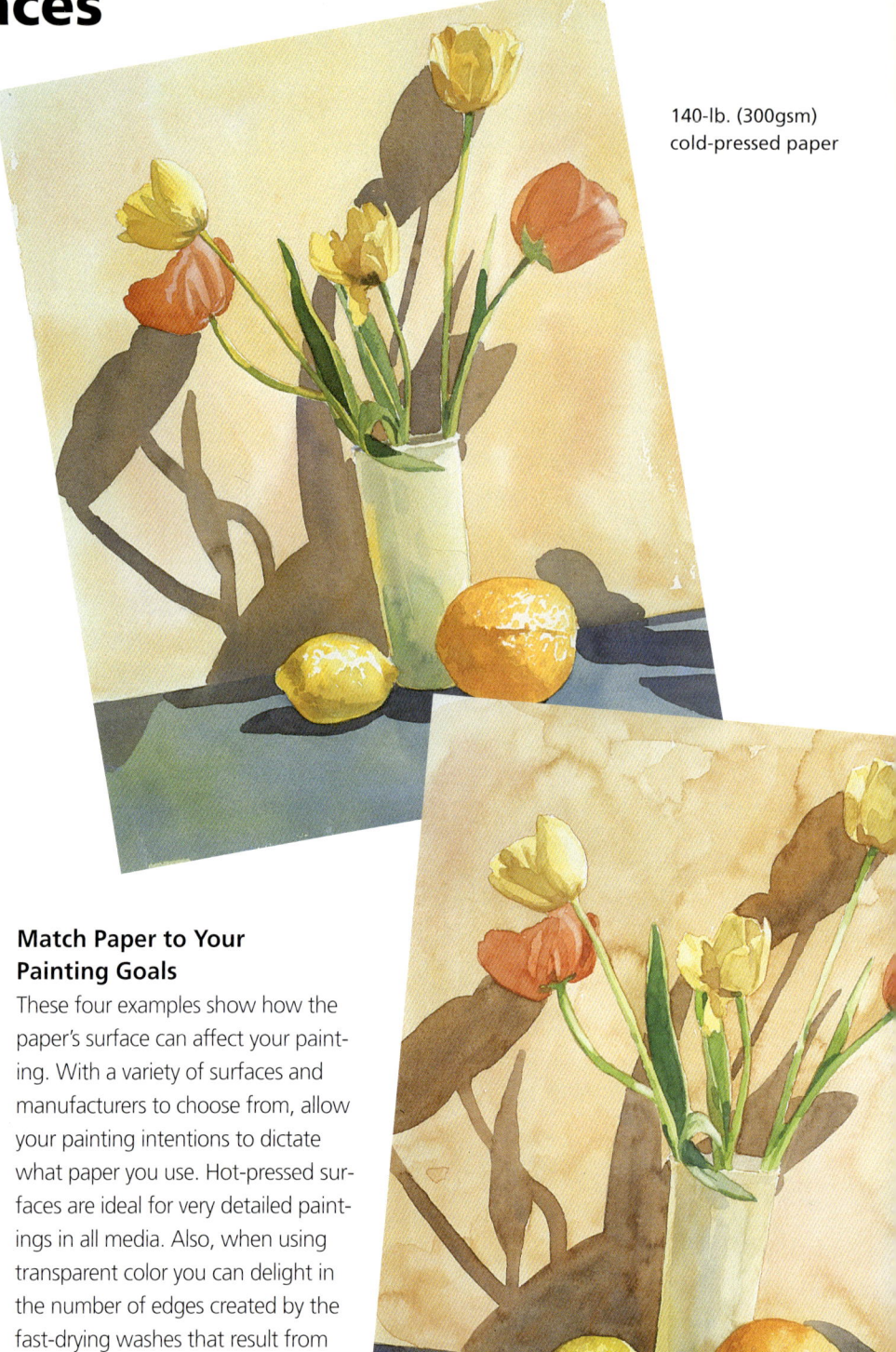

140-lb. (300gsm) cold-pressed paper

140-lb. (300gsm) hot-pressed paper

Match Paper to Your Painting Goals

These four examples show how the paper's surface can affect your painting. With a variety of surfaces and manufacturers to choose from, allow your painting intentions to dictate what paper you use. Hot-pressed surfaces are ideal for very detailed paintings in all media. Also, when using transparent color you can delight in the number of edges created by the fast-drying washes that result from working on this surface. Cold-pressed surfaces can allow you some detail and precision as well as more textural effects. If your painting subject has many interesting textures, a rough paper may be the ticket.

media. Try different brands to see what you like.

Working on Gesso-Coated Paper

For another interesting surface, coat cold-pressed paper with a couple layers of thinned acrylic gesso. The gesso keeps the paper from absorbing the washes. This allows unlimited lifting of watercolor. If the absorption of color bothers you when you use acrylics on watercolor paper, this surface might be the answer.

Paper Stretching

You will find that 140-lb. (300gsm) paper buckles when painted with very wet washes. To avoid this problem, stretch your paper as follows.

First, soak the sheet in a bathtub or container large enough to let the sheet lie fairly flat. Allow 10 to 15 minutes for the paper to become completely saturated. At this stage it is like a wet cloth. Pull the paper out and let the excess water pour off, then immediately lay it on a wooden board. (I use an old pine drawing board to which I've applied several coats of varnish so the water won't soak in and warp the wood.) Staple the sheet to the board every 1 inch (25mm) or so along the edges and let it dry. The paper will shrink as it dries and you will get some tearing along the staples. After 24 hours, remove the staples and you are ready to paint.

I stretch paper only if I know that I will be using large washes that could cause buckling. For drier techniques, you can get away without stretching. Or you can use 300-lb. (640gsm) paper, which doesn't require stretching.

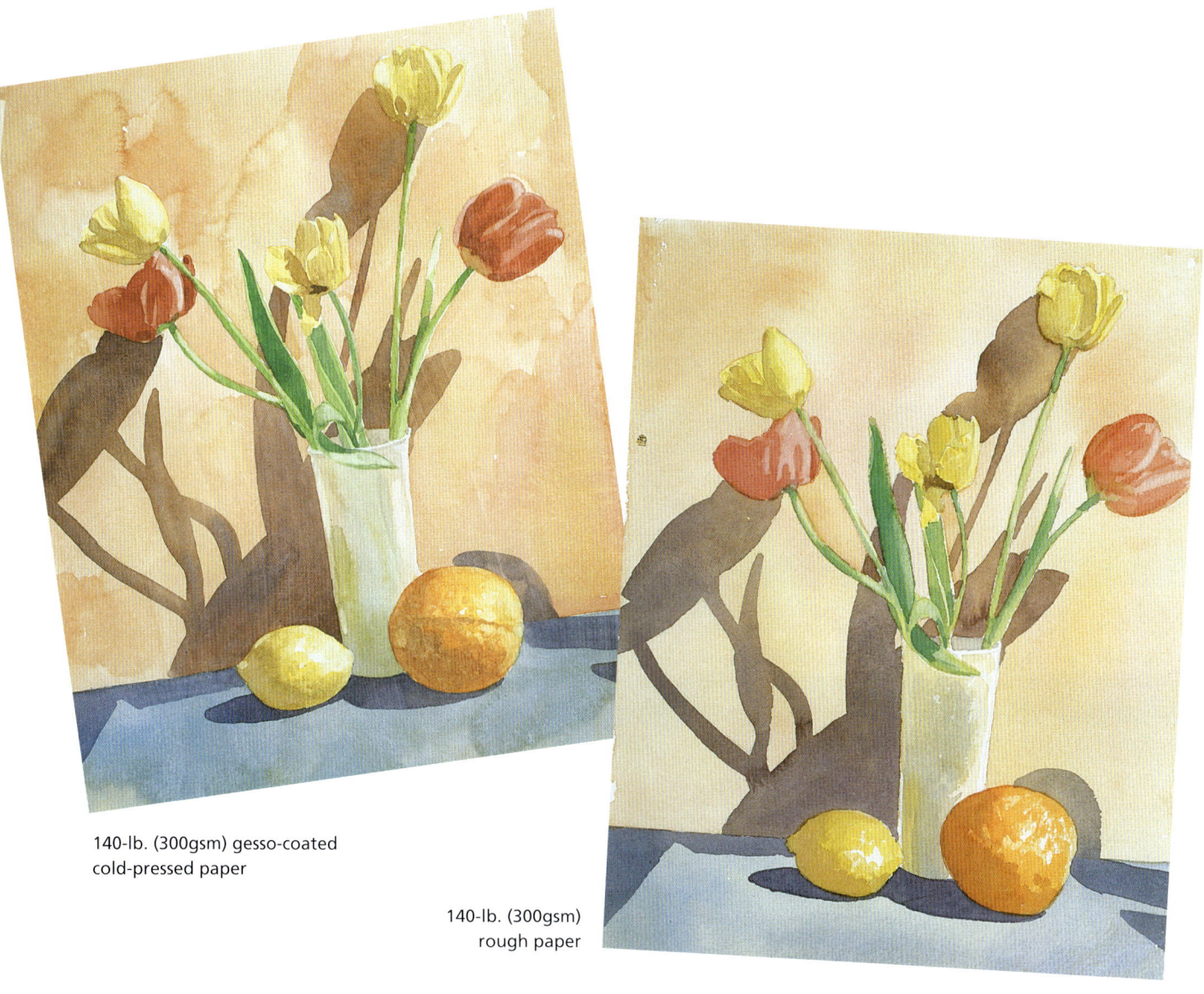

140-lb. (300gsm) gesso-coated cold-pressed paper

140-lb. (300gsm) rough paper

Other materials and studio setup

Pencils and Kneaded Erasers
I use pencils such as HB, B or 2B for my final drawings on watercolor paper. The medium hardness of these pencils is ideal for drawing on watercolor paper. Pencils that are too soft tend to blend with washes and muddy the colors, and harder H pencils can dent the paper. When you wash over these indentations, pigment settles into them and leaves a dark line that cannot be erased.

A soft kneaded eraser is a good tool because it effectively erases while being gentle to the paper. Also, if you happen to make your drawing too dark, you can press this eraser over your drawing several times to lift the excess graphite.

For preliminary sketches, use a soft pencil (4B to 8B) that can give you a wide range of values. You might also want to try a pen like a Sanford Uni-Ball or Sakura Pigma Micron. These pens are a cross between a marker and an ink pen. They are filled with permanent ink and have a hard, durable plastic or metal nib that works great for sketching. They come in a variety of line sizes.

Water Containers
Use two large water containers: one for rinsing your brushes and the other for adding clean water to your palette or paper.

Paper Towels
Keep your watercolor palette clean to achieve clean, bright colors. Use several folded paper towels beside your painting as a convenient way to wipe excess water from your brushes. This will help control the amount of water in your mixes.

Mounting Board
Tape your paper to a lightweight board that can be easily moved around. Foamboard, Gator board and Masonite all work well. Masonite can get rather heavy in larger sizes so I usually use it only for smaller paintings. Mounting your painting on a board will help you control the flow of a wash and find comfortable angles as you work on different parts of your painting.

Hair Dryer
One of the axioms of watercolor painting is "Let it dry." If you work with a lot of wet-into-wet washes and like to really soak the paper, you may have quite a wait if you don't use a hair dryer.

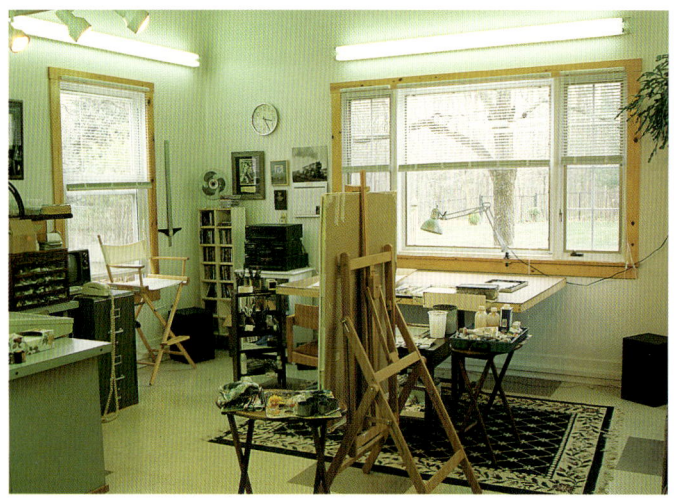
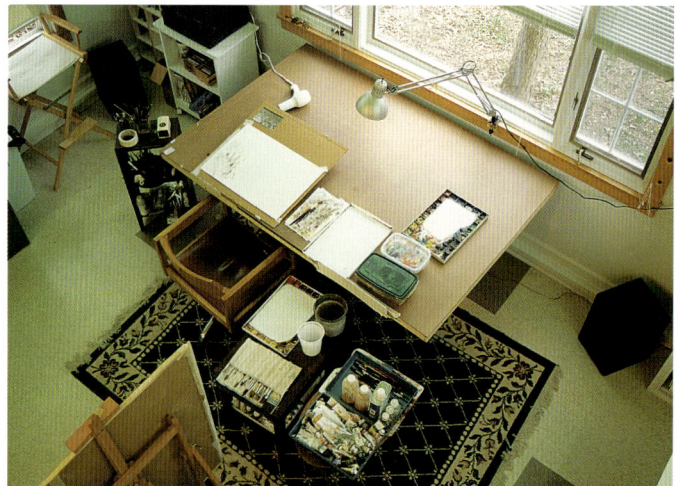

Welcome to My Studio
For years I worked in dark basement studios. I made the most of those situations but always dreamed of having a studio with natural light and plenty of space for larger works and for storage. A few years ago I finally got my wish, and I have enjoyed working "above ground" ever since.

I try to centralize my painting area. I have a large table for watercolors and acrylics. Beside that I have an easel for oils, pastels and large acrylics. Often I will have two paintings in progress, and I can easily turn from one to the other. My studio setup is about having everything within arm's reach. The more comfortable and convenient you can make your work environment, the more you can concentrate on your painting.

Working outdoors

Nothing compares to working on location. You see so much more than in a photo, and you experience the subject with all your senses. Unfortunately, my schedule doesn't always allow me to work en plein air, and I often have to rely on photos and quick sketches. Because of this, I cherish every opportunity I get to paint outside.

Convenience is the name of the game when it comes to choosing your materials for plein air painting. The easier it is to transport and set up your stuff, the more time and energy you will have to paint. I like to have almost everything in my bag or strapped to my bag so I can throw it over my shoulder; then the only thing I have to carry is my foamboard or block of watercolor paper. The key is to find a bag that is comfortable and large enough to carry what you need.

I use an old book bag, which usually contains:

- Watercolor and acrylic palettes
- Brushes
- Paper towels
- Plastic bag (to hold my used paper towels)
- Masking tape
- Small sketchbook
- Three water bottles (one filled with clean water, one empty for storing dirty water to discard later, one filled with drinking water)
- Water container
- Pencils (4B and 6B for sketching; HB for drawing on watercolor paper)
- Erasers
- Roller ball pens
- Extra tubes of paint

I use various sizes of foamboard for mounting my watercolor paper. I tape a large manila envelope to the back to hold extra sheets of paper. I use different-sized boards depending on the size of paper I will carry into the field. Sometimes it's more convenient just to carry a watercolor block. I usually buy the smaller sizes for carrying convenience.

I carry a lightweight collapsible chair and a portable aluminum easel. I strap both to my bag with bungee cords. I also carry a bath towel. Sometimes it is convenient to sit on a rock or a log, and a folded towel can soften a hard seat.

keep your brushes healthy

Acrylics can be tough on brushes in the studio and can ruin them in the field. Be sure to aggressively rinse your brushes and wrap them in a damp paper towel after you're done painting on location. When you get home, give them a good cleaning with soap and water.

try india ink

A fun technique to try while you are out in the field is an India ink study. Try combining washes along with some linework. Use a reed pen, a crow quill pen or even the handle of your brush to create lines. See the lively drawings of van Gogh for inspiration. Note: Use older brushes since ink dries quickly and can beat up a newer brush.

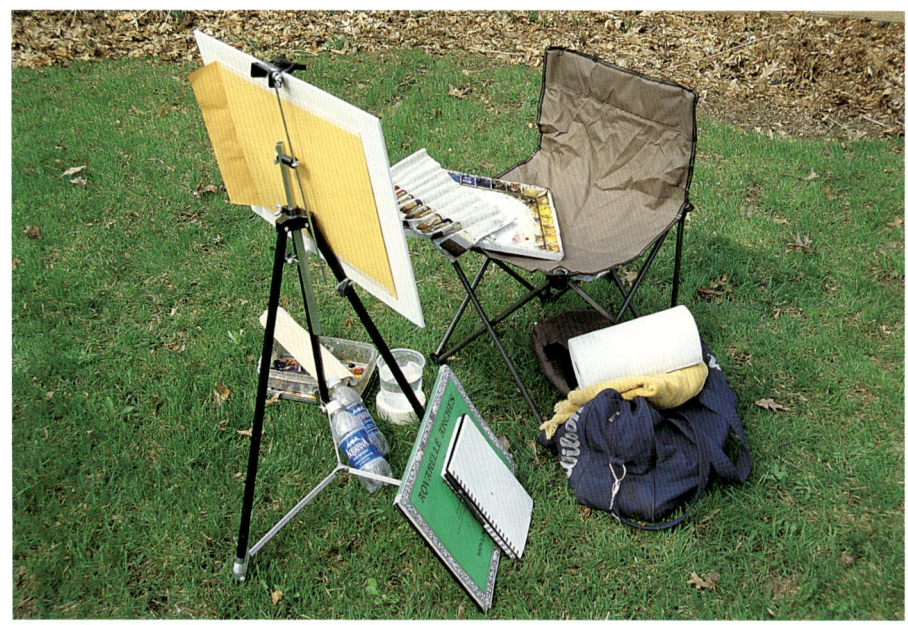

My Outdoor Setup
If I know the subject and the area that I will be painting, I might decide to take only my watercolors or my acrylics. If I am exploring a new area, I usually take everything. Sometimes situations present themselves where I can work close to my van. In that case, I pull out only the materials that I need.

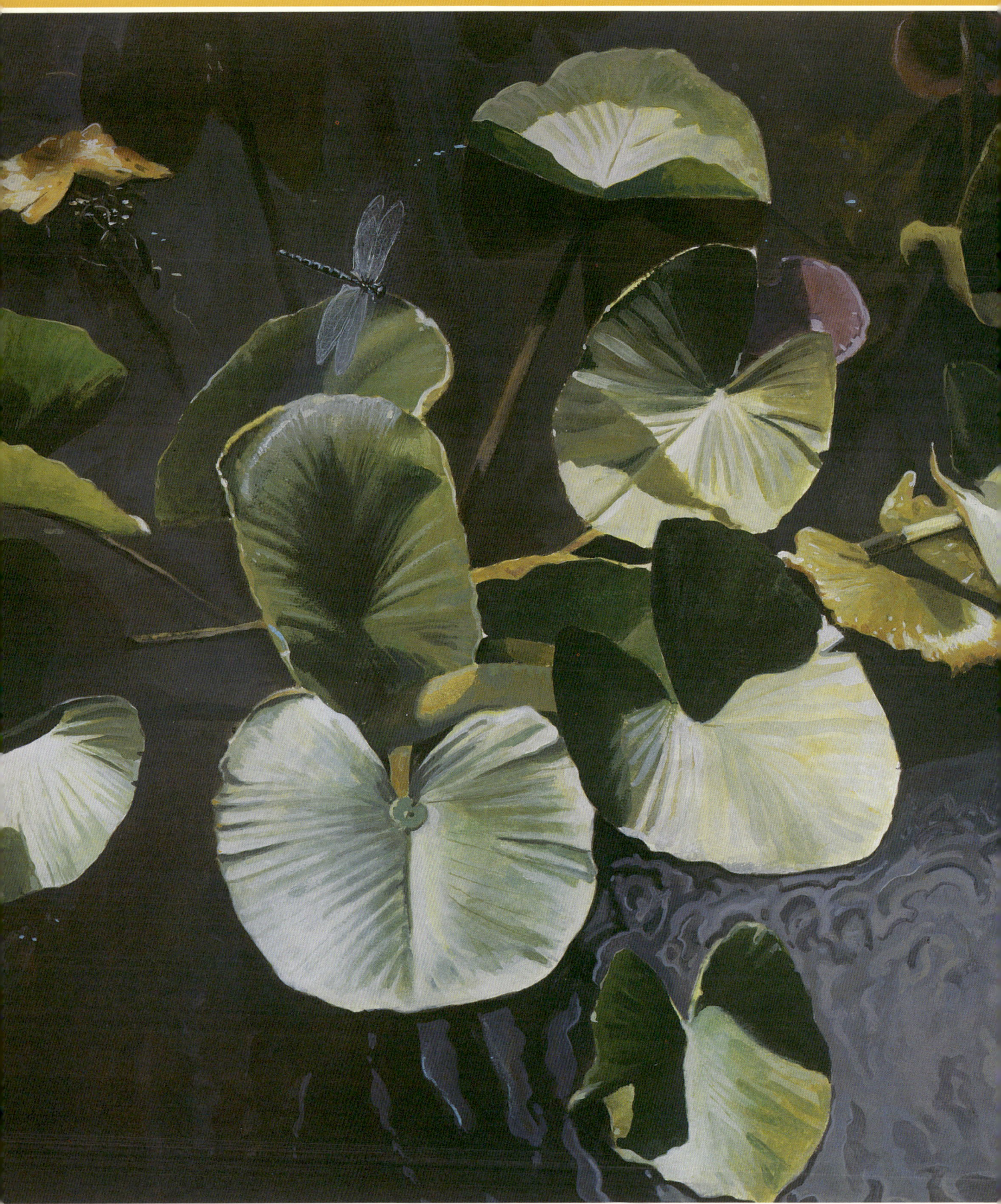

Where Dragons Roam » Acrylic on cold-pressed watercolor board » 16" x 20" (41cm x 51cm)

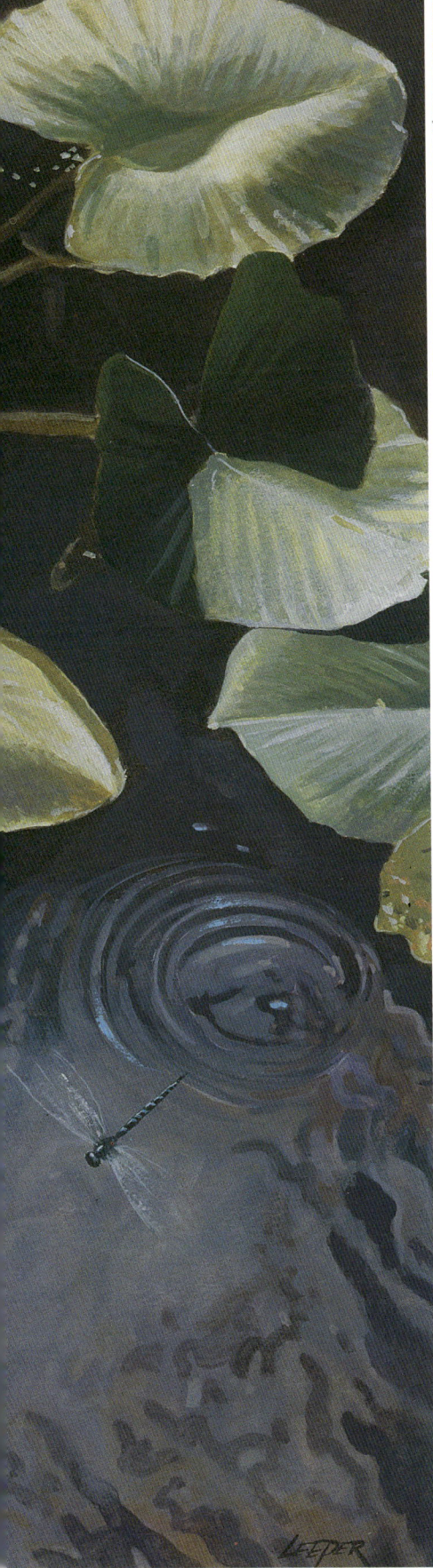

2 »
plan values for impact

Of all the art elements that make up a representational painting, value can be considered the most important. Without interesting value relationships, the most wonderful colors and techniques are wasted. Composing with value lets you build your painting upon a solid foundation. If your value relationships and composition are sound, you will be well on your way to a successful painting.

The importance of value

Value is the lightness or darkness of an object. In this book, I often refer to a painting as having a "dynamic" or "full" value range. This means a painting contains values from the lightest to the darkest on the value scale. This will be your goal for most paintings. A painting with this range usually has interesting shapes, contrasts and emphasis.

A dynamic value range can benefit your painting in many ways. It creates within your composition a strong structure that allows you to emphasize color and texture without compromising your composition. It allows you the freedom to explore interesting and often dramatic color relationships. And composing with value gives you the freedom to move and combine value shapes to create new and exciting compositions that are filled with mood and drama.

Start With a Sketch

A fresh white sheet of watercolor paper can be intimidating. The best way to break this barrier is to start with a small rough sketch or thumbnail. I start every painting with a series of thumbnails. Even if I am going to work closely from a photo, I still have to interpret the colors, shapes and forms of the photo into a workable composition for my painting.

I carry a sketchbook with me just about everywhere and fill it with small value sketches. Such sketches are the beginning of the painting and design process; use them to explore various compositions and value arrangements.

design for your format

All the sketches in this chapter are contained within a drawn box or format. The format is the ratio of height to width. This is when you decide whether your painting will be vertical, horizontal or square. You cannot compose without relating the subject to the format in which it will be painted. You can start with a drawn format, or you can create a boundary around the subject once you have sketched the basic shapes.

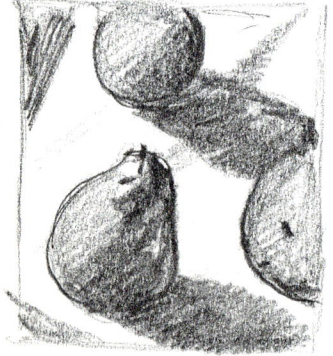
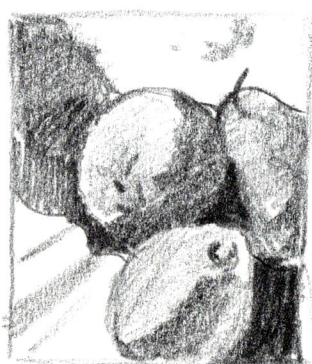
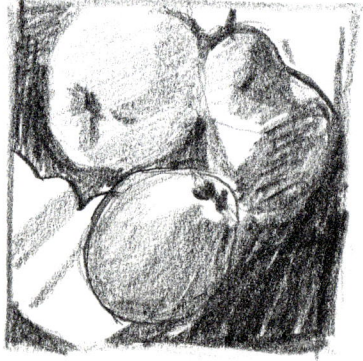
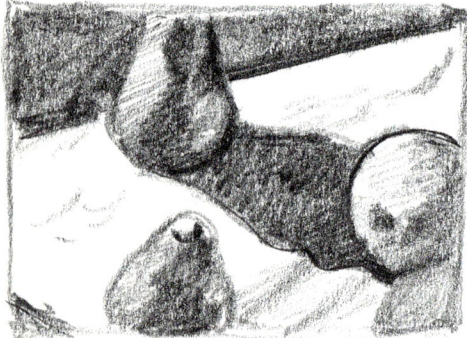
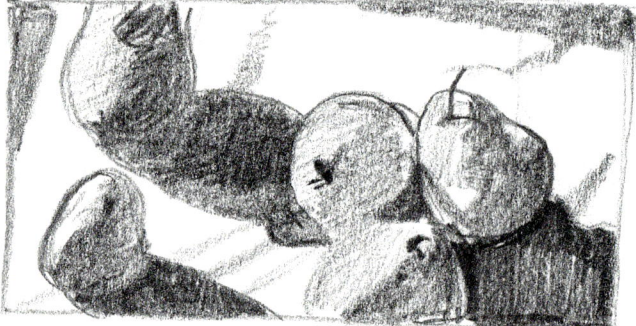

A Rough Beginning
These rough sketches are the beginning of the planning process. Rough sketches let you not only interpret values but also work out composition ideas. These were done with a 5B pencil.

Look for value patterns

Whether you are painting en plein air or working from a photo, finding the pattern of lights and darks is the key to understanding the value structure of your subject. Our world is made up of thousands of values. Trying to interpret all of them is an impossible task. But if we group similar values into shapes, we begin to simplify and clarify our understanding of complex forms.

When you make your value sketch, try to compose with only four values: white, light, middle and dark. With this limited value scale you will be able to create the basic patterns and shapes of your composition without getting bogged down by detail.

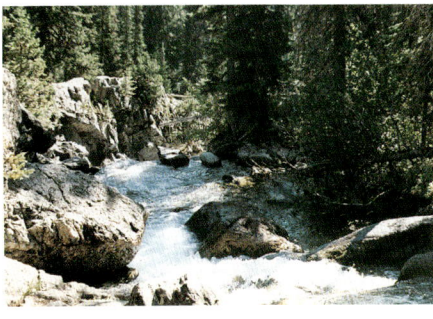

Reference Photo
I took this photo when visiting Grand Teton National Park in Wyoming.

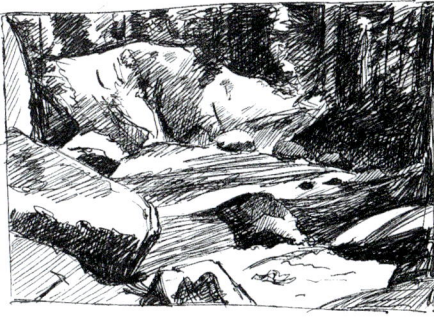

Value Sketch
This sketch was done with a roller ball pen. I like the rich value range that can be quickly established when using a pen. My main concern was finding the basic value pattern. Because the subject was fairly complex, this helped me to understand the main value shapes that would dictate my composition.

go ahead . . . squint to see values

Have you ever watched an artist or photographer while he was looking at his subject? He will often squint as if looking at the sun. The reason for this is that he is trying to see the basic value pattern of the subject. By squinting, you eliminate details and see only the basic shapes and values. I tell my students it's the "Clint Eastwood" look. Very cool!

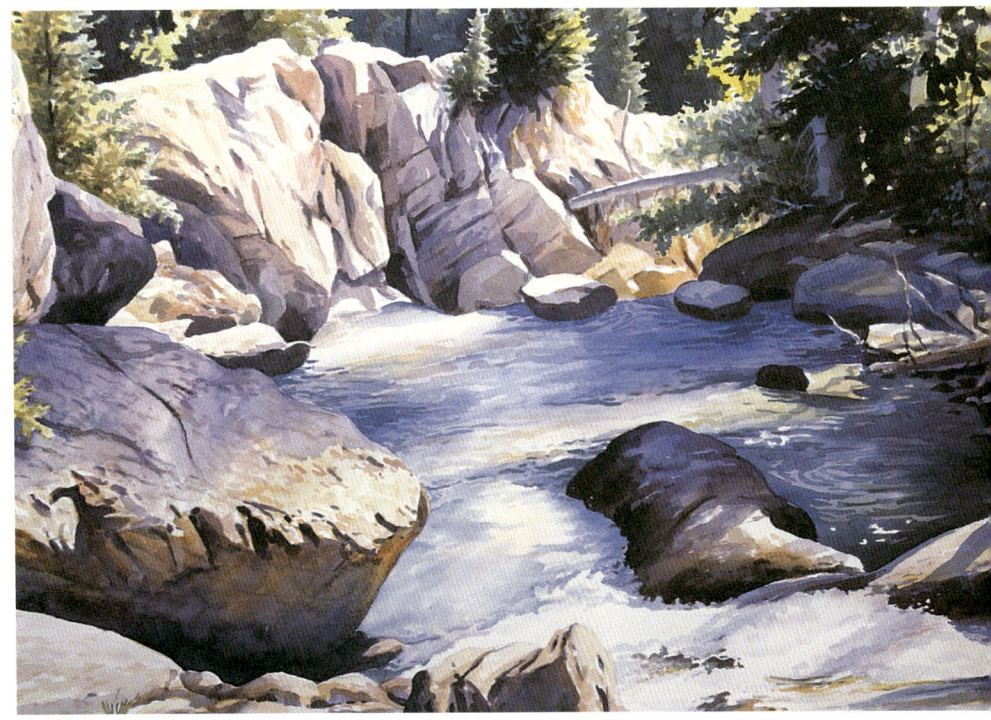

Start All Paintings With a Strong Value Pattern
Notice the editing and simplifying of the small complex shapes in the rocks and water. After establishing a strong value pattern, you can add or subtract as much detail and texture as you want.

Cascading Stream » Watercolor on 140-lb. (300gsm) cold-pressed paper »
20" x 30" (51cm x 76cm)

Value is relative

A value is light, medium or dark in relation to the values surrounding it. This relationship helps us understand form and shape. It also enables us to create mood within our compositions.

Using a full value range as your starting point, you can shift values to the darker or lighter side of the scale to create a different mood or emphasis. High-key paintings have values predominantly from the lighter side of the scale. Low-key paintings have values from the darker end of the scale. The important aspect of these types of paintings is articulating subtle value shifts. This is where your value sketch will help. You can work out several versions until you get the right feeling for your painting.

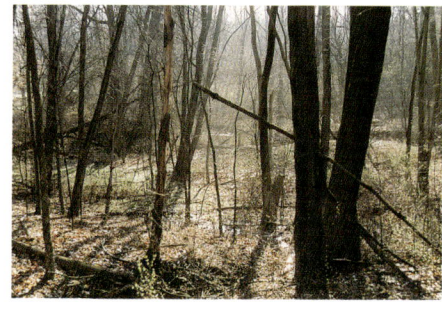

Reference Photo
I took this photo behind my studio on a bright March morning. I was attracted to the sense of light that filled the woods and the strong value contrasts of the trees.

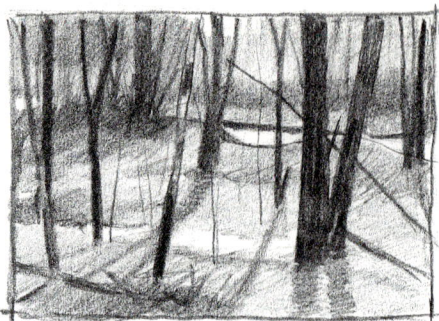

Value Sketch
This was going to be a relatively low-key painting, and I thought it would need a few light areas to make the value range more dynamic. This is why I made the stream and standing water a larger presence in the composition.

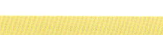

value check

If you are dissatisfied with the value structure of your painting, the problem may be a lack of contrast. Usually, adding more medium-dark to dark values can solve the problem. Also, make sure that either the lights or the darks dominate.

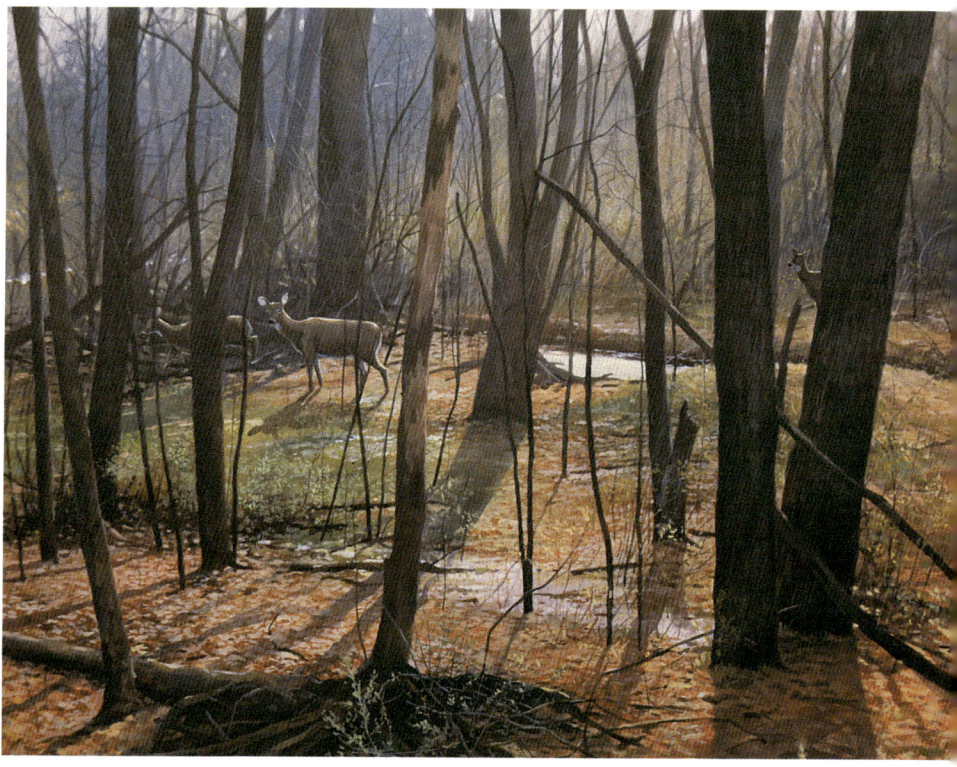

A Low-Key Finish
I started this painting without the deer in mind. Halfway through the painting I saw a few deer walk behind my studio and thought they would be a nice addition. I wanted to show the deer as we commonly see them—quietly blending into their surroundings.

Early Morning Whitetails   »   Mixed media on 140-lb. (300gsm) cold-pressed paper   »
22" x 30" (56cm x 76cm)

Common value problems and solutions

The following paintings show some of the mistakes often made when it comes to value. Notice that a common thread for improving value structure is to broaden the value range from light to dark and to consolidate shapes, which then improves the composition.

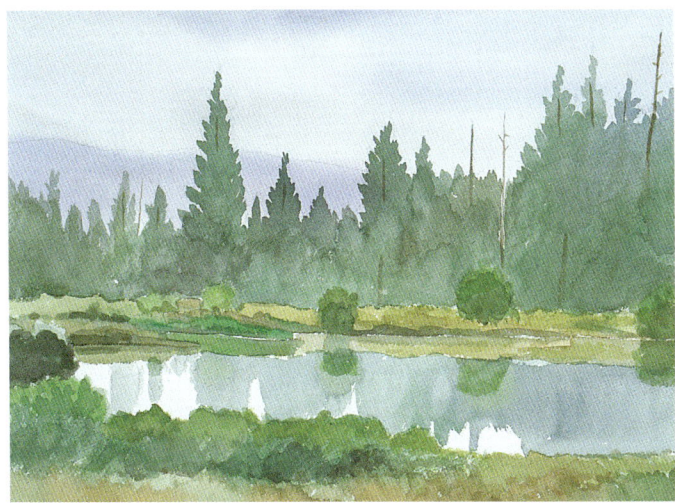

Problem: A "Wishy-Washy" Watercolor
Many beginners are afraid to commit to darker values. I tell my students to err on the side of strong value and color. Even if the value relationships and colors aren't perfect, you will still have a bold statement to build upon. This painting also shows the danger of using Burnt Umber as a main color in mixes—it tends to gray them out, leaving drab, lifeless colors.

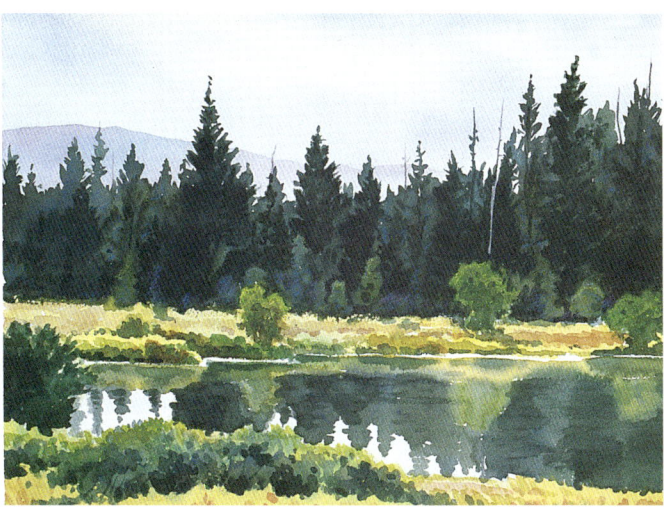

Solution: Create Contrast
Strong value contrasts and distinct color notes coming from the trees and grasses greatly improve this watercolor. The pines were painted with various mixes of Phthalo Blue, Alizarin Crimson, Emerald Green, Green Gold and a touch of Burnt Sienna; the grasses, with a mix of Aureolin, Rose Madder Genuine and Cobalt Blue. Touches of light blue and yellow colored pencil add color variety in the pines.

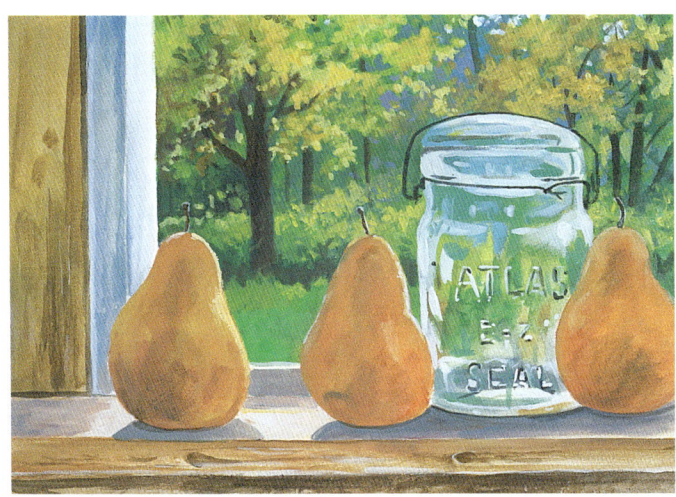

Problem: Value Monotony
The main problem in this acrylic painting is that there is a lack of emphasis since everything is calling for our attention. The pears, jar, window frame and background all read as separate middle-value objects that don't relate as a whole. This reduces the sense of light and of any spatial illusion. Also, too many loud color notes can actually defeat any clear sense of color and light.

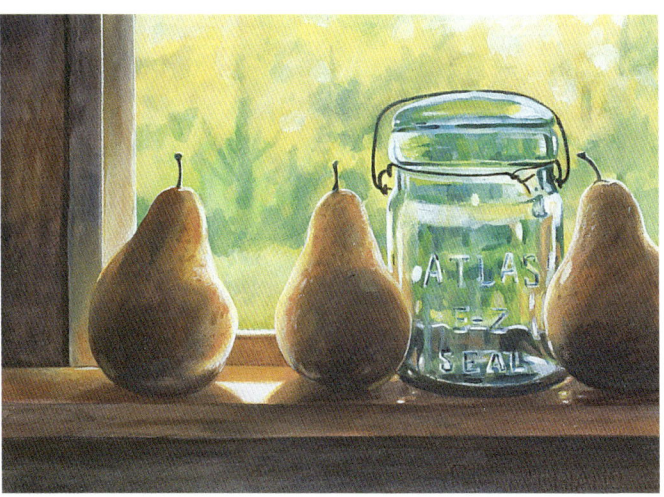

Solution: Create a Value Hierarchy
Joining the pears, jar and window frame into a large, dark shape contrasts well with the lighter, simplified background. The emphasis is now on this large shape, and it gives a sense of light and space. Because some of the color is neutralized and simplified, especially in the shadows and the window frame, the remaining colors are more vibrant and interesting.

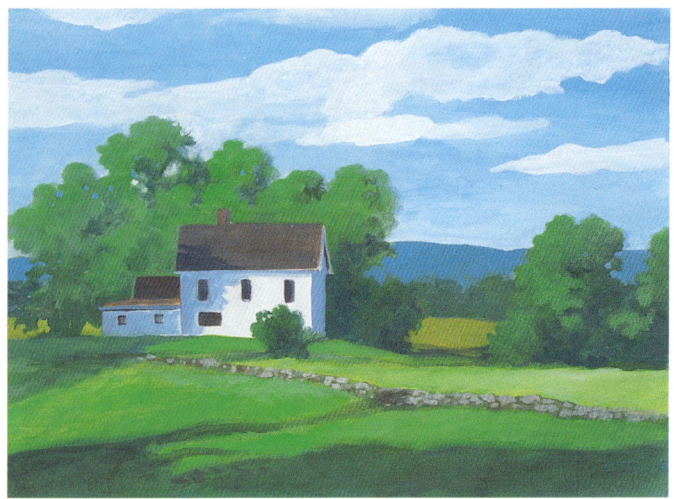

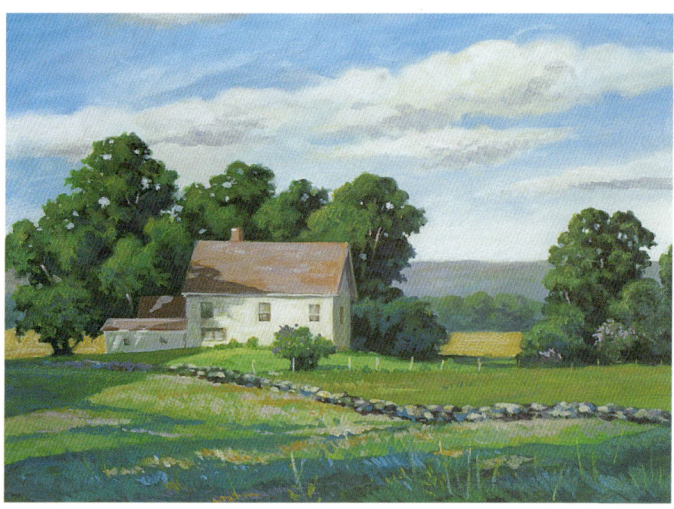

Problem: Too Much Local Color
Each object in this acrylic painting has been painted with a boring local color, which in turn created a series of poor value relationships. In watercolor, this problem often goes hand in hand with tentative value choices. Here the value range is fairly wide, but the relationships are harsh.

Solution: Create Better Value Relationships With Interesting Color
We can turn to the Impressionists for a solution to this value problem; their landscapes demonstrate how color can be used to create dynamic value relationships. They understood that light and atmosphere affect local color, and they played up these interesting changes.

There are many subtle but helpful value shifts created by using interesting color. Touches of blue and pink in the grass soften the value contrasts of the shadows. Also, warm colors have been added to the stark white of the clouds and the house. This slightly reduces their value contrast and increases our sense of sunlight hitting them.

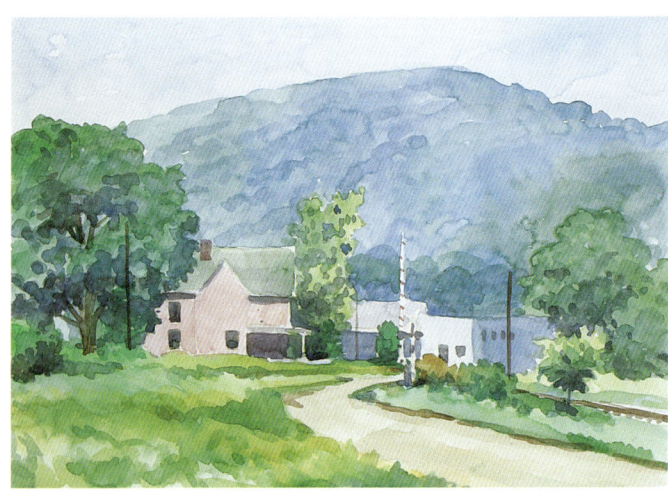

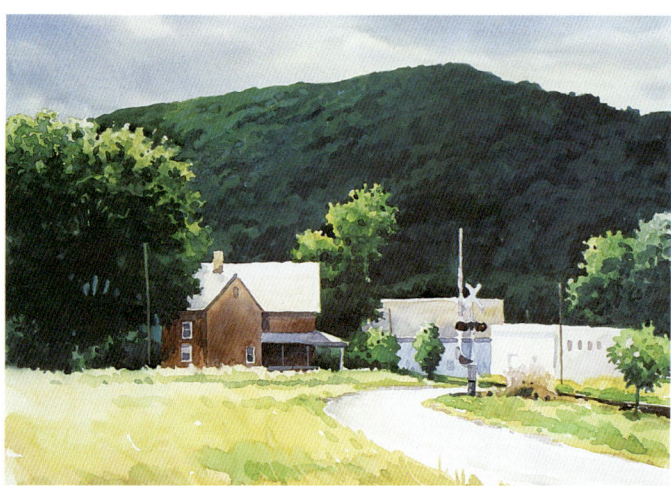

Problem: No Value Punch
In this watercolor painting, the color and values are not too bad. The problem is the lack of a strong visual statement. The overall value range is fairly wide, but the value relationships could be much more dramatic.

Solution: Increase the Drama
The large hill rising behind the building is quite imposing. Why not take this shape and this feeling of imposition and really play them up? A consolidation of values creates strong shapes and value contrasts. Increase or diminish the shapes and values of a scene as needed to strengthen the composition.

A limited palette holds unlimited benefits

Limited-palette studies are more involved than a rough value sketch but not as involved as a full-blown painting. The value sketch gets you thinking about the values and composition of your painting. The limited-palette study adds to this knowledge and helps you work out more problems.

When dealing with a complex subject, understanding the value structure can be quite difficult. Often we need to create paintings with subtle value shifts and just the right amount of value contrast to make things work. Since this subtlety is often difficult to achieve, it's helpful to render these values free of color concerns. This is also a good way to work out various value compositions with a little more detail than rough sketches provide. Another benefit is that it alerts us to issues we may not have anticipated.

My limited-palette studies are rarely larger than a quarter sheet (11" × 15" [28cm × 38cm]). I want to decide as much as possible about the value structure of my full-color painting, but I don't want to spend a huge amount of time on this rendering. I like to use Ultramarine Blue and Sepia watercolors for these studies. When mixed, these two colors have a wider value range than when they are used separately. Some artists prefer using other two-color combinations, or simply black. You may want to experiment with a few combinations. As an added benefit, it will increase your knowledge of the two colors that you choose.

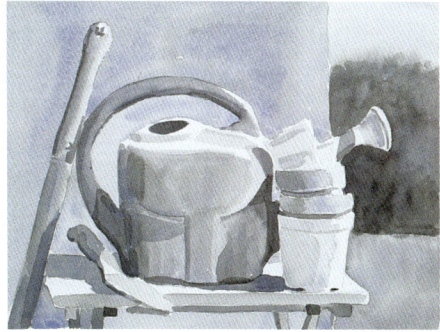
This value structure is the closest to what was happening in reality.

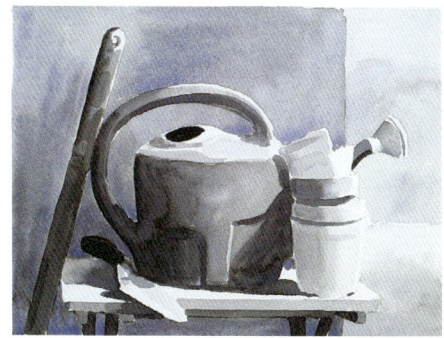
The value presence of the far-right background is diminished, and the value contrasts of everything else are deepened.

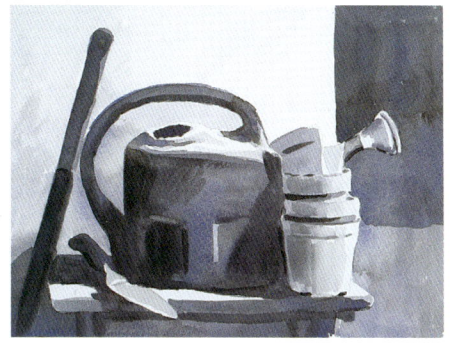
This version tries some interesting positive and negative shapes.

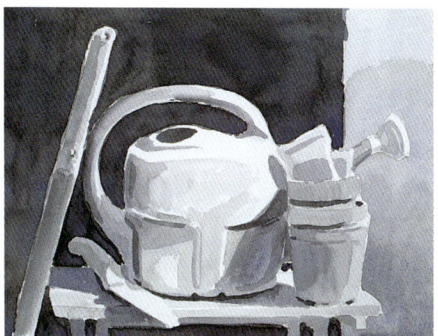
Same here, but the contrasts are reversed.

Value Options
The examples above show ways value can impact a composition. Do you have a preference?

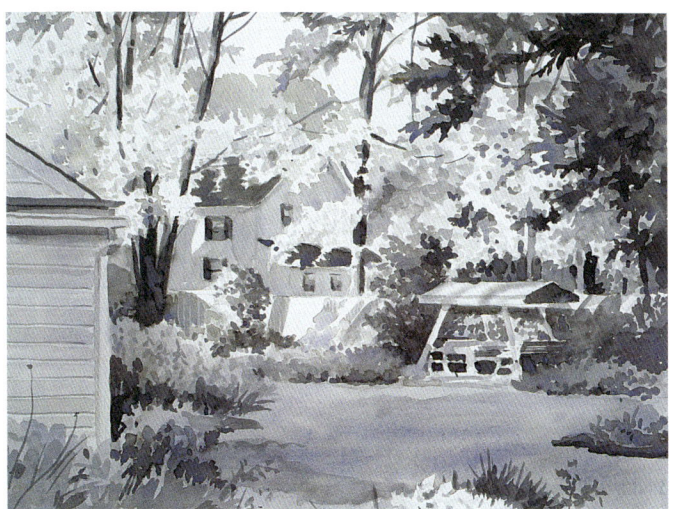

Value Plans Simplify Complex Scenes
The complexity of the late-afternoon light and shadow made this subject a prime candidate for a limited-palette painting. After completing this study I had a great deal more confidence about tackling the larger full-color version.

mini-demonstration » watercolor

Try a Limited-Palette Study

The complexity of this subject, a small stream, calls for a limited-palette study before tackling a full-color painting. As I completed this study, I realized that when doing the final painting I would need to spend extra time studying and drawing the reflections if I was to competently render them. Working out the values in a limited-palette version ahead of time allowed me to concentrate on painting the complex reflections later.

For this study we'll use Sepia and Ultramarine Blue.

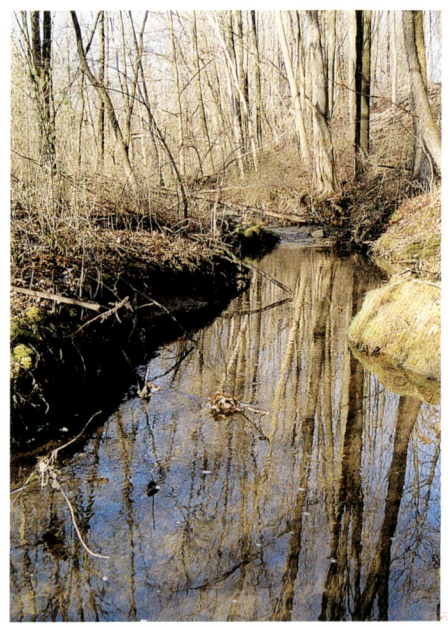

Reference Photo
The subject of this study is a small stream that runs behind my house and studio.

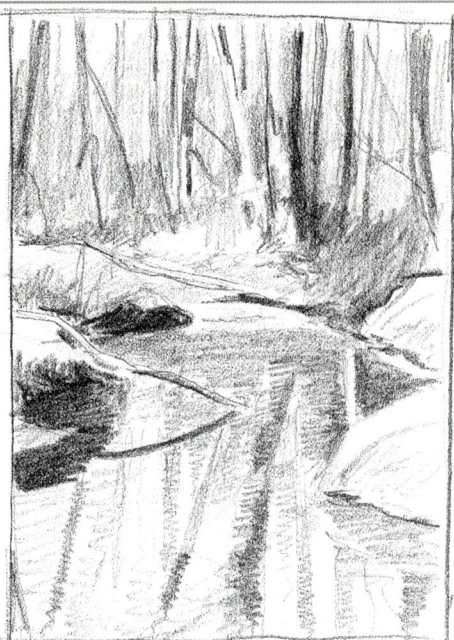

Value Sketch
The sketch establishes the composition and basic value structure.

1 Start With the Lightest Values
Using a mix of Ultramarine Blue and Sepia, wash in the lightest values over a simple pencil drawing and let it dry. In watercolor, always start light and end dark.

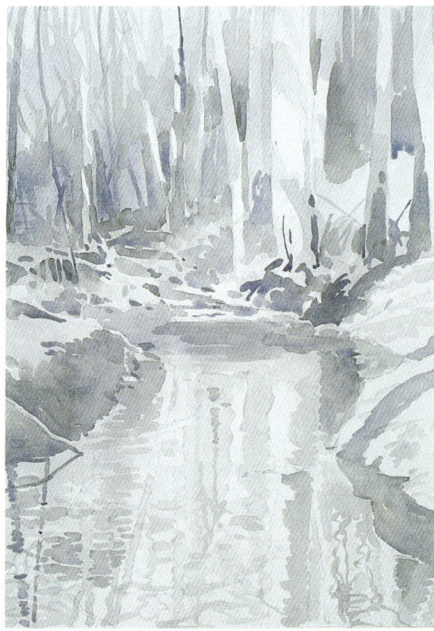

2 Add the Light Middle Values
During this step you can begin to structure the shapes within your composition. Let this dry.

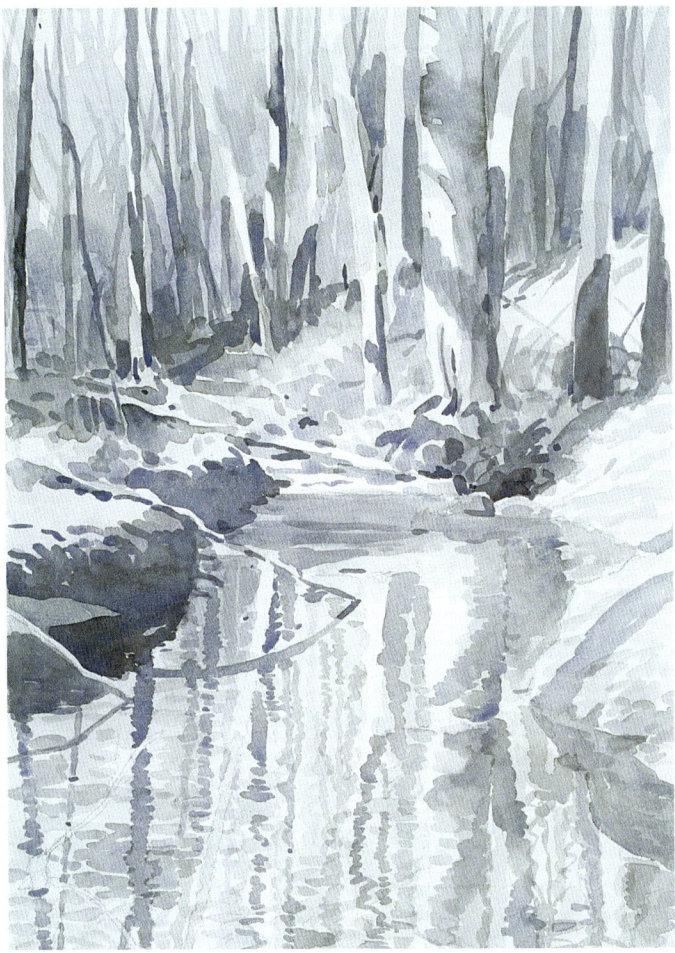

3 Add Darker Values
Add another wash to establish the middle and darker middle values. Make the background a bit darker to contrast against the shape of the hill. This sloping diagonal shape strengthens the composition.

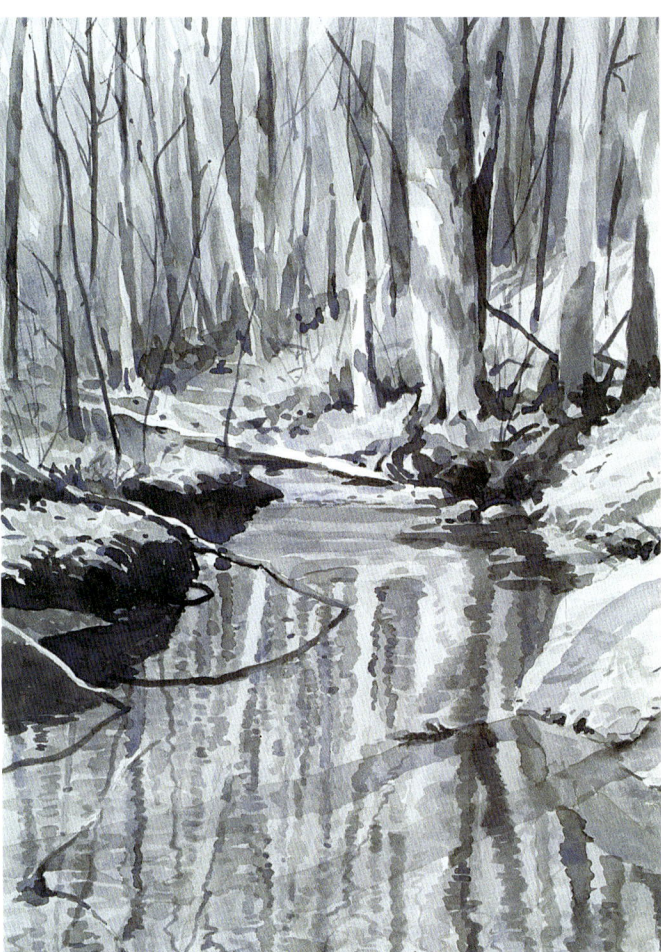

4 Finish With the Darkest Values
Add the darkest values and reinforce the shadow shapes. Because a reflection is darker than the object being reflected, the water and reflections need to be slightly darker than the woods, so apply a light wash over the entire stream. After this is dry, establish the darkest reflections.

achieving darks in watercolor

It's often tough to get those really rich, dark values in watercolor. Here are a few tips that should help:

- **Use fresh color out of the tube.** Place fresh color on your palette when you plan to create some rich color passages in your painting.

- **Mix more color than you think you'll need**. That puddle of color never goes as far as you think it will.

- **Use as large a brush as you can handle.** Bigger brushes mean more color with each brushstroke.

- **Be direct**. The fewer washes you put on your paper, the more vibrant your darks will be. Too many layers create dense color that may come across as dull and heavy.

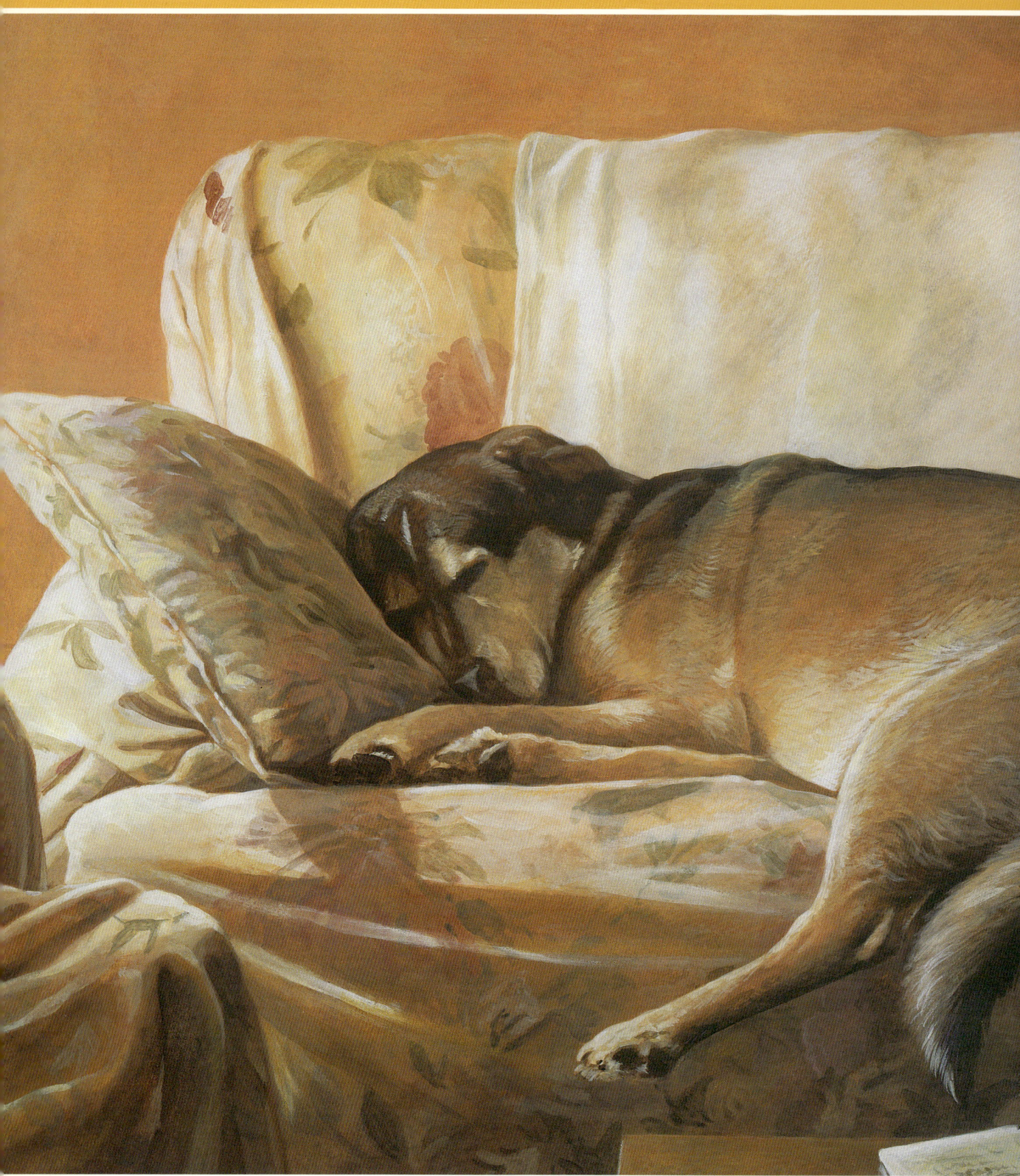

Sleeping Betty » Watercolor on 140-lb. (300gsm) cold-pressed paper » 11" x 16" (28cm x 41cm)

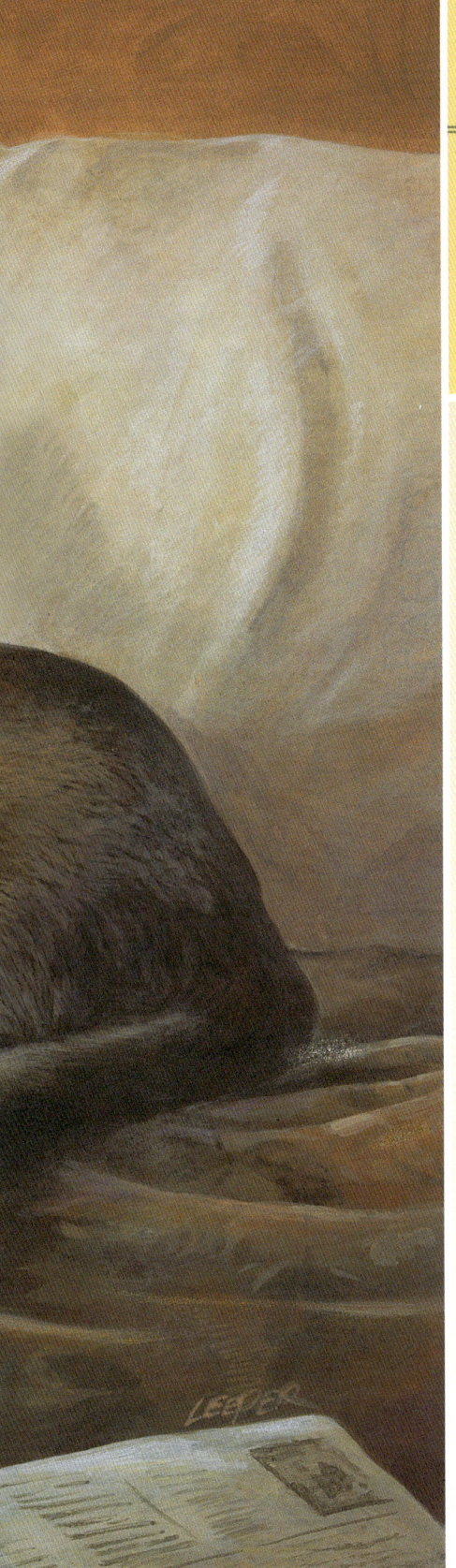

3 »
painting from life

There is no better way to gain an understanding of your subject than to paint it live—and, if working outdoors, en plein air. However, the wealth of visual information can sometimes be overwhelming. Successful paintings from life demand that we simplify the scene, edit the details and use techniques that let us record as much information as possible as quickly as possible. Whereas studio paintings can take several hours, days or even weeks to complete, on-location paintings are usually done in one sitting. This brevity makes them fun to do as well as refreshing to look at.

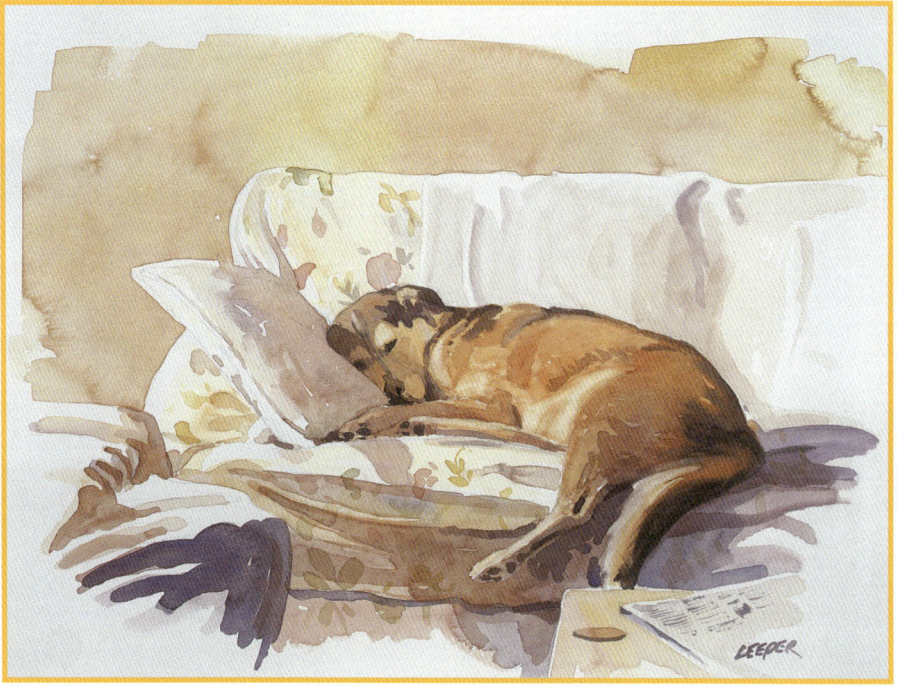

A Simple Beginning
Here is the first quick watercolor I painted of Betty before developing the scene further in the studio painting.

mini-demonstration » watercolor

Create a Symphony of Edges

Hot-pressed surfaces are ideal for working on-site. Washes dry quickly, so you can easily establish forms and shapes. Don't fight the edges; enjoy the myriad interesting patterns created by fast-drying washes.

I like intricate, almost chaotic scenes of nature. Swamps and marshes are among my favorite places to find such scenery. Since the light and shadow of this scene changed as I worked on the following painting, I tried to paint rapidly with smaller washes so that I wouldn't have to wait long for my paper to dry. This process left many wash edges that added to the unmistakable hot-pressed character of the piece. This painting, *Frog Pond*, took about an hour and a half to complete.

materials

paper
140-lb. (300gsm) hot-pressed paper, 11" x 15" (28cm x 38cm)

watercolors
Alizarin Crimson • Aureolin • Burnt Sienna • Burnt Umber • Cobalt Blue • Emerald Green • New Gamboge • Phthalo Blue • Quinacridone Gold • Ultramarine Blue • Winsor Red • Winsor Yellow

brushes
Nos. 12, 6 and 4 rounds

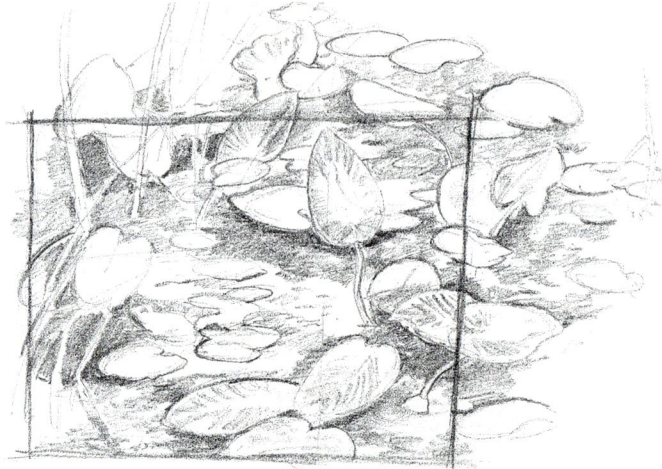

Find a Composition
Dealing with a multitude of shapes and forms can be overwhelming. A rough sketch allows you to clearly define your composition.

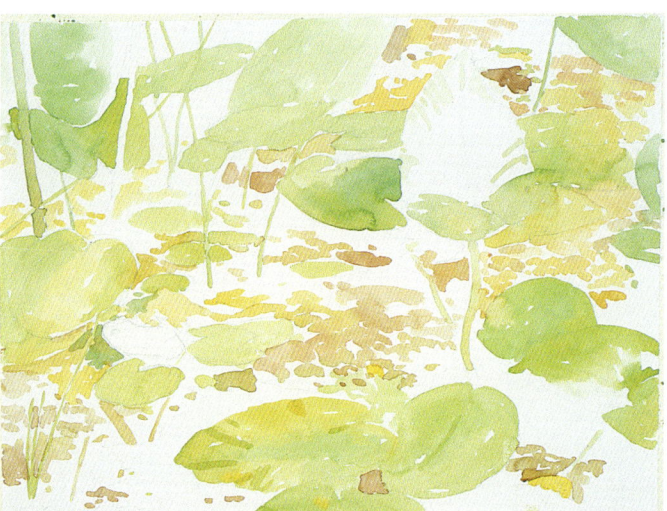

1 Wash In Warm Local Colors
Establish your main shapes with warm washes of local color. Warm colors will shine through the cool washes applied later and help give a sense of sunbathed foliage. Paint the lime green areas with a mix of Quinacridone Gold, Aureolin and a little Phthalo Blue. The tan color was put in with a mixture of Quinacridone Gold, Burnt Sienna and Cobalt Blue.

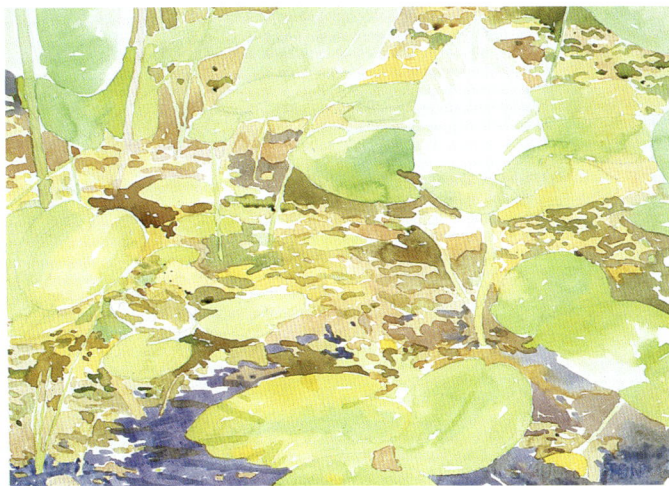

2 Create Textures
Using a smaller brush than you would normally use for such a large area, put down dozens of interconnecting marks to begin forming the underwater weed bed. (Using a smaller brush also makes it easier to paint around the lily pads and grasses.) When painting such textures, load the brush with color, use a light touch and avoid overbrushing. Use variegated washes of Alizarin Crimson and Ultramarine Blue as well as a mixture of Burnt Sienna, Quinacridone Gold and Phthalo Blue.

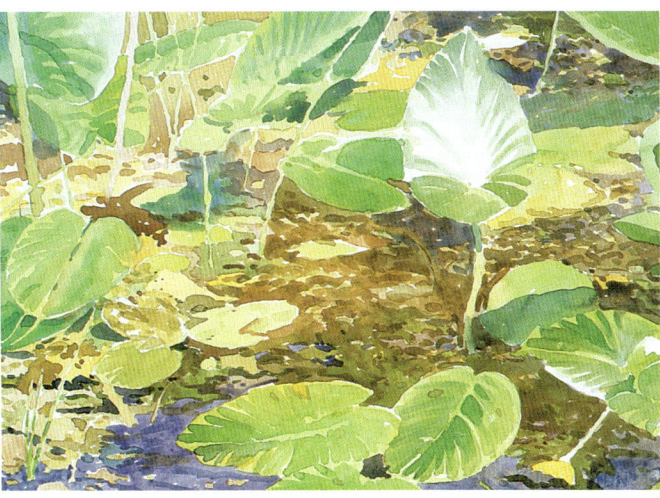

3 Build Value and Color
Use transparent washes to increase value contrast, deepen color and create more textures. Paint the deeper greens with mixes of Winsor Yellow, Phthalo Blue and Emerald Green. Create the browns and rust colors of the weed bed with mixes of New Gamboge, Quinacridone Gold, Burnt Sienna and Alizarin Crimson. With the light changing and the shadows moving, wash in shadow color with mixes of Alizarin Crimson and Cobalt Blue.

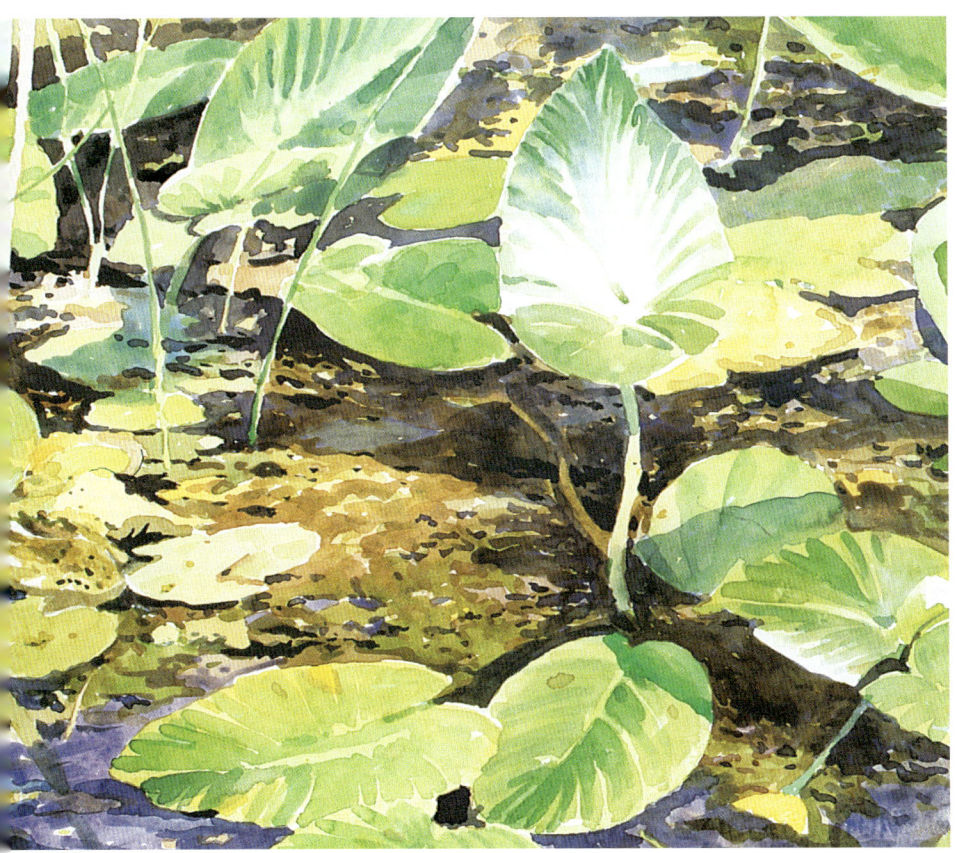

4 Add Darkest Values to Create Exciting Contrasts
Using intense but relatively transparent mixes of Phthalo Blue, Winsor Red and Burnt Umber, establish the darkest shadow values. These washes push forward the lighter value lily pads and give the painting a crisp sense of light.

mini-demonstration » watercolor

Practice Addition by Subtraction

Gessoed paper allows color to be lifted easily and is a perfect surface for rendering textures like the rocks in this painting. The only disadvantage to working on a gessoed surface in the field is that the paint lays on the surface and takes a bit longer to dry. If you are trying to capture a changing lighting effect, this could be a problem.

When I began sketching this scene, the weather was hazy, but there was no fog. Within minutes the fog rolled in from the ocean and hung in thick layers above the water and tree line. This painting, *Valley Cove, Maine*, took about an hour to complete.

applying gesso to your paper

Gesso can be applied easily with a large bristle brush, foam brush or roller. Create a half-and-half mix of acrylic gesso and water and apply two to three coats. Make sure each coat dries between applications. Your paper will buckle during the process, so staple or tape it down.

materials

paper
Gessoed 140-lb. (300gsm) cold-pressed, 11" x 15" (28cm x 38cm)

watercolors
Burnt Sienna • Burnt Umber • Cobalt Blue • Emerald Green • New Gamboge • Phthalo Blue • Quinacridone Violet • Ultramarine Blue • Winsor Red • Yellow Ochre

brushes
Nos. 10, 8, 6 and 4 round
Stiff bristle brush

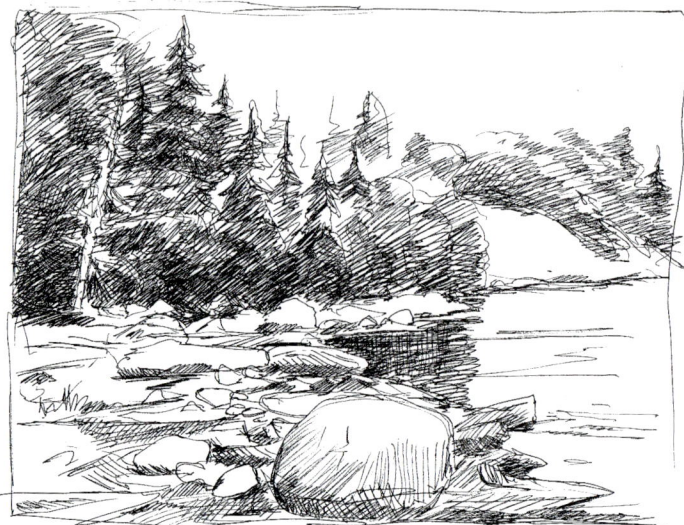

Preliminary Sketch
Try using an ink pen for sketching. It will allow you to quickly establish the values in your composition.

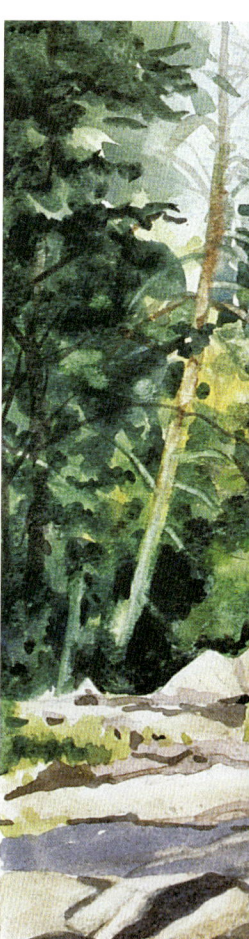

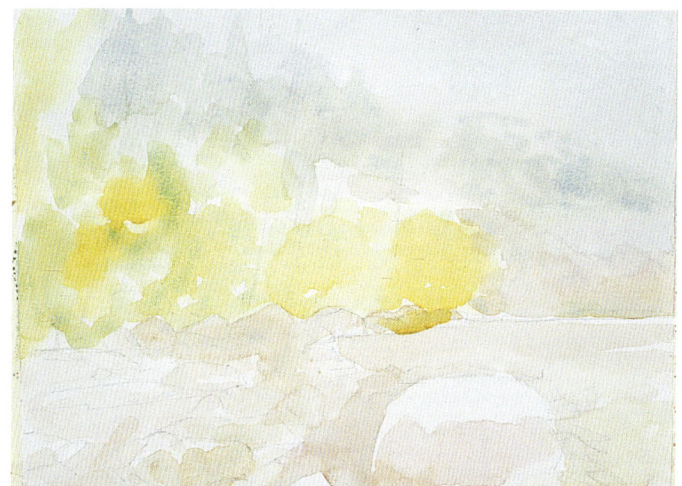

1 Lay Down the First Washes
Lightly draw the composition on your paper. Since the fog obscures much of the background trees, lay down a simple wet-into-wet wash to establish the distant hill. Use a variegated mix of Cobalt Blue, Ultramarine Blue, Burnt Sienna and a bit of Yellow Ochre for this wash. With warm washes of yellow (New Gamboge, Yellow Ochre and Emerald Green) and pink (Winsor Red, Burnt Sienna and Yellow Ochre), establish the base tones of the trees and rocks.

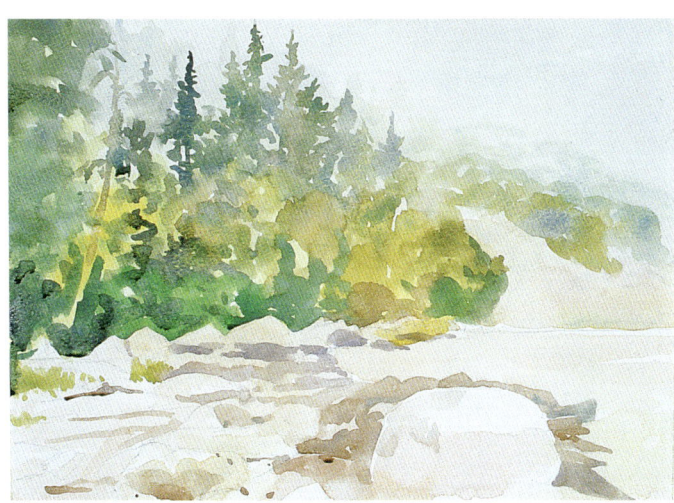

2 Further Define the Tree and Rock Shapes
Create a nice gray-green with mixes of Ultramarine Blue and New Gamboge to paint the darker trees. Paint the truer green trees on the far left with mixes of Emerald Green, Phthalo Blue and Burnt Sienna. Using variegated washes of Winsor Red, Burnt Sienna, Yellow Ochre and Cobalt Blue, further develop the rock shapes.

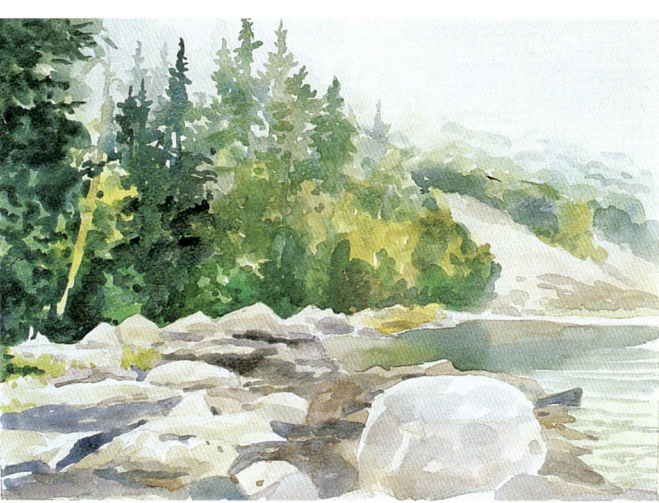

3 Deepen Values and Establish Textures
Wash in darker values and establish textures in the trees and rocks. Paint the darker colors in the trees with variegated washes of Phthalo Blue, Burnt Sienna and Burnt Umber. Paint the darker rocks with variegated washes of Cobalt Blue, Quinacridone Violet and Burnt Sienna.

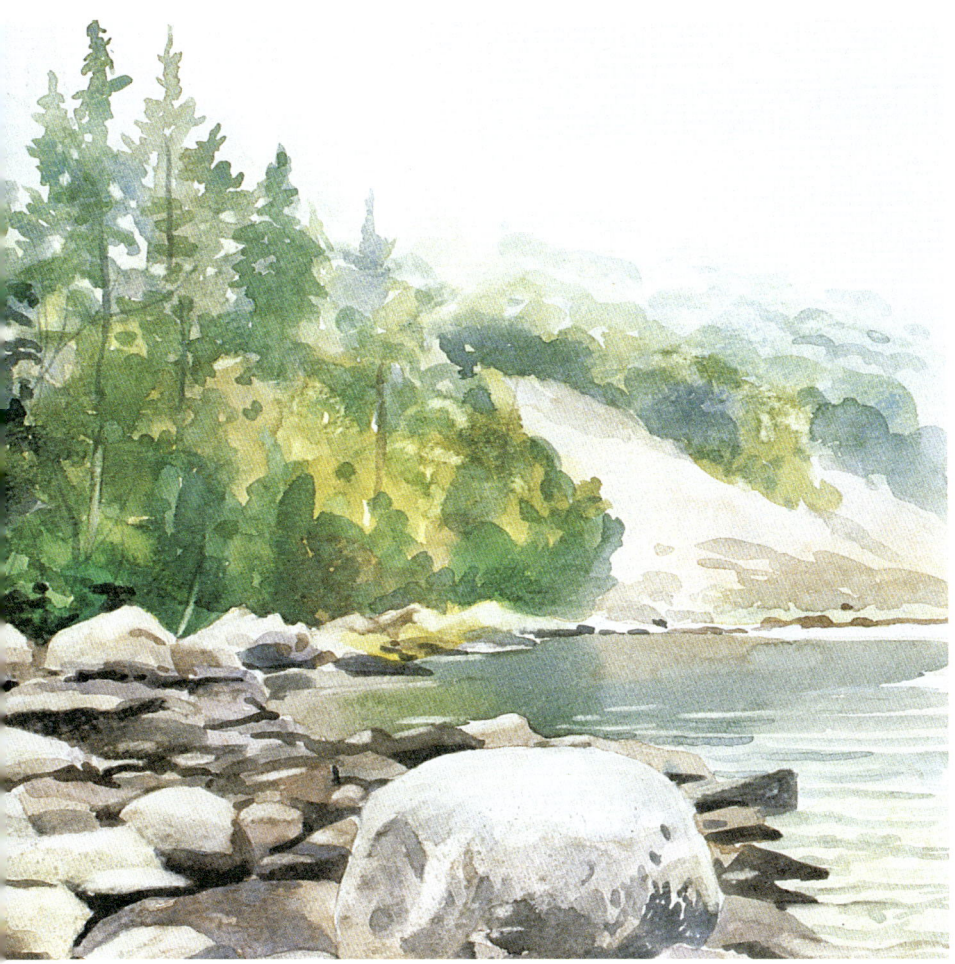

4 Add Deeper Values and Lift Color
Lifting color is the unique and fun part of painting on gessoed paper. However, before lifting color from the rocks, put in the darkest shadow values with mixes of Ultramarine Blue and Burnt Umber, and layer more washes of the blue-violet-sienna mix from the previous step. Spatter some of this mixture onto the rocks to give them additional texture.

Once these washes are dry, use a damp brush to lift color and create the lightest values. Any brush will work, but a stiff bristle brush is really effective. You can also lift some of the wet color with a paper towel to get down to the white paper. Last, lift some tree trunk forms in the background.

mini-demonstration » acrylics and colored pencil

Create a Bold Impression on Location

Try acrylics for bold and lively plein air paintings. The combination of transparent and opaque color gives you versatility in rendering textures and values. Colored pencils are easy to carry and allow you to add final touches quickly.

This painting was done on an unseasonably warm February day. The recent snowmelt created a muddy and puddle-filled farm road.

materials

paper
140-lb. (300gsm) cold-pressed, 15" x 22" (38cm x 56cm)

acrylics
Brilliant Blue • Burnt Sienna • Burnt Umber • Cadmium Yellow Medium • Dioxazine Purple • Indo Orange Red • Naphthol Crimson • Titanium White • Ultramarine Blue • Yellow Ochre • Yellow Orange Azo

colored pencils
Orange

brushes
No. 8 round
¾-inch (19mm) flat
Sable rigger

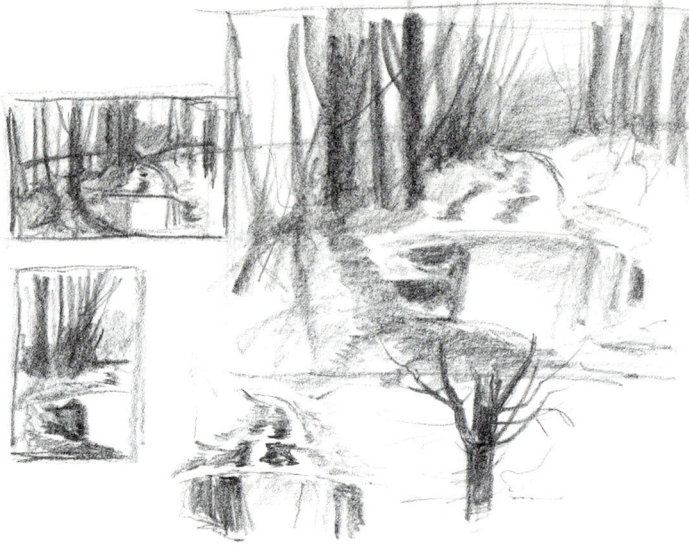

Try Soft Leads for Quick Sketches
A 6B or 8B pencil can help you quickly establish value patterns and composition ideas.

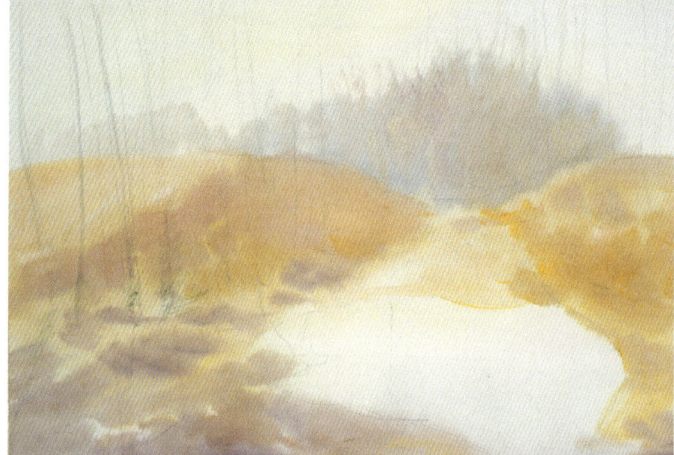

1 Start With Bold Wet-into-Wet Washes
Since there would be applications of transparent and opaque color, this drawing was done quickly and made darker than you might do for a traditional watercolor. After making your drawing, use warm wet-into-wet washes of Yellow Orange Azo, Cadmium Yellow Medium and Burnt Sienna to establish the large forms. Lay in the background trees and foreground with mixes of Ultramarine Blue, Brilliant Blue, Naphthol Crimson and Burnt Sienna.

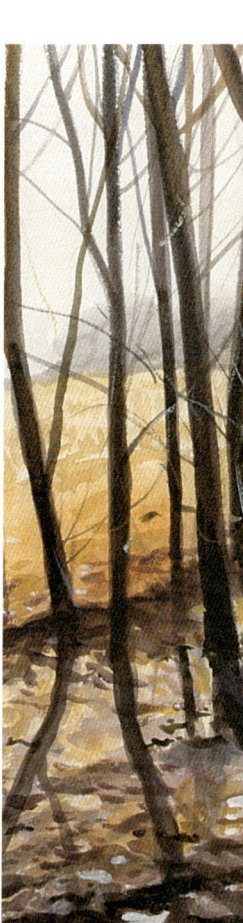

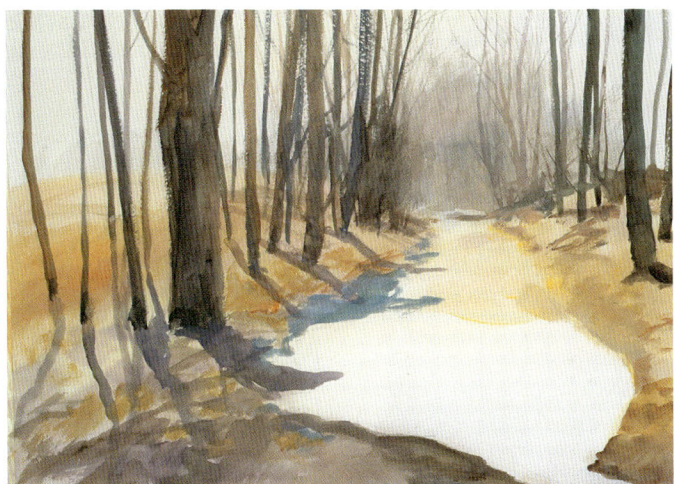

2 Establish Bold Tree Forms and Darker Values

Use a thin mix (equal parts water and paint) of Ultramarine Blue and Burnt Umber with a bit of Naphthol Crimson to create the dark tree color. Wash in background trees with a transparent mix of Brilliant Blue and Naphthol Crimson. Paint the foreground with the same dark tree mix, but with Dioxazine Purple added and Burnt Umber used sparingly. Add a bit of Brilliant Blue and Titanium White along the road for more color variety.

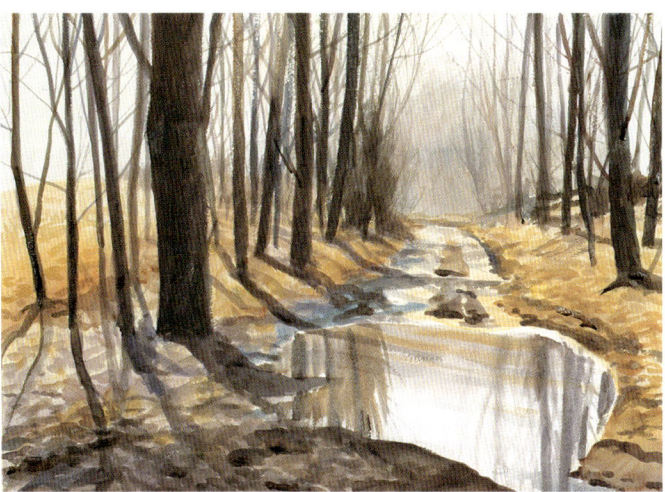

3 Establish Textures

Brush on the ground clutter and road textures with transparent color. Wet the puddle area with clean water and paint the reflections wet into wet, using the same colors that you used for the background and trees. Deepen the value of the darker trees and add more limbs. Paint the ground shadows with a transparent mix of Ultramarine Blue, Dioxazine Purple and a bit of Burnt Umber to gray the colors slightly. Establish leaf textures on the ground with transparent washes of Indo Orange Red, Yellow Ochre and Burnt Sienna. Use opaque Titanium White around the edge of the puddle and on the road to add some reflective texture.

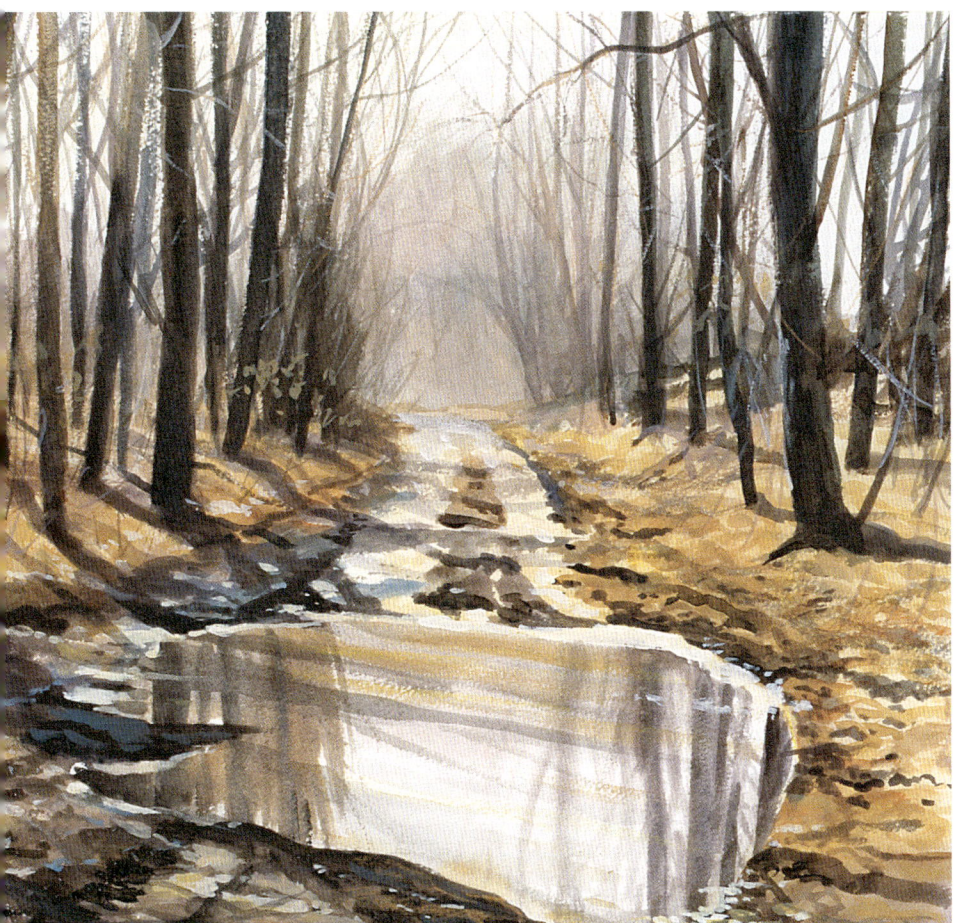

4 Establish the Darkest Values and Opaque Textures

The richest colors and values will make everything pop. Use a mix of Burnt Umber and Ultramarine Blue for the darkest markings on the road and in the woods. Wash over the shadows one more time to establish their final shapes and values. Use the same mix for shadows across the puddle. Drag and dab an opaque mix of Brilliant Blue, Ultramarine Blue and Titanium White across some of the darkest shadow areas. Do the same with an opaque mix of Yellow Ochre and Titanium White, and use the same mix to create more tree limbs and branches.

Add textures in the road and trees with an Orange colored pencil. This final bit of color adds variety in a rather limited-palette painting.

From plein air to the studio

Plein air paintings can be wonderful fresh statements that stand on their own, or they can act as visual road maps for studio paintings. Besides fully realized paintings we can create rough composition sketches, field sketches, nature studies and value-study paintings. All of these can add to one's understanding of the subject. Plein air work can be your sole source of information for studio paintings, or it can be supplemented with reference photos.

Combine Text and Visuals

Sometimes it isn't always convenient to paint en plein air. In these cases, spend time critically observing your subject and making a few sketches with written notes. I like to imagine that I am an early explorer documenting my subject for the first time. Make notes about colors, shapes, forms and actions or anything that will help you back in the studio. The more you know about your subject, the more you can edit or amplify in the studio.

Make a Nature Study

Nature studies are more-involved sketches or paintings concerned not with composition or design but only with the physical presence of the subject—its textures, colors and details. The value of a nature study is the wealth of information you learn about your subject while doing a detailed rendering. Look at the work of the nineteenth-century pre-Raphaelites for some beautiful and engaging studies.

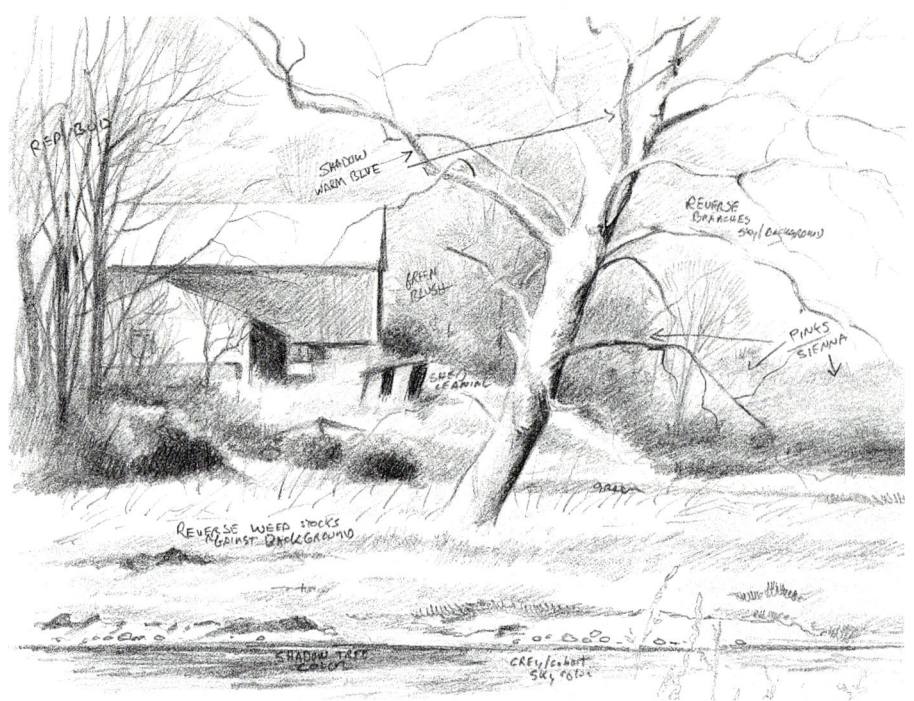

Observe and Take Notes

This is an example of a sketch with notes about colors, shapes and values. Combining visual and written observations allows you to recall much more when painting the subject in the studio.

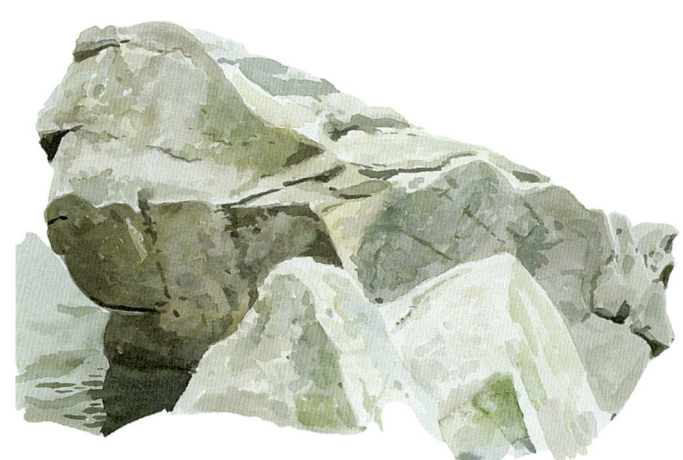

Study and Render Nature's Details

In these small watercolor studies of pink granite and a trout lily there is no concern for composition; the only goal is to describe the physical nature of each subject.

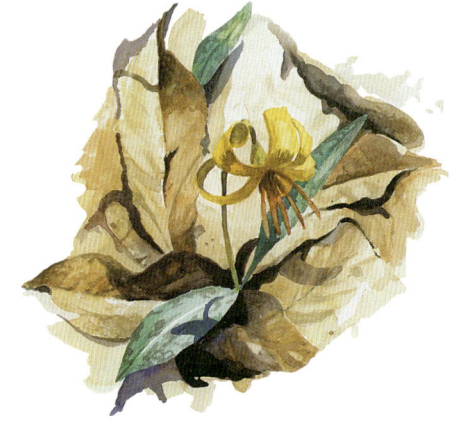

Map Out Your Values

Before you begin a full-color painting, create a couple value studies of the scene. These don't have to be complex but should convey the general sense of shape and form that you will be rendering. They can also be used to quickly explore various compositions before starting your larger painting. Try rendering them in watercolor, ink or pencil.

Get the Most Out of Your Subject

A quick way to work through ideas is to make several thumbnail sketches. If you have time, create a couple paintings on the spot. The additional time spent with the subject will impart more information as well as inspire additional paintings. I have started one painting and ended up making four or five because each additional composition shows new possibilities and ideas.

Put It Together in the Studio

When you begin your studio painting, spread all your reference material out in front of you and try to identify what sparked your interest. It may have been interesting shapes or forms, a certain lighting effect or maybe just the look of the subject. This is what you should emphasize as you create your larger work. Use your photos for specific information about details, but lean on your plein air paintings and studies for the overall sense of design and mood.

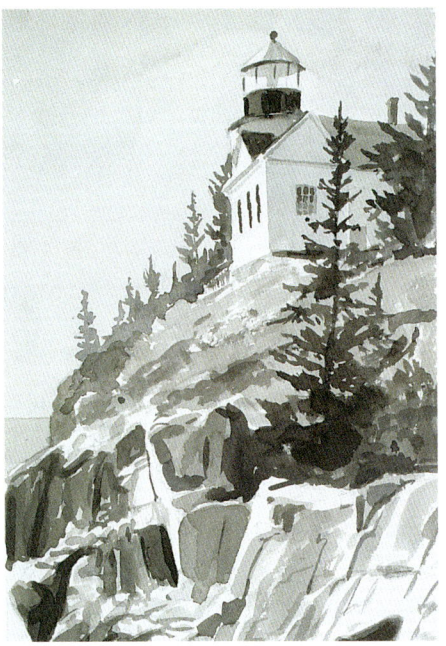

Make Value Studies in the Field

Value studies can assist you in understanding the value construction and composition of your subject. This value study was completed in watercolor.

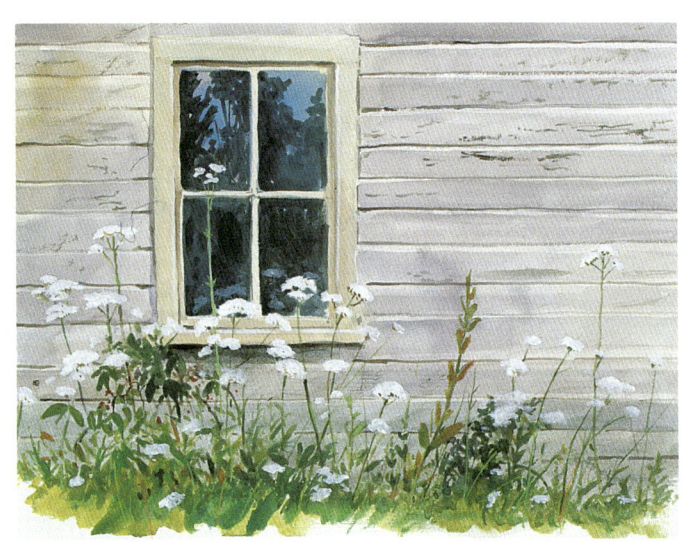

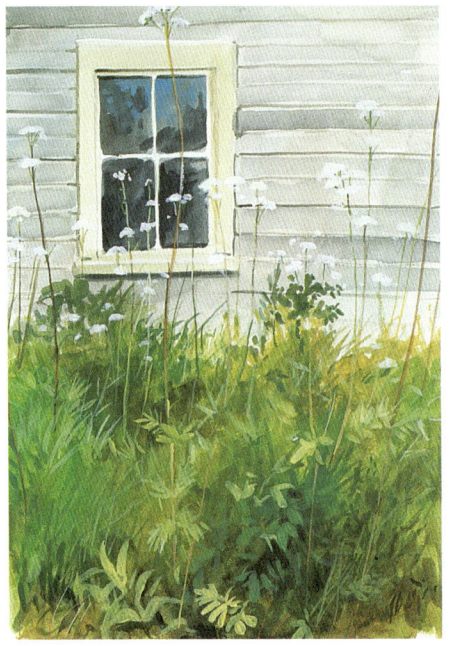

Think Ahead: Alternative Compositions

Consider all the compositional possibilities when you approach a subject in the field. I edited some of the tall flower stalks in the first painting so the emphasis was on the building. The second painting, besides having a vertical composition, emphasizes the tall stalks. I really liked the vertical line rhythm of these tall flowers. These acrylic studies were completed on cold-pressed paper.

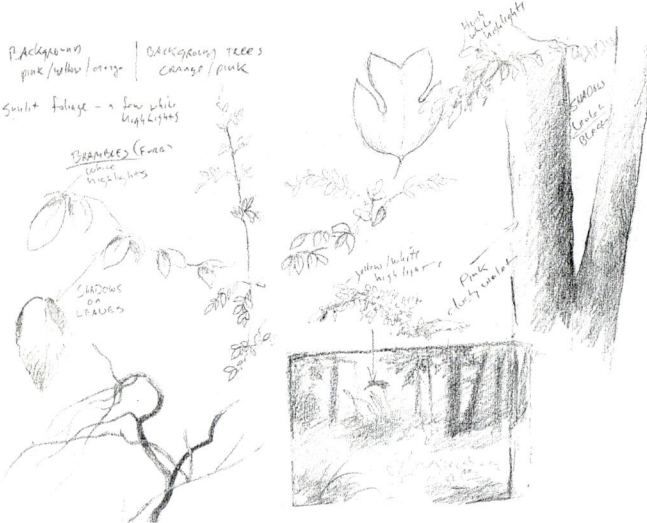
Pencil Study

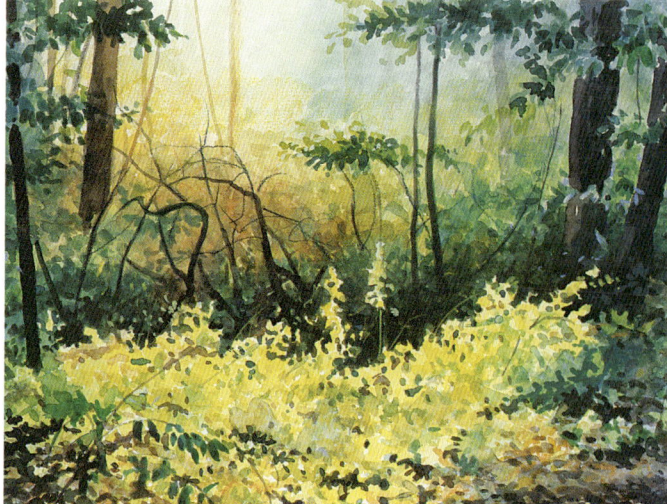
Watercolor Study

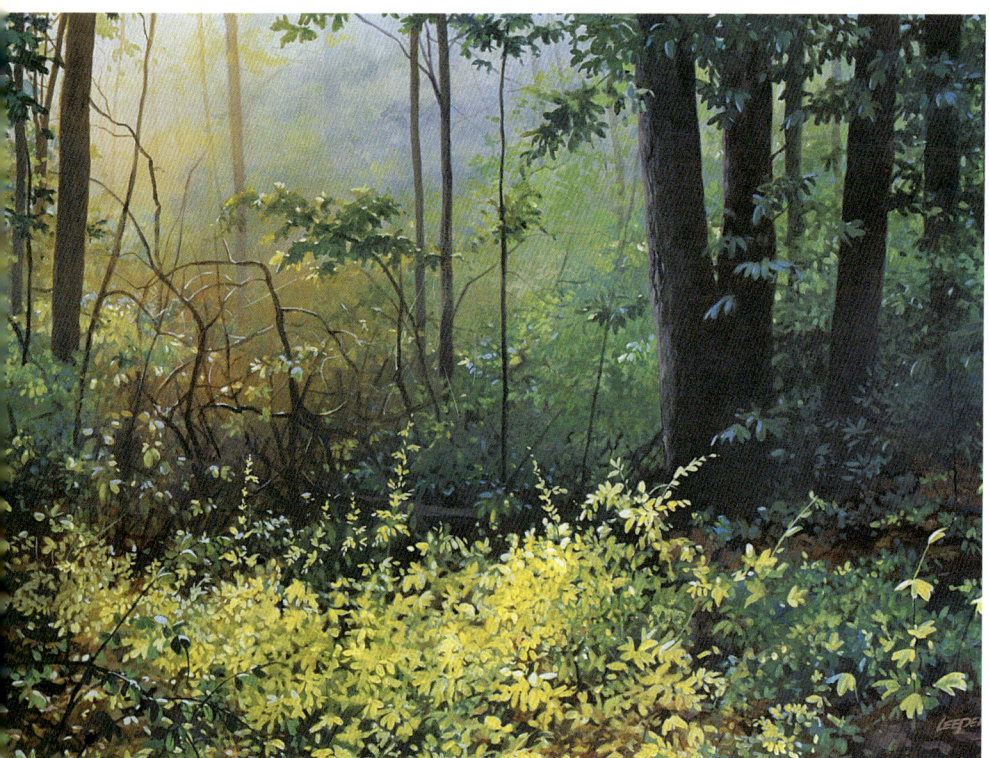

Carry Your Inspiration Back to the Studio
You can combine sketches, studies, plein air paintings and photos to create your larger and/or more finished studio paintings. *Woodland Sunset* was created from the small watercolor and from sketches made on location. The watercolor study also includes some colored pencil.

Woodland Sunset » Acrylic on 140-lb. (300gsm) cold-pressed paper » 20" x 30" (51cm x 76cm)

prepare for mother nature

Here are some tips for painting in the great outdoors.

- **Carry rain gear if straying far from shelter.** Don't get stuck unprepared in a downpour!

- **Bring sunscreen and bug repellent.** Insects seem to be big art lovers.

- **Never paint with the sun shining directly on your paper.** It's harder to judge the correct values, and the glare is brutal on the eyes.

- **Secure your setup on windy days.** A slight gust of wind can blow easels down and scatter paper and materials.

- **Leave with what you brought.** That includes your dirty water.

- **Be aware that the humidity in the air will affect your work.** High humidity causes washes to dry slowly, and very hot and dry conditions will make them dry almost instantly.

Be prepared for a surprise subject

Sometimes a great subject will sneak up on you. As you head to your intended painting location, keep an eye open for new and sometimes even better subjects.

This is an example of an unintended subject. I was walking back to my car after painting along a beautiful stream in Pennsylvania when I noticed this field edge. I liked the way the sun was backlighting the field. I did a quick watercolor on a block of cold-pressed paper and then a pencil sketch on the same paper. I also photographed the scene.

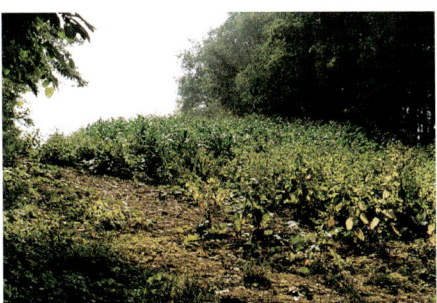
On-Location Photo

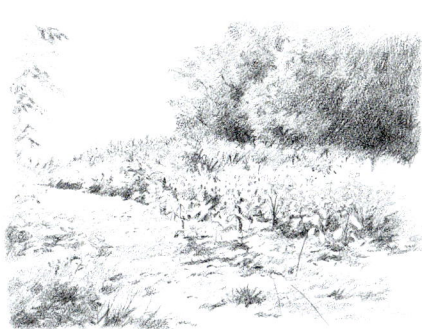
Pencil Sketch

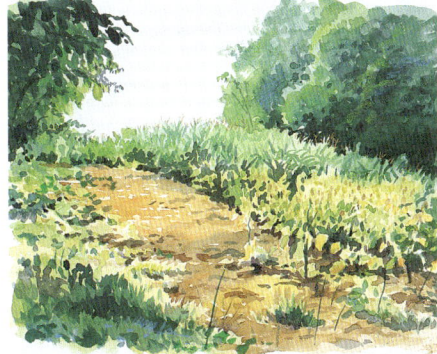
Watercolor Study

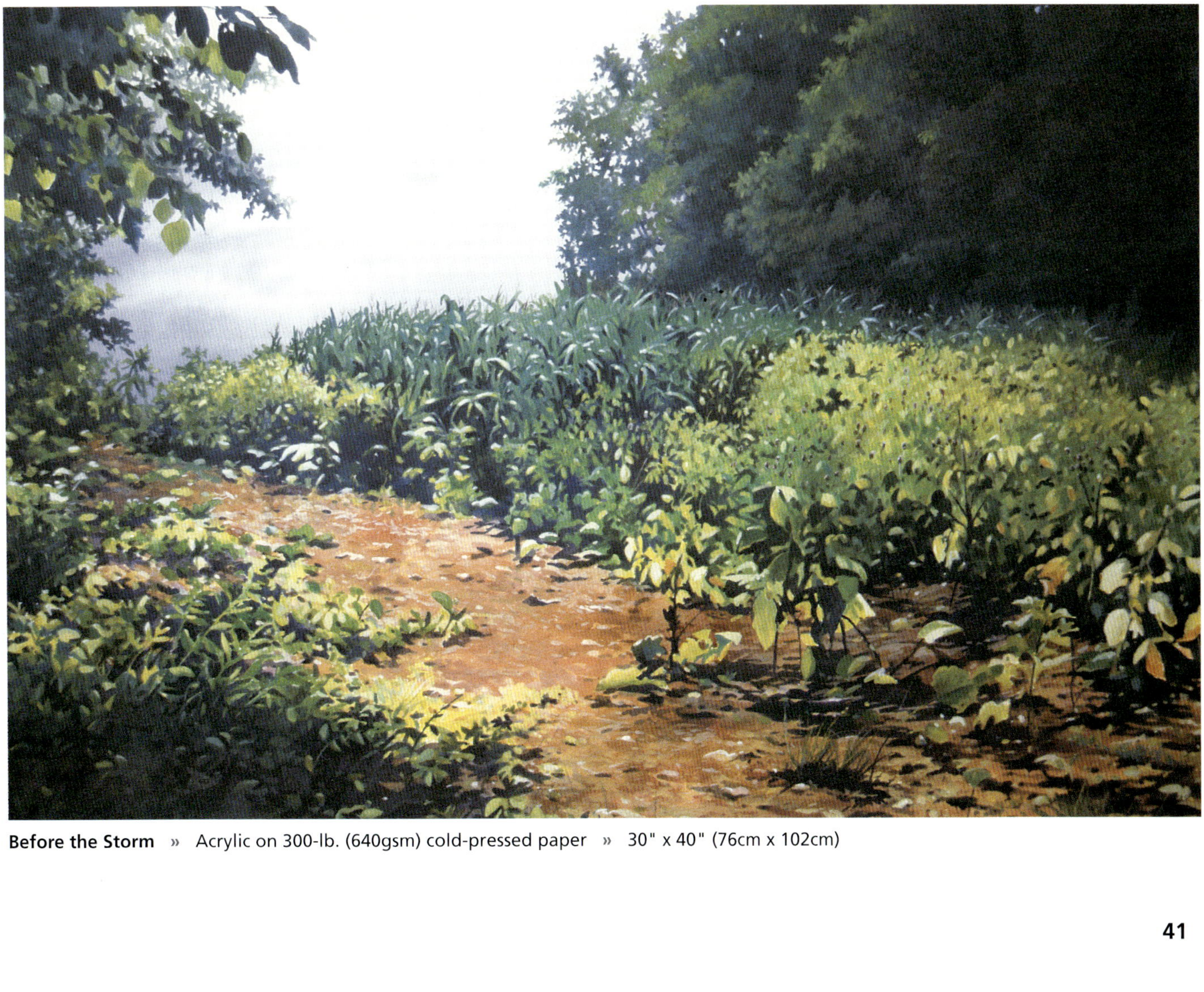

Before the Storm » Acrylic on 300-lb. (640gsm) cold-pressed paper » 30" x 40" (76cm x 102cm)

Back in the studio: enliven watercolors with acrylics

When we paint on location, we are vulnerable to the whims of Mother Nature as well as our own busy schedules. As a result, sometimes our plein air watercolors might not meet our painting goals. You can chalk it up as experience and toss the paintings on the shelf, or you can try to give them new life by adding acrylics. You can use acrylics to accent a watercolor that needs an extra touch, or you can totally rework a painting with a more-opaque application of color.

when should I add acrylics?

Base your painting's need for acrylics on how close you came to achieving your goal. There was something about the subject that inspired your painting. Think about what is needed to fulfill your vision. Usually it's the values, colors or textures that need adjustment. Or it might need just a few opaque touches to solidify a shape or form. The last reason to add acrylics might be a desire to produce a more concise, detailed image. Adding acrylics allows you to do this without making the painting look overworked.

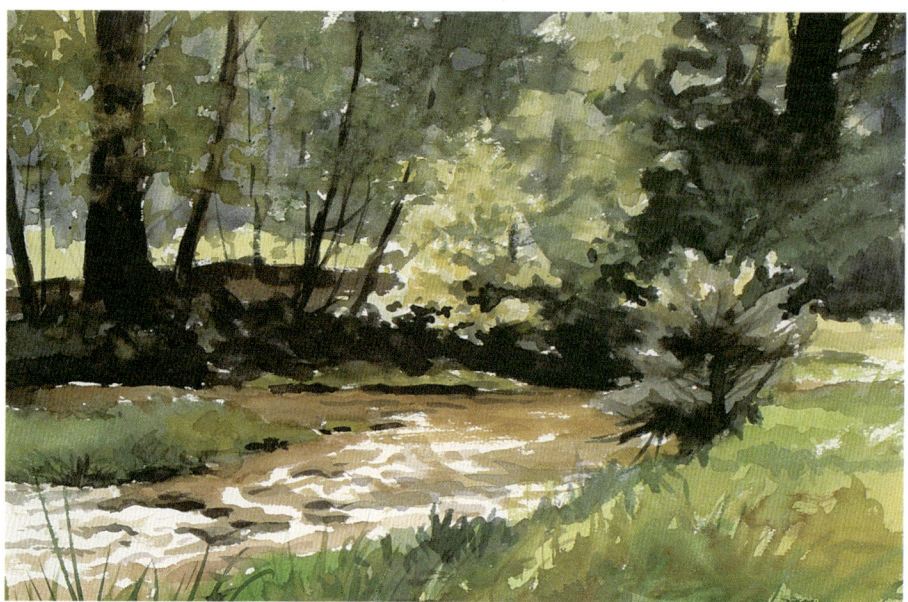

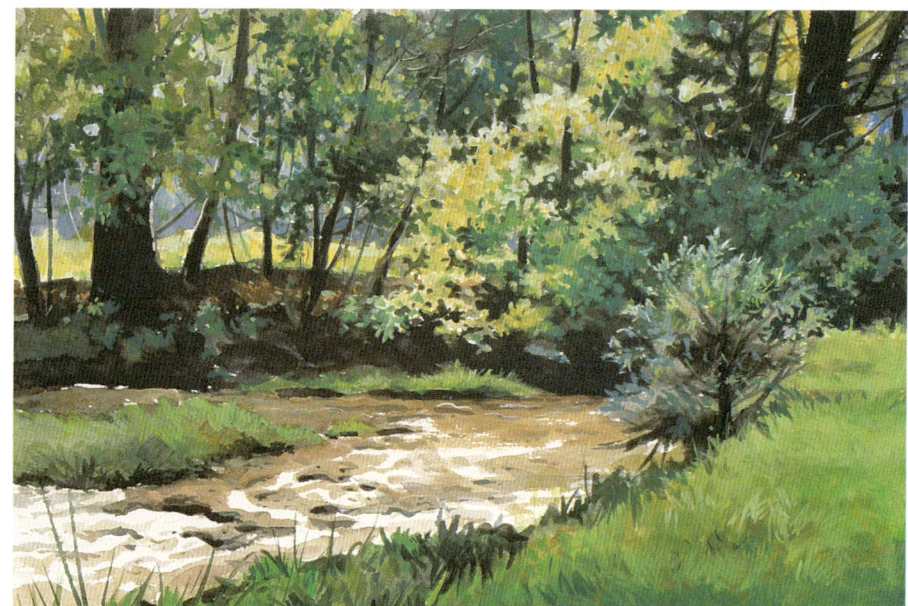

Energize Your Colors

Sometimes you may not capture the color as vividly as you see it. Adding acrylics gives you the opportunity to capture and even play up the colors in your plein air painting. Because of a brewing storm I quickly rendered this rain-swollen stream and created a painting that was a bit lacking in color. I made many changes back in the studio. The sunlit foliage became lighter and more colorful, violets and blues were added into the background, and the grasses were enriched.

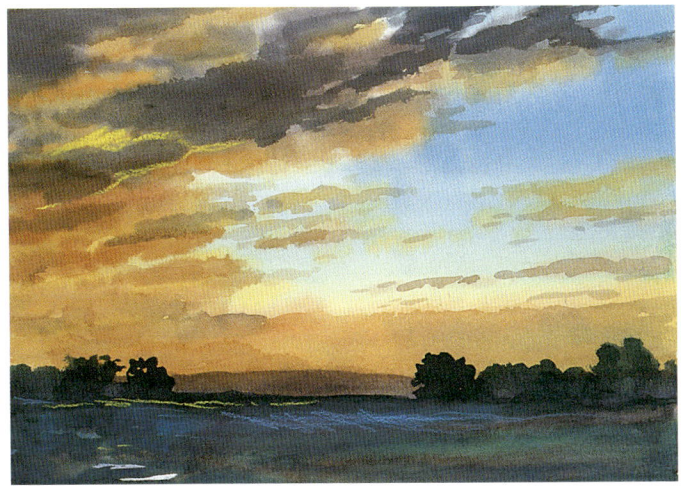
Plein air painting

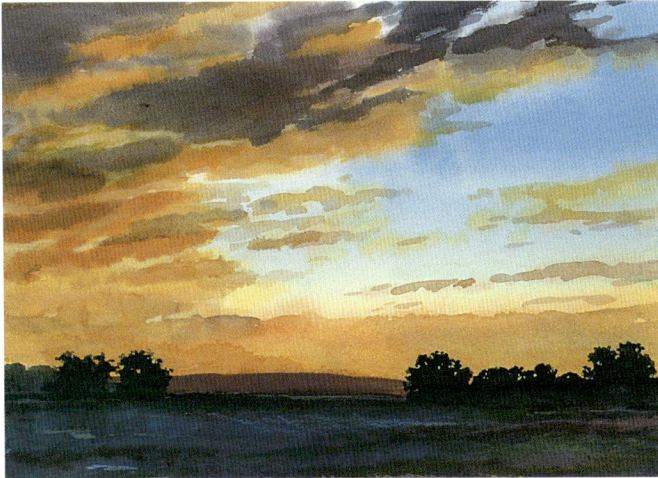
Revised painting

Add Accents
Often a few opaque touches or washes of acrylic will improve a painting's value and/or color scheme. This study already had some pastel marks to add color. I solidified these marks and the darker values in the tree line and field by washing over them with transparent layers of Dioxazine Purple and Phthalo Blue.

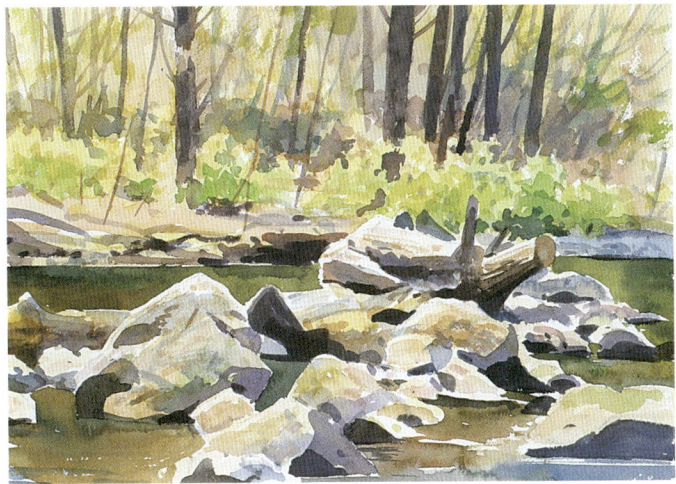
Plein air painting

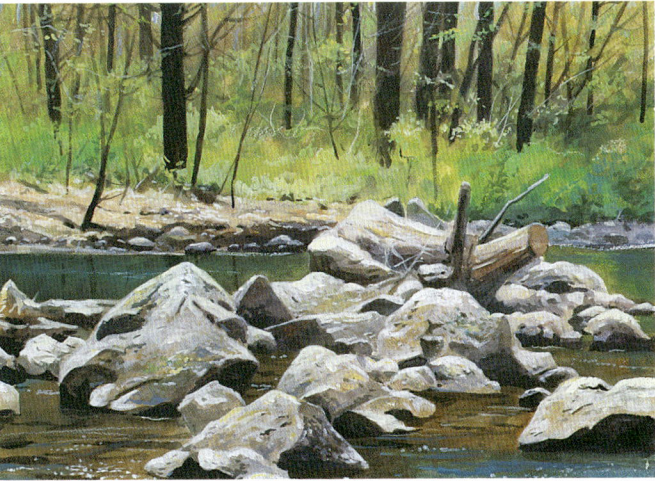
Revised painting

Make Wholesale Changes
Sometimes a painting just completely misses the mark. That's when you can approach it with a devil-may-care attitude and attack it with acrylics. This study of a stream shows what can happen when you let the sun shine on your painting as you work. I just couldn't position my paper out of the sun's glare and decided to forge ahead. When I returned to the studio, I was disappointed with my efforts. I felt that the forms looked rather flat, and although there was some nice color, it didn't work to solidify the composition.

I decided to revise just about the entire painting with acrylics. I used a photo taken of the stream as reference. I deepened values and modeled the rock forms with layers of opaque and transparent color. I also washed over the entire background and attempted to more evenly distribute the color and value and to add more detail. I even threw in some touches of colored pencil to create more-interesting textures.

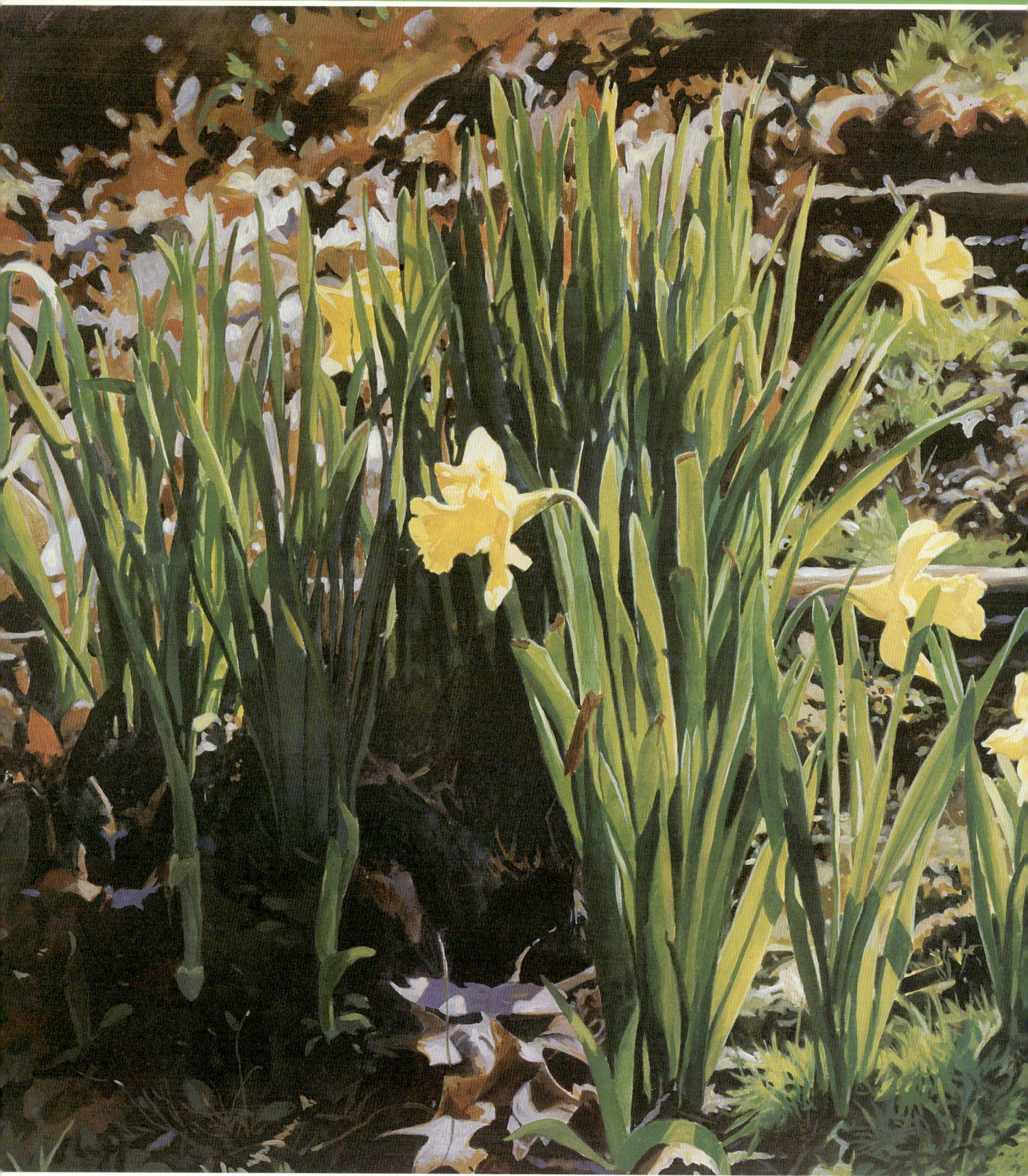

Backyard Daffodils   »   Acrylic on 140-lb. (300gsm) cold-pressed paper   »   22" x 30" (56cm x 76cm)

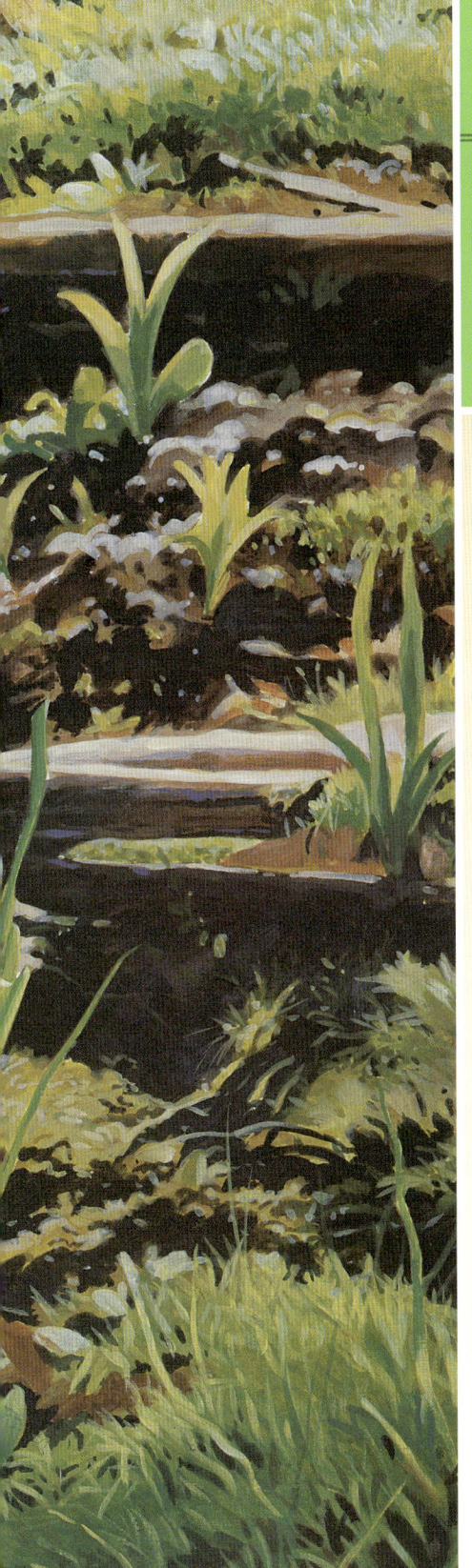

4 » painting from photographs

Since the late nineteenth century, artists have been using photographs as references for their paintings. Today, artists can choose from traditional film, digital photography and computer-enhanced imagery. The advancement of new photographic technology gives artists powerful tools for understanding and interpreting a subject. The key is incorporating these tools into your painting process so that they support but do not overwhelm your painting goals.

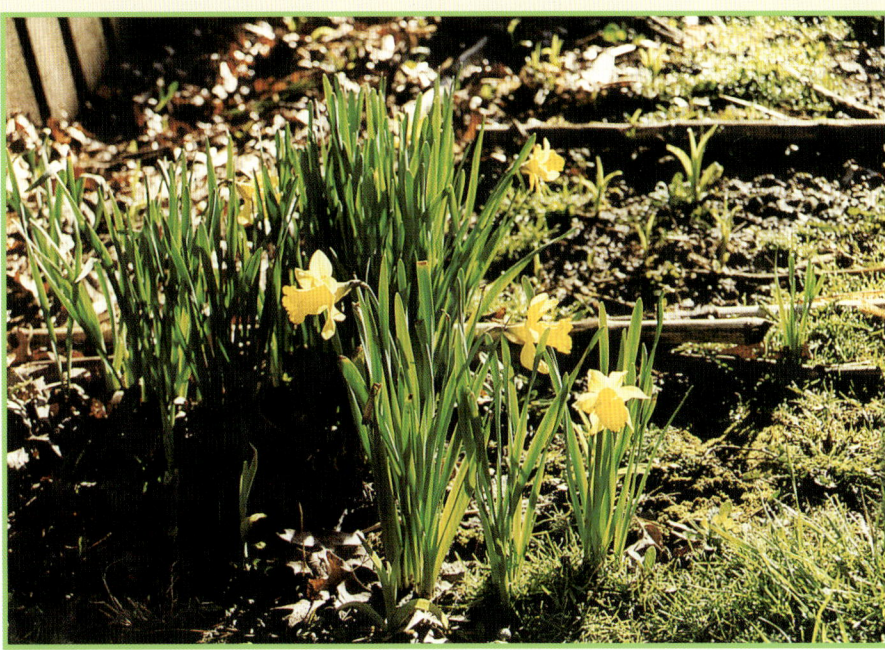

Reference Photo
I stuck fairly closely to the photo as reference. I did, however, paint the background a bit more loosely. This put the emphasis on the flowers.

Pros and cons of using photos

Regarding reference photos, it is helpful to understand their advantages and limitations. The most obvious advantage is a detailed record of your subject. Our minds can recall an amazing amount of visual information, but when we need more information than we can remember, a photo certainly helps. Another advantage is convenience. When working on location is not feasible, a photo can provide a visual record for you to reference later. Along these same lines is the ability of a photo to capture a transient moment, such as a moving subject or a changing weather or lighting effect.

A common problem with using photos occurs when we rely on the sometimes flawed visual information they provide. Cameras can distort and flatten space, shift colors and change the value structure of a subject. Recognizing these issues when you translate the information into a painting is all that's needed to avoid problems.

The good news about these distortions is that they often spark a painting idea. An exposure that flattens a form or changes its color may inspire you to find new shapes or colors in your painting. I have had many inspiring moments while looking at some of my worst photos. Obviously, this is the exception, and an understanding of photographic techniques is a great help.

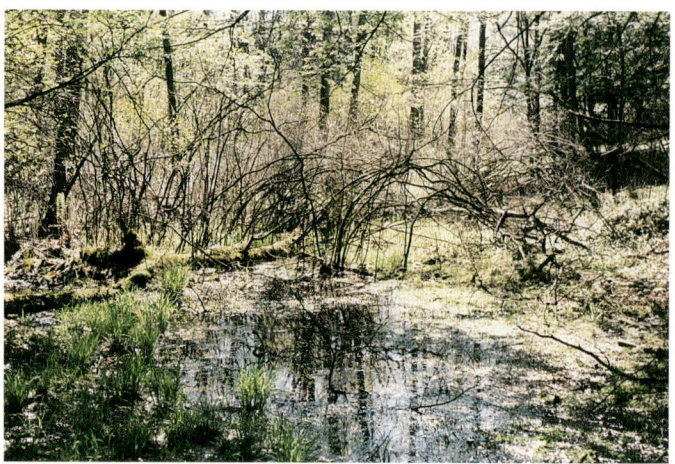

Reference Photo
This photo was taken during a spring fishing trip. I was attracted to the contrast of the strong morning light and deep shadows. This part of the woods was very wet, and everything glistened.

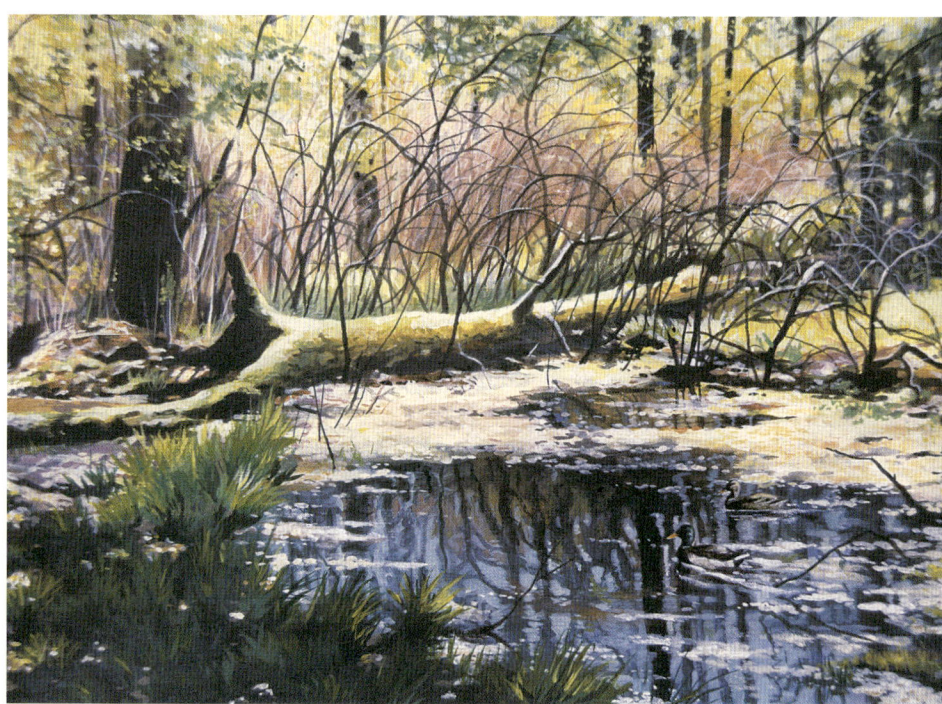

Simplify the Photographed Subject
This is a good example of simplifying a complicated photo. I tried to see past the surface details and emphasize the overall value pattern. Once that was established, I could put in enough details to describe the scene. The ducks added a sense of scale.

Backwater » Acrylic on 140-lb. (300gsm) cold-pressed paper » 9" x 12" (23cm x 30cm)

Working from a projected image

Many of our most respected and well-known realist painters work from a projected slide. This may seem like a simple way to translate photographic information onto paper or canvas; however, this technique presents its own set of problems and issues that must be dealt with before a successful painting results.

First, the original photo or slide must be strong enough visually to stand on its own. Second, projecting a slide usually gives more information than you need. A drawing made from a projected image sometimes ends up looking like a crazy jigsaw puzzle. Translating and assimilating all the shapes into a cohesive painting can be a daunting task. Finally, the distortions present in many photos can cause problems if they are not recognized and adjusted as the drawing is developed.

Occasionally, I have worked from a projected negative (a negative that is cut and mounted into a slide frame). Usually, I have done this if the subject is very complex and if that complexity is one of my painting goals, or if the print doesn't contain enough information. This process works successfully for many artists but is not my favorite way to design a painting. I find the issues listed above can make this process tedious and exhausting.

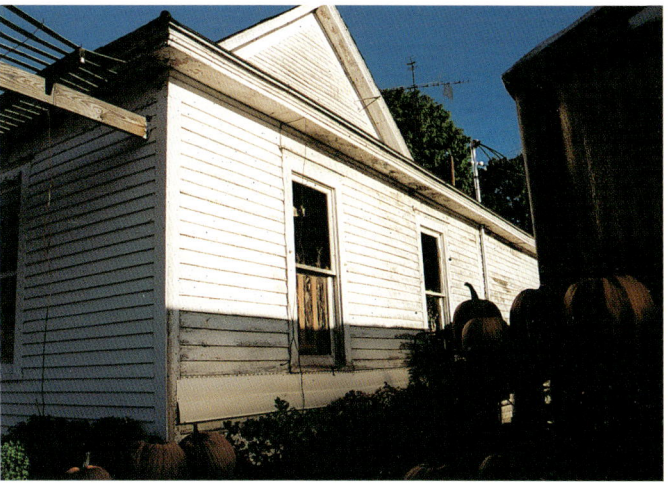

Reference Photo
This photo was from a roll of film I shot of a roadside market and greenhouse. The weathered buildings and strong afternoon light made for many interesting photos.

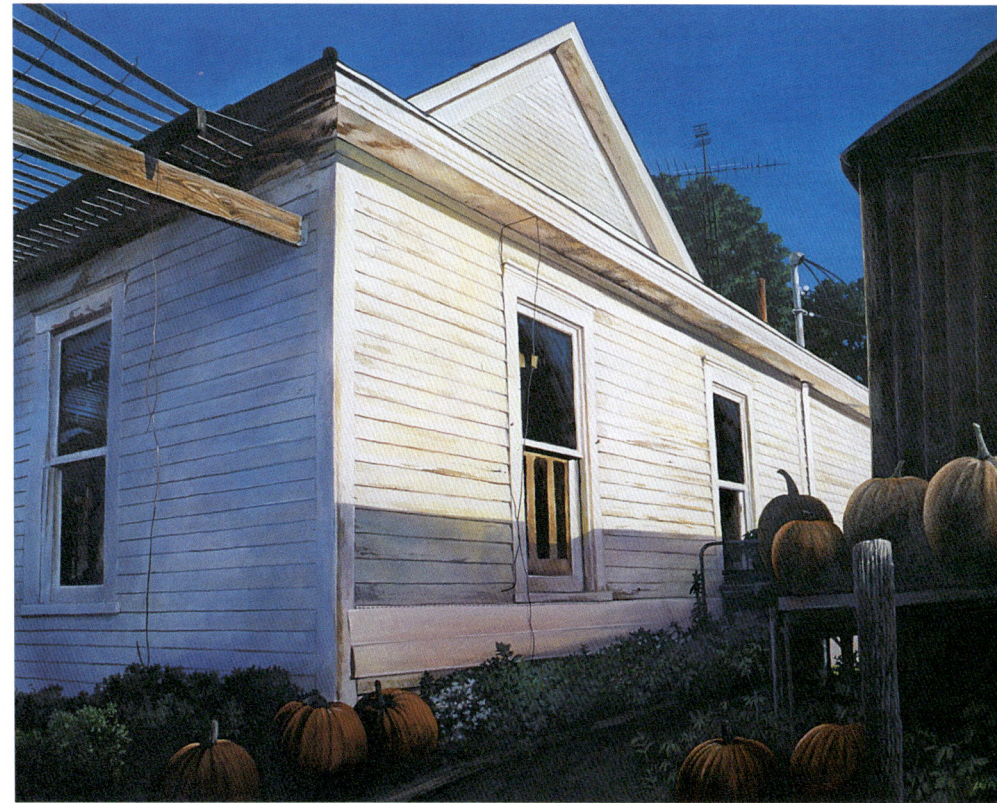

Be Aware of Photo Distortions
I used a projected negative for my drawing since the negative contained a great deal more information in the shadow areas than I could see on the print. However, because I made my drawing directly from the photo, I created a painting that projects a strong sense of foreshortening common in photos taken with a telephoto lens. I like this painting for its sense of place and color, but its photographic source is not very transparent, which bothers me. I would prefer that the viewer just enjoy the painting as it is rather than having to consider its source or process.

Pumpkins Electric Blue » Acrylic on 300-lb. (640gsm) cold-pressed paper » 30" x 40" (76cm x 102cm)

Photograph with painting in mind

Since I rely on photos a great deal, I almost always photograph with painting in mind. This doesn't mean that each photo will become a painting; each photo provides some bit of visual information I may be able to use later. If a subject presents itself, I try for a well-composed shot done with bracketed exposures (a regular exposure plus one lighter and one darker). Most often, however, I take photos just to document as much information as possible. In these cases, I rely on the auto-exposure mode on my camera and fire away.

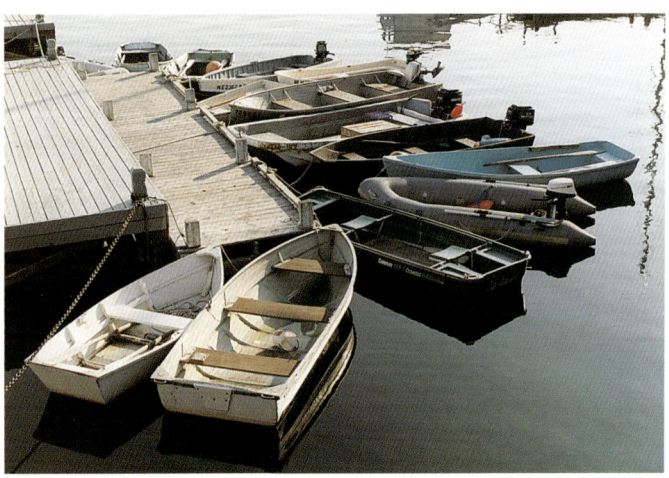

Try for a Great Photo
Shot in Maine, here is an attempt at a well-composed photo. I purposely framed the subject thinking how the entire view through the camera lens would translate into a painting.

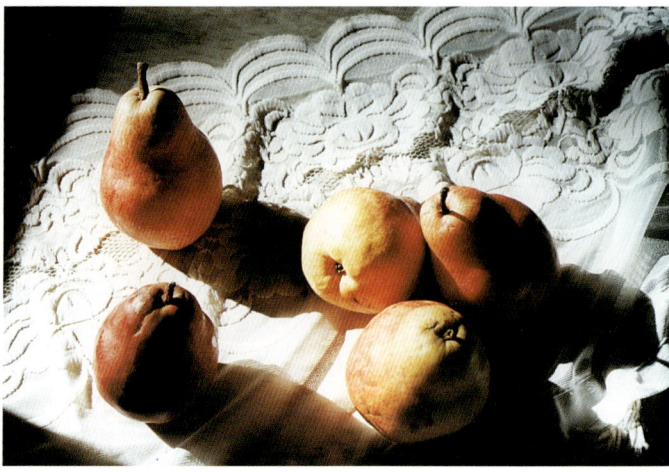

Photograph a Still Life Setup
My wife, Kathy, had been to a farmer's market and bought several pears. There was a patch of early-morning light hitting my studio floor, and I thought of how the pears would look sitting in that light. I shot them with different fabrics laid on the floor. This photo shows them sitting on some old drapery.

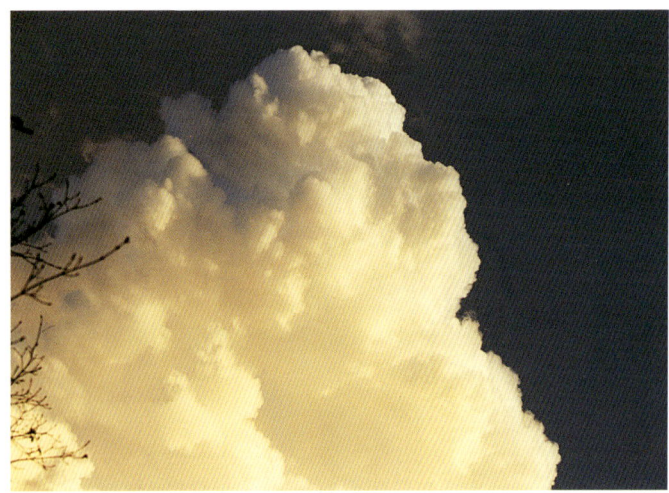

Photograph the Unexpected
Sometimes a subject presents itself and begs to be photographed or painted. This thunderhead was photographed at first light one early-spring morning. I was still half asleep when I noticed the strange light reflecting off my garage. The sun had just peeked above the horizon and was striking the cloud tops. The photo was about documenting these clouds. It won't translate directly into a painting but can be used as a future reference.

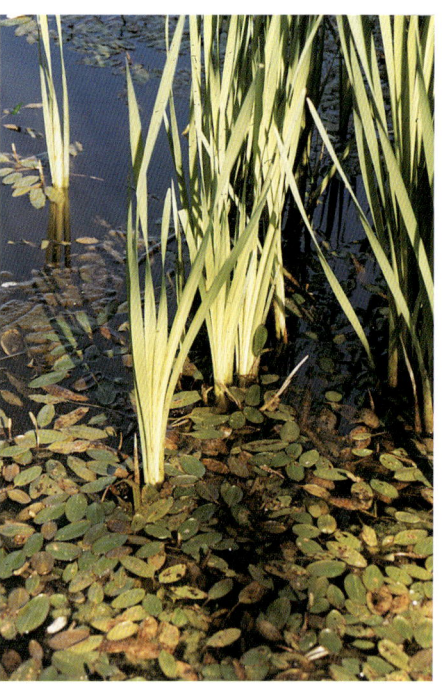

Photograph Nature's Details
I have accumulated a large collection of reference photos like this one. (The cloud photos also fall into this category.) Over the years, I have saved many hours of research by finding a photo in this collection. The hardest part is keeping them organized; I have often joked that I need to hire a reference librarian.

Edit your photos

Unless you work as a photorealist, most of your photo references will be edited as you translate them into paintings. Occasionally you can stick close to the photo, but most times you will be making changes and adjustments as your painting takes on its own identity.

Simplify What You See
Translating all the information a photo provides can be daunting. The easiest way to translate that information is to simplify it. Look for the major shapes and forms and make a value sketch before beginning your painting. Just as we squint at a subject while painting on location, we can squint at our photos to help eliminate details and see the basic pattern and design.

Reference Photo
I took this photo at a friend's family farm. I liked the way the diffused light flattened the forms. I immediately thought of how appealing it would be to paint them using large areas of color without concern for textures or aerial perspective.

Watercolor Sketch
Overcast skies tend to reduce color contrasts, and this farm seemed like a good subject for a monochromatic painting. I explored this idea with a few small Sepia watercolors. When I did my larger painting, I changed my mind and used the full palette. The colors were subdued, and I figured the effect would be about the same.

I liked the idea of creating a composition that was heavily weighted to one side, yet balanced. This was accomplished by understanding the concept that distance and space have visual weight that can counterbalance the center of interest.

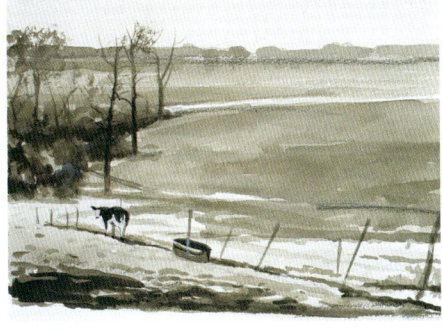

The added green foliage reduces the contrast of the once-bare trees, which would have taken away interest from the cow.

The distant field was made lighter and warmer to connect with the middle filed and harmonize with the warmth of the foreground.

Simplify the Composition for a Mood-Filled Painting
I liked the mood created by simplifying this composition. Removing the cows on the right side created a sense of isolation. Combined with the subdued color, this makes for a rather melancholy painting. Among the other changes made, notice how the leaning trees were not added. I felt that this distracted from the cow.

Gray Day Cow » Acrylic on 140-lb. (300gsm) cold-pressed paper » 15" x 22" (38cm x 56cm)

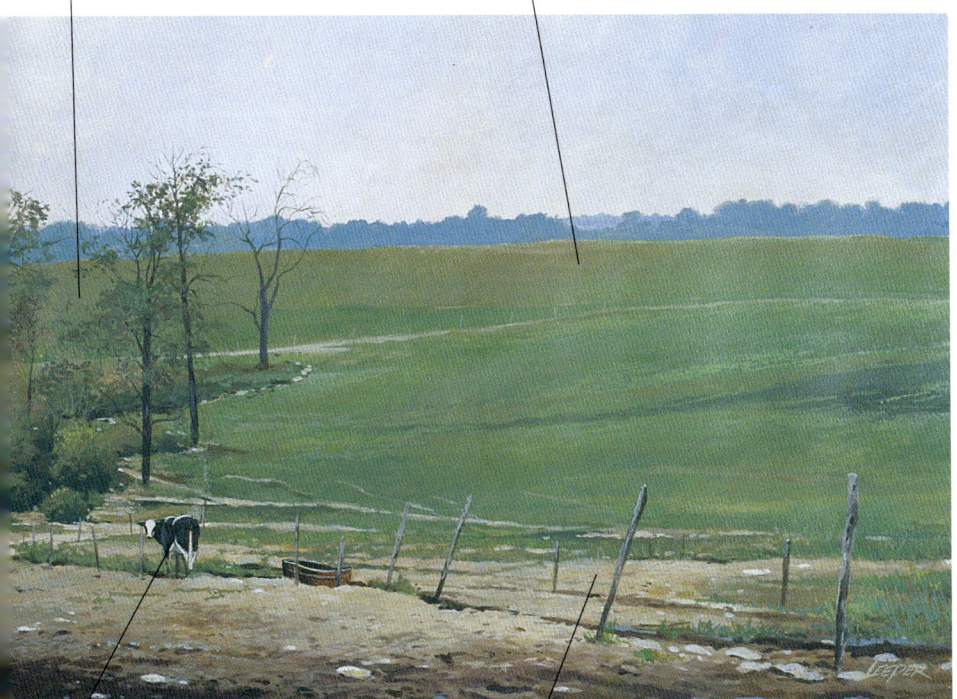

The center of interest contains the lightest and darkest values.

The dirt shapes were strengthened in contrast and simplified in detail to better support the simple field shapes.

49

Crop or Change Elements

Often a photo can provide great visual information but must be cropped to make a solid composition. Moving, adjusting or eliminating some elements within the photo can also improve a composition. A rough compositional sketch is invaluable in these situations.

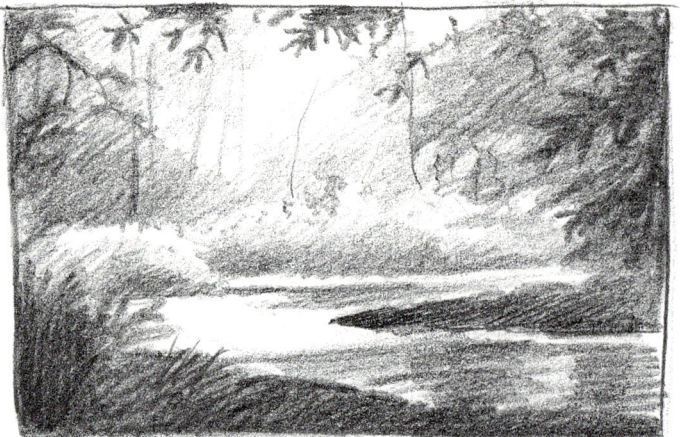

Pencil Sketch
This rough sketch focused on finding the composition by cropping the top and bottom of the photo and making the center of interest the sparkling stream and the filtered light coming through the trees.

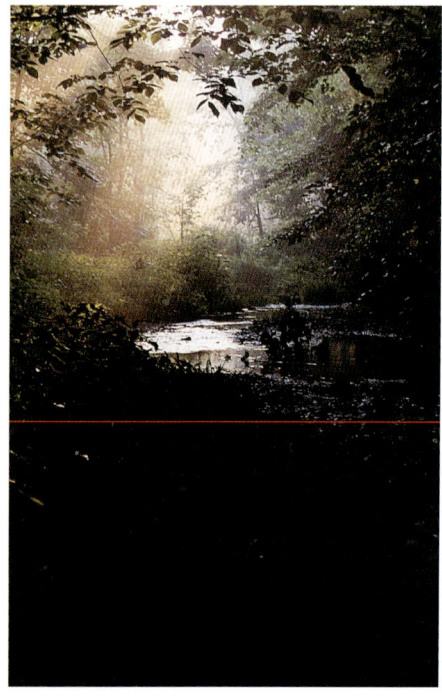

crop

Reference Photo
We had just experienced a violent thunderstorm after a day of intense heat and humidity. When the sun came out, everything glistened and the moist air seemed to practically glow. I grabbed my camera and headed for the nearby woods.

What I remember most about that day besides the beautiful sunlight effects was the number of deerfly bites I suffered while shooting three rolls of film. This photo is certainly not a great exposure; however, I felt that by cropping the photo I could come up with a workable composition.

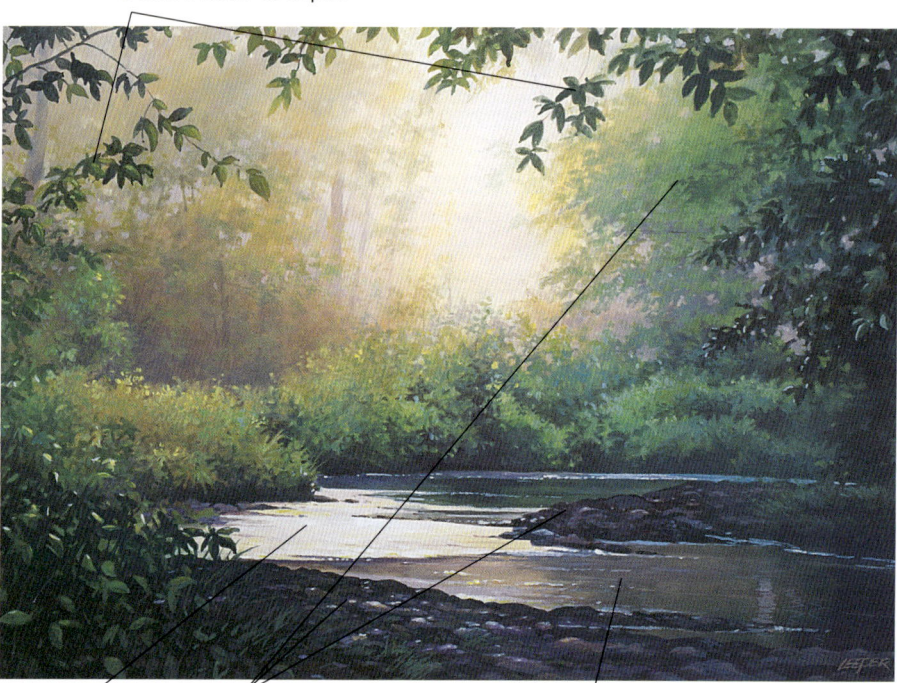

The limbs were carefully positioned to create a sense of depth.

Center of interest   These shapes were simplified.   Some elements were eliminated from the reference photo to further simplify the scene.

Improve the Photo's Composition
Once I had established a new composition based on my sketch, I proceeded to push the color and contrast to support my center of interest. I paid extra attention to the tree limbs framing the composition. I wanted to create a sense of layered depth as the viewer moved toward the glowing background.

Sunshine After the Storm » Acrylic on 140-lb. (300gsm) cold-pressed paper » 20" x 30" (51cm x 76cm)

Combine Photos

Combining elements from multiple photos can create an exciting new composition. This takes some planning, and a few compositional and value sketches may be needed to make things work. Using photo editing software such as Adobe Photoshop can help in this endeavor (see page 56).

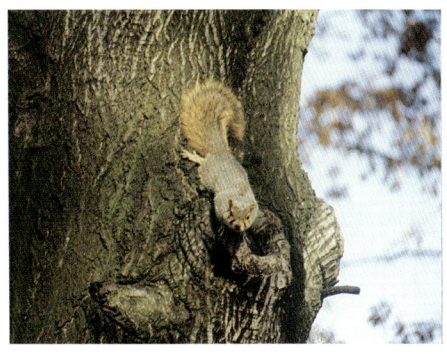
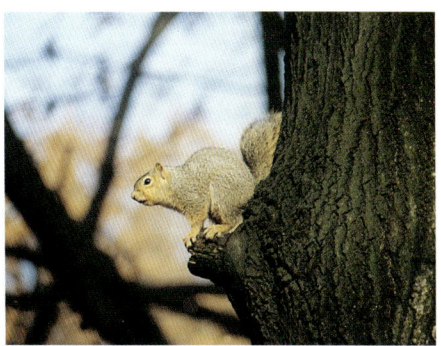

Reference Photos
I used three photos as references to come up with *Looking for Trouble*, the painting on the next page. The squirrels were photographed in my backyard, and the trees were photographed at a nearby park. The painting was done a couple years after the photos were taken. A squirrel that sat outside my studio window was the inspiration for the painting. I didn't have photos of him but knew my files contained plenty of reference material.

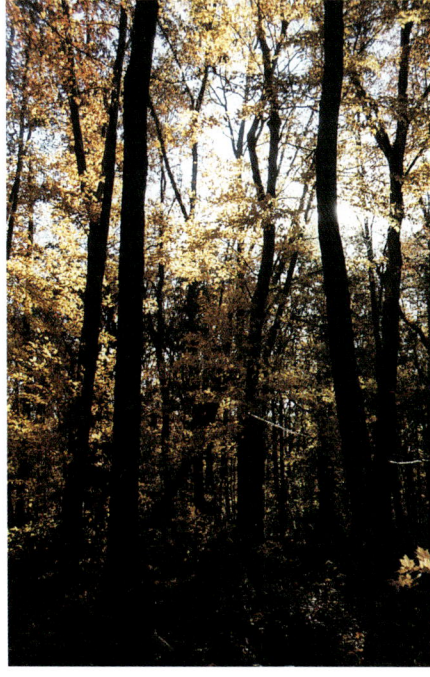

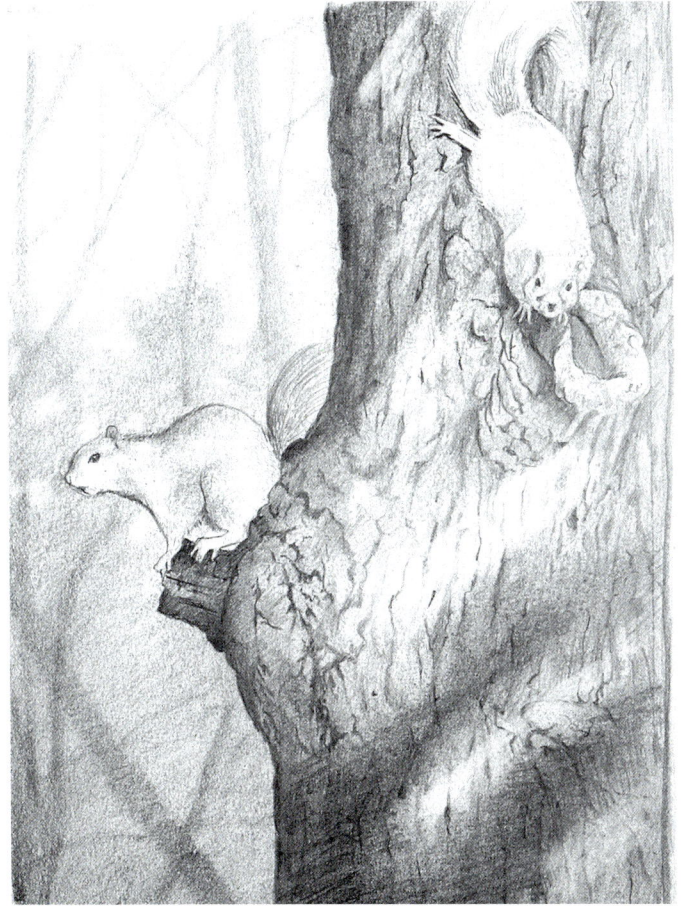

Pencil Sketch
I made several thumbnails before creating this larger sketch. Using multiple reference photos forces you to make a more detailed and complete preliminary sketch. This sketch then becomes your main reference, and the photos support individual elements within your painting.

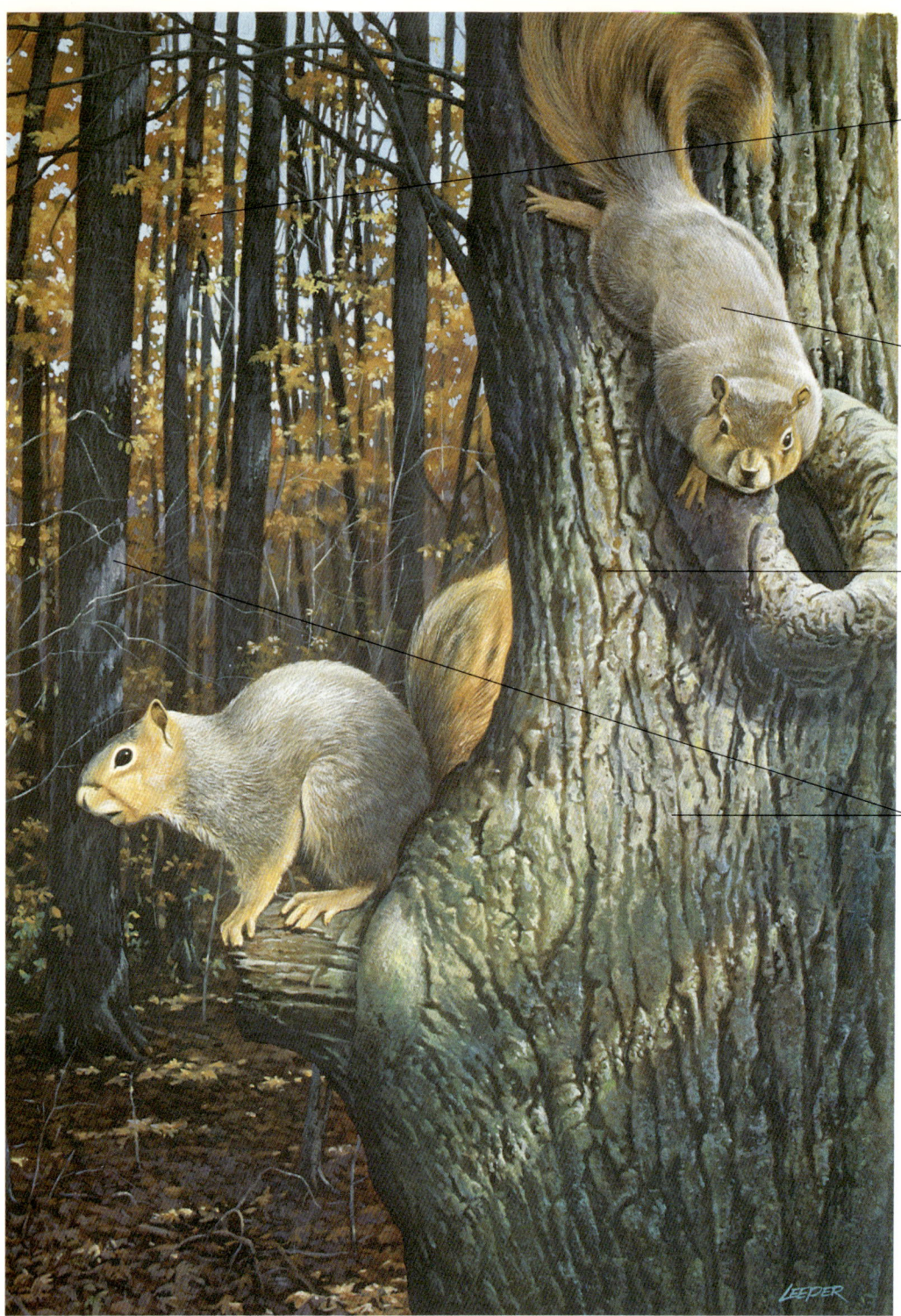

The background is inspired by a reference photo but not copied

Gouache was used for rendering the final details.

The bark texture is similar to photos but not copied.

The pattern of light and shadow was invented.

Combine Photo References

This painting was a lot of fun. Squirrels can be quite comical and curious, and I wanted to capture a sense of whimsy with their postures. For the composition, I stayed pretty true to my sketch. I increased the sense of light and shadow that was present in the squirrel photos. This diagonal pattern of light and shadow is an important element because it helps move the viewer's eye through the composition. The painting is a combination of watercolor, acrylic and gouache.

Looking for Trouble » Mixed media on 140-lb. (300gsm) cold-pressed paper » 30" x 20" (76cm x 51cm)

Take multiple approaches to the same photo

Using one photo as the basis for multiple paintings, each with a different painting goal, is a great exercise. Besides allowing you to get the most out of your photographic resources, it helps you expand your artistic vision and take chances with your paintings. By manipulating the basic art elements of color, value, shape, line and composition, you can explore an endless variety of new paintings.

Change the Color Scheme
Think of the possibilities of adjusting or completely changing the color scheme of a photo. A scene can be rendered using warm colors, cool colors, a limited palette or complementary schemes, to name just a few. A small color sketch is helpful for working out these ideas.

Change the Value Structure
Adjusting the values of photographic elements can generate many new and exciting compositions. Starting with a photo that has a dynamic value range gives you the most possibilities. Of course, value sketches are a must in this circumstance.

Crop the Photo to Find a New Composition
Cropping a photo with a viewfinder is a great way to discover a new composition. You can use practically anything that has straight edges to experiment with different cropping ideas. I like to use two L-shaped pieces of card stock; they can be adjusted easily to find any compositional ratio. Many paintings can be created from one photo.

Let's complete a series of small watercolor studies based on this reference photo to see which approach works best for a final painting.

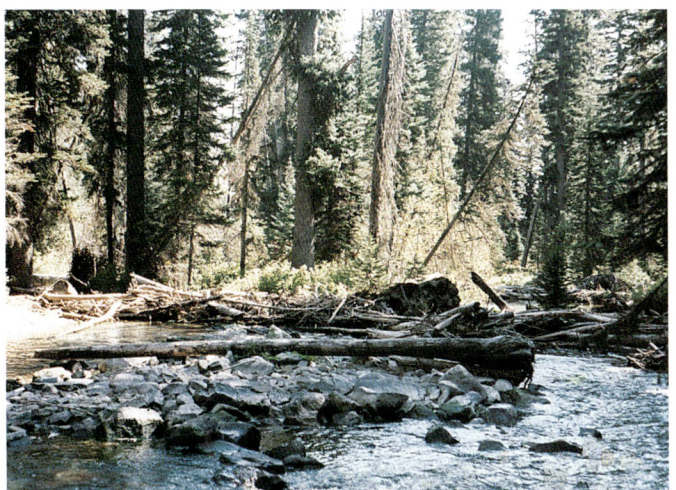

Reference Photo
I photographed this scene in Grand Teton National Park. The complexity of the tangled woodland along with the strong afternoon sun provided me with a challenging subject.

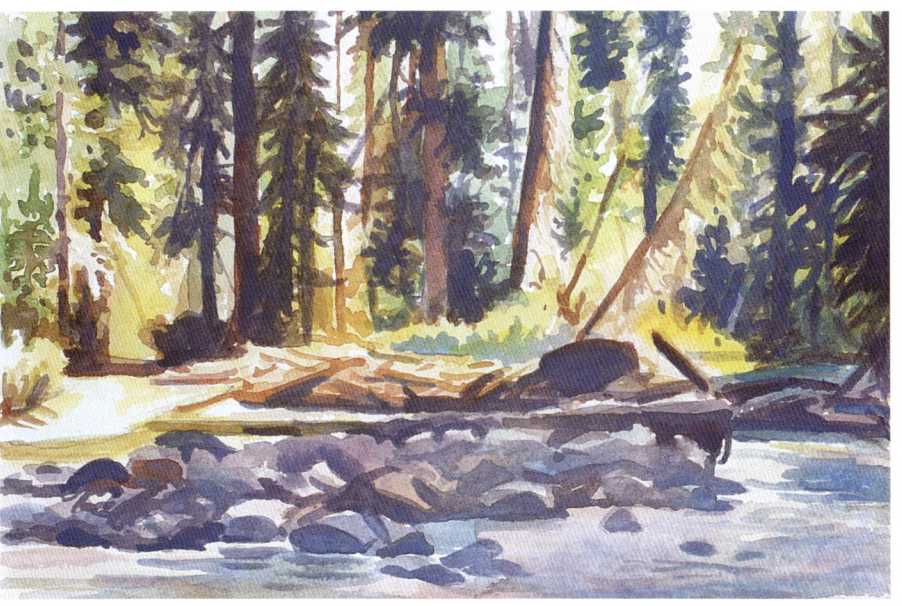

Try Warmer Colors
Using John Singer Sargent's watercolors as inspiration, I decided to try a study using a much warmer palette than the reference photo shows. The value structure is pretty consistent with the photo, but I replaced some of the greens and blues with yellows, oranges, reds and violets.

Teton Shadows (Study #1) » Watercolor on 140-lb. (300gsm) cold-pressed paper » 6" x 9" (15cm x 23cm)

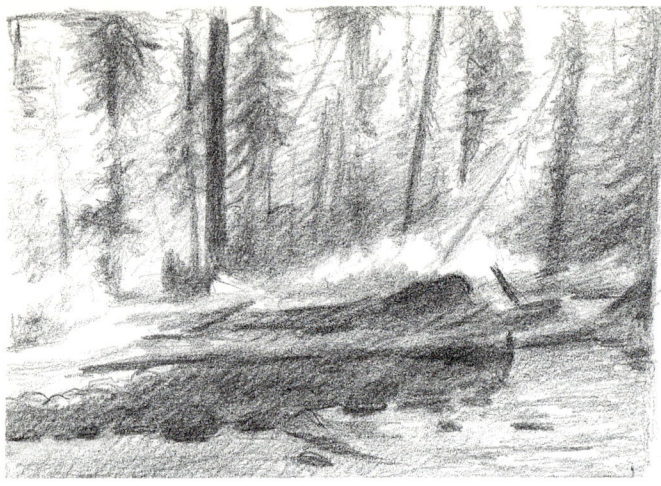 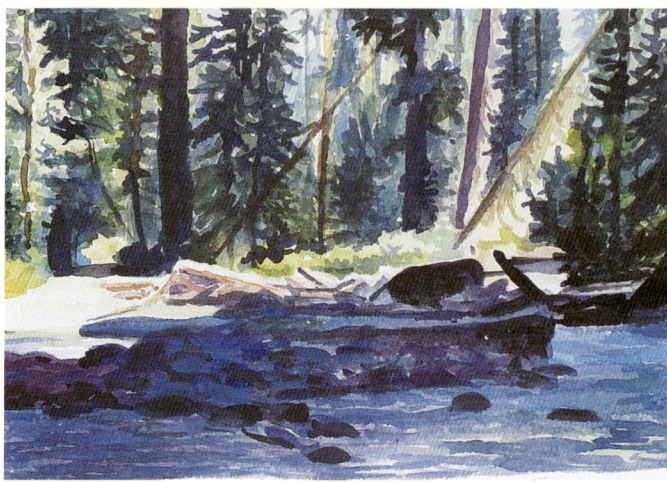

Change the Value Pattern

In this study, I wanted to create a more dramatic lighting effect than the photo shows. I deepened the value of the rocks and water and kept the sunlit trees and middle ground lighter. The grouping of the light values created a spotlight effect that reminded me of a theatrical setting.

Teton Shadows (Study #2) » Watercolor on 140-lb. (300gsm) cold-pressed paper » 6" x 9" (15cm x 23cm)

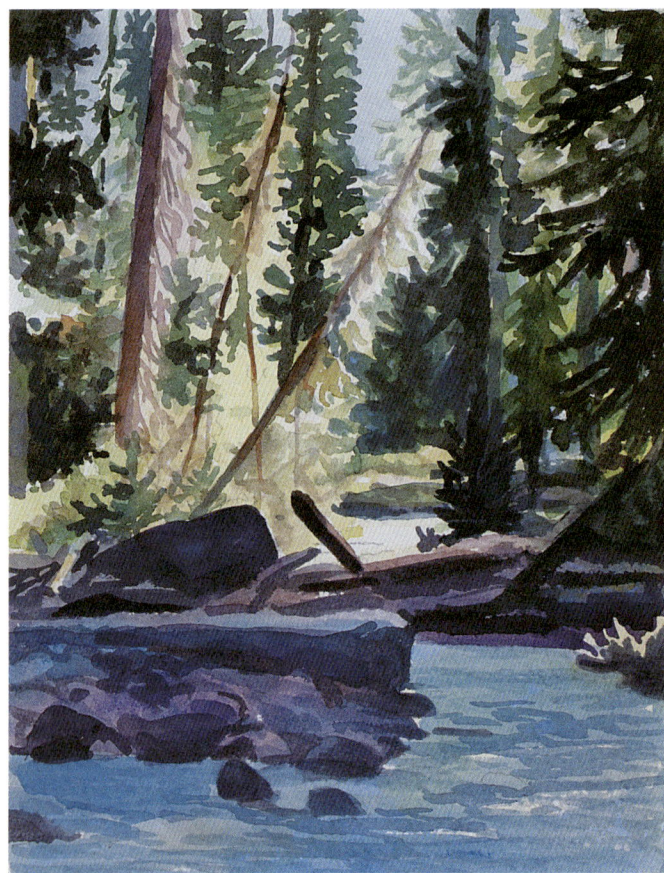 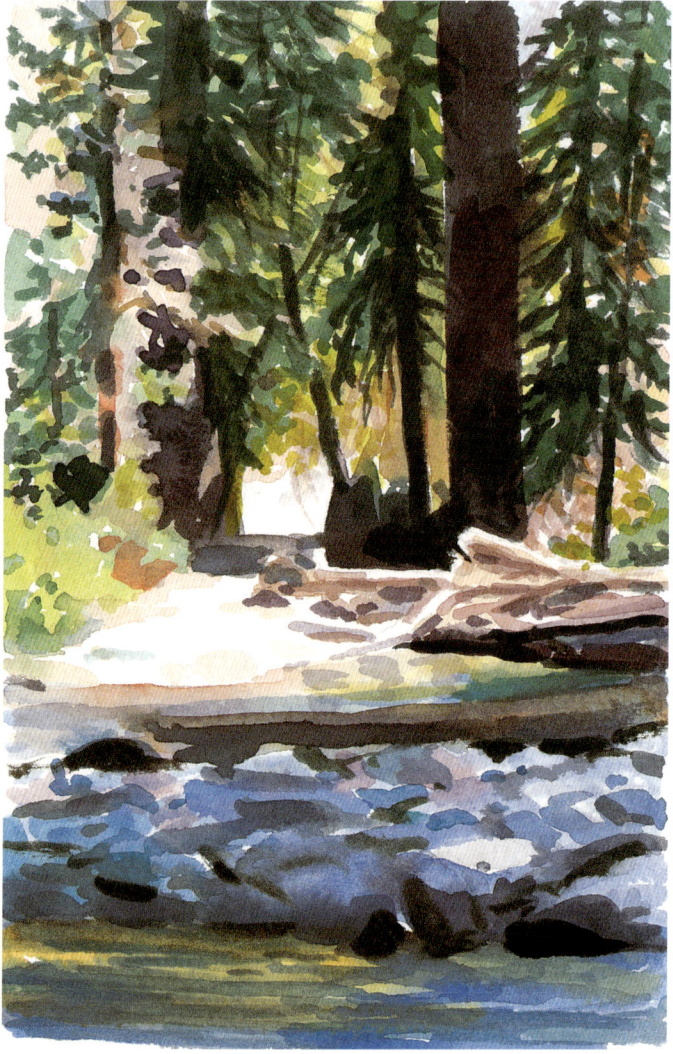

Create New Compositions

These compositions have an intimate feel. Notice how the large tree and boulder shapes are used as the dominant elements in the compositions.

Teton Shadows (Study #3) » Watercolor on 140-lb. (300gsm) cold-pressed paper » 8" x 6" (20cm x 15cm)

Teton Shadows (Study #4) » Mixed media on 140-lb. (300gsm) cold-pressed paper » 8" x 5" (20cm x 13cm)

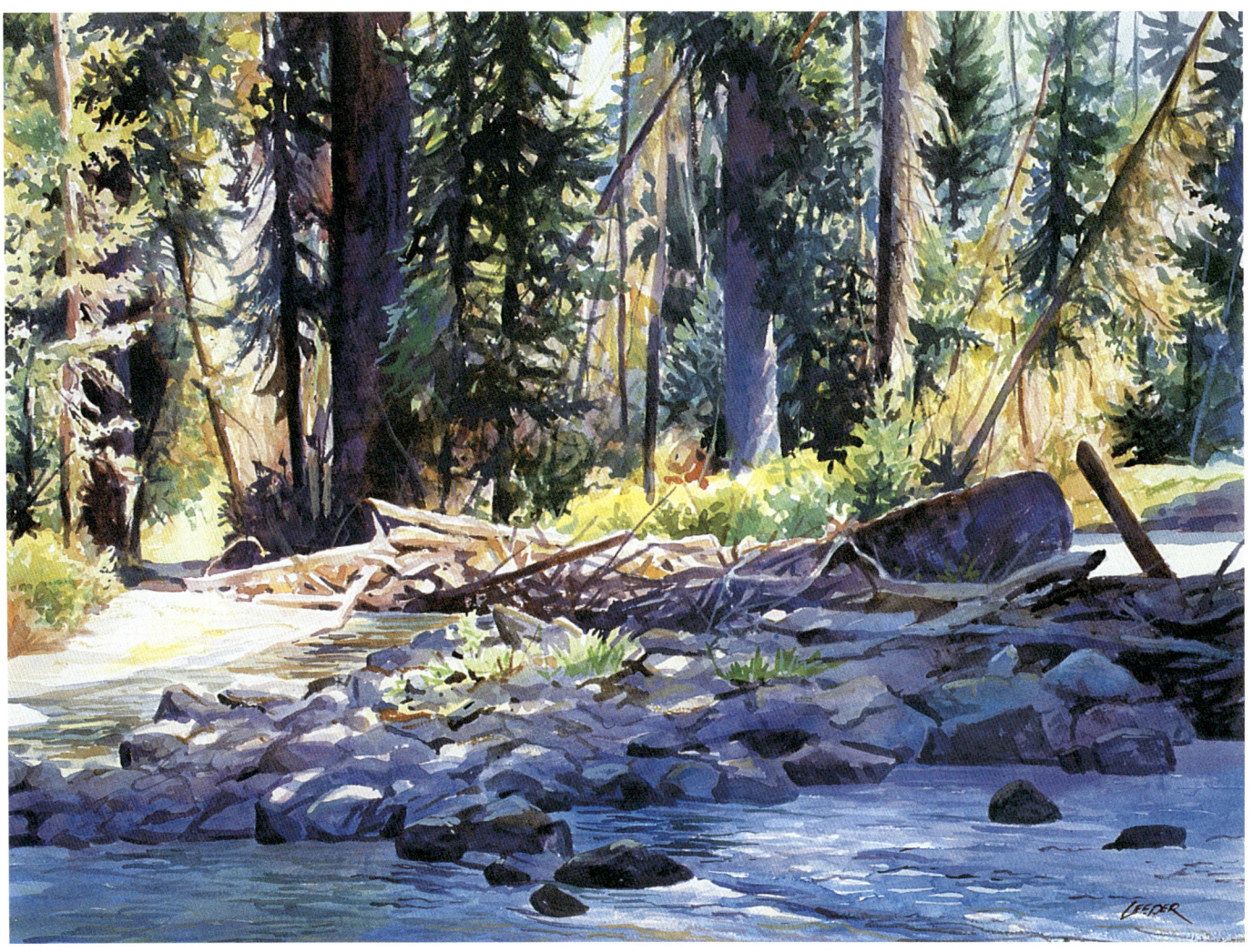

Combine Studies to Create the Final Painting
I chose the general composition of the first and second studies, used some of the warmer colors in the first study and borrowed some of the deeper values from the second study. I eliminated the fallen log since its strong horizontal shape seemed distracting and static. The combination of warmer colors and deeper values made for a more dynamic painting.

Teton Shadows   »   Watercolor on 300-lb. (640gsm) cold-pressed paper   »   21" x 29" (53cm x 74cm)

Use your computer to create exciting compositions

The personal computer has become an integral part of most people's lifestyles. This is no different for the artist. Using powerful photo editing software such as Adobe® Photoshop®, the artist can explore an endless variety of visual solutions.

I think of this process as a playful exercise: It is great fun, and when a painting comes from it, I think of it as a bonus. Because of the immediacy of this process, you can quickly create a number of images on the computer that range from the sublime to the outrageous.

Testing an idea on the computer before committing to it in a painting can save you time and aggravation. Ideas about color, value and composition can be tried out. Many times my original design is reaffirmed and I can proceed with confidence. Other times, a new idea works, or on occasion something unforeseen emerges and the painting takes off in a new direction. I have saved many a painting from disaster by first trying out an idea on my computer.

There are many photo editing software packages to choose from. I prefer Adobe Photoshop because of the powerful options it offers the user. What you choose to use will depend on what you can afford and the options you want. Scanners and digital cameras often come with some kind of photo editing software that may work very well for you.

Following are just a few of the ways you can use photo editing software to your advantage.

Manipulate Color and Value

One of the most common uses for photo editing software is adjusting

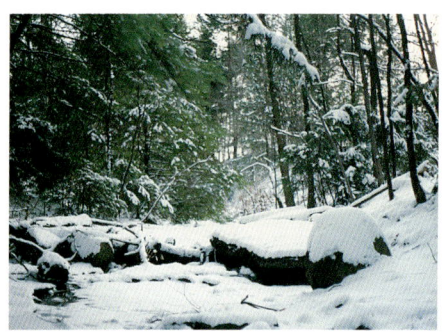

Reference Photo
When I shot this photo, the sun was just beginning to set and a soft, warm light was falling on the back corner of our family farm. The photo didn't seem to capture the warmth that I remembered.

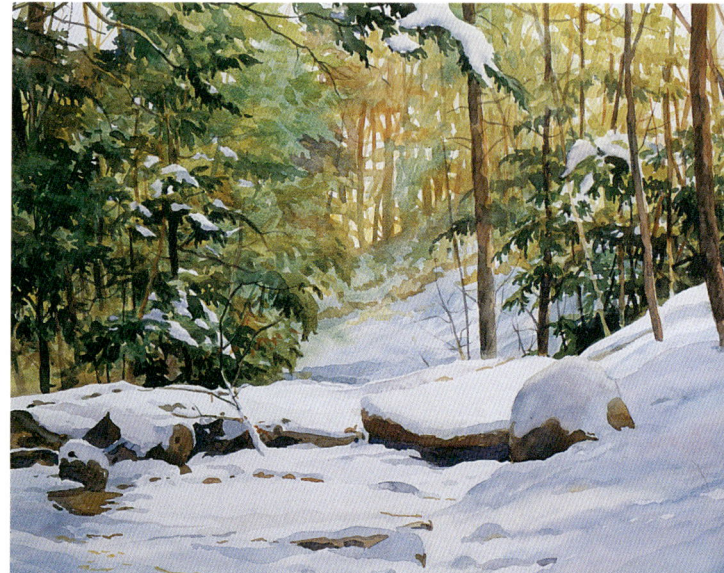

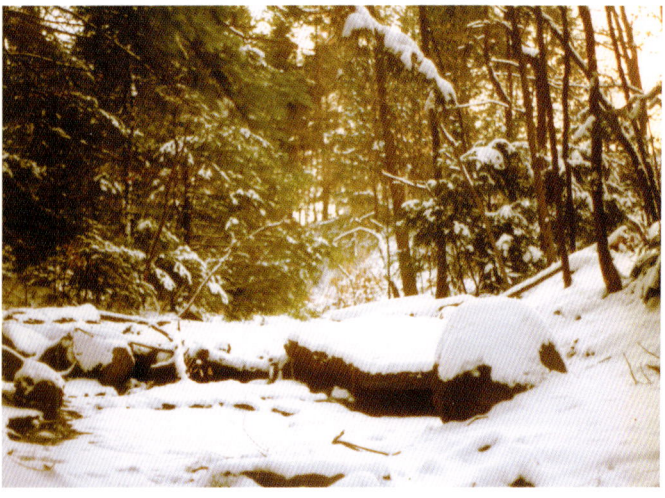

Computer-Altered Photo
I decided to warm things up by adjusting the color balance in Adobe Photoshop.

Play With Color
Using just the ink-jet printout of the manipulated photo, I really pushed the warm-color palette. I lost some detail in the conversion, but I chose to disregard my reference photo and instead let the digital photo guide my painting decisions. The idea was to create a painting with a completely new identity from that of the photo.

I worked on Strathmore Imperial paper because of its bright white surface and because color doesn't soak in or fade very much on this paper. I figured I would be lifting out color to render the snow clumps, but I ended up painting them fairly directly with very little surface manipulation.

Frozen Stream » Watercolor on 140-lb. (300gsm) cold-pressed paper » 22" x 30" (56cm x 76cm)

the color balance or values of a photo. This tool can be used to dramatically change the feeling or mood of an image, or it can be used to make slight adjustments to individual areas.

Combine Photos
One of the most useful features of photo editing software is the ability to combine multiple images for a new and often unique composition. With some practice, you can produce amazing results and save yourself the time and effort of piecing together physical photos.

Make Corrections
A digital camera is a great help in this situation since most scanners cannot accommodate a painting larger than 8½" x 14" (22cm x 36cm). Working with your painting on screen, you can test solutions to problems before committing paint to paper.

Create a Whole New Composition
I occasionally use additional photo editing software features to create a whole new image. You can paint using a virtual airbrush, or you can rubber-stamp textures and colors from one part of an image to another. The list goes on and on. When you combine these special features with photographic images, you really can invent a whole new composition to work from.

Reference Photo
This photo had a nice chiaroscuro effect—containing a wide range of values that clearly reveal the forms—but I wanted to create a bright, warm painting of these oranges.

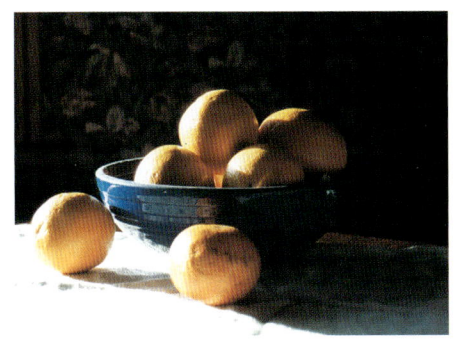

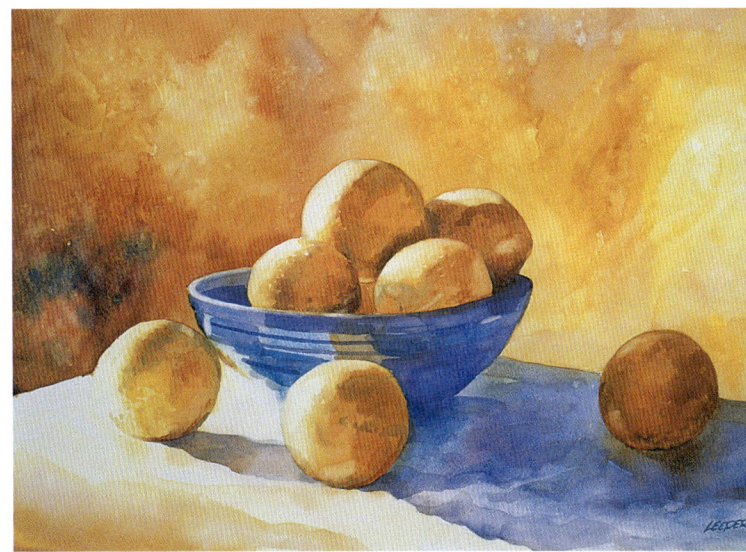

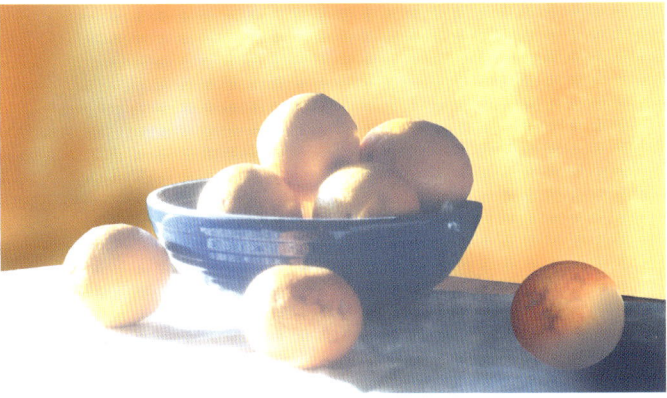

Computer-Altered Photo
I used the airbrush tool in Adobe Photoshop to create the background. To improve the composition, I copied one of the oranges and moved it to the right side. Since it was in shadow, I adjusted the value density and added a few shadow colors with the airbrush tool. This example isn't a radical change, but it shows some of the potential of photo editing software.

Dramatically Change the Photo
As I was beginning this painting, I thought I might try for a really high-key sun-filled look, but as I worked, my love of rich, saturated color took over. Strathmore Imperial paper worked well for this painting, as I could easily lift color to get the highlights and texture on the oranges. The colorful and textured background was easy to achieve on this paper as well.

Splash of Orange » Watercolor on 140-lb. (300gsm) cold-pressed paper » 15" x 22" (38cm x 56cm)

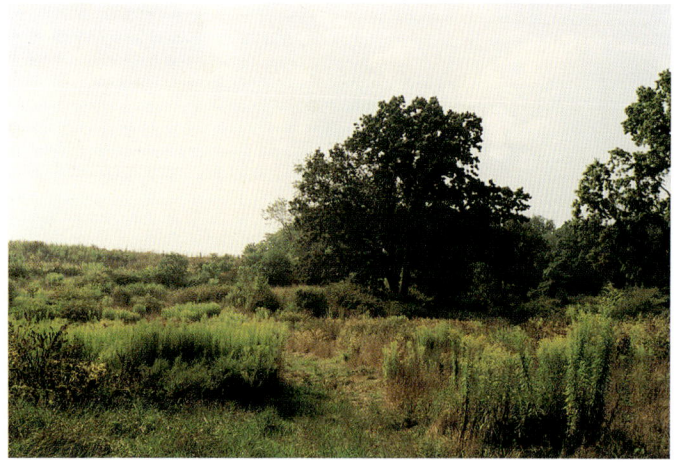
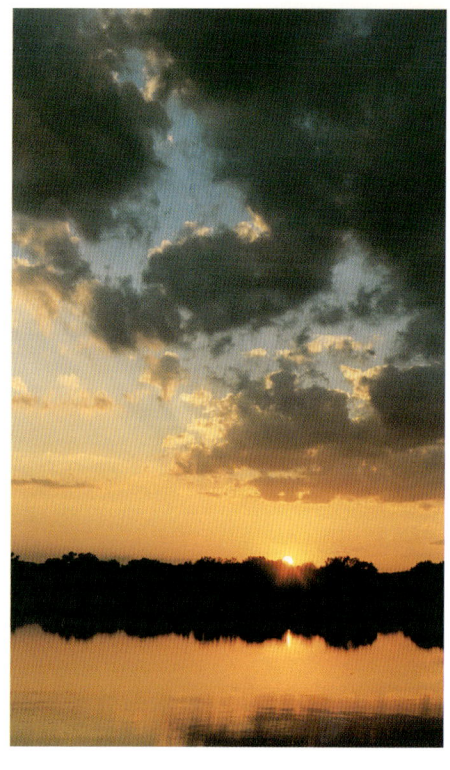

Reference Photos
Combining landscape photos and sky photos is one of the easiest Adobe Photoshop tricks.

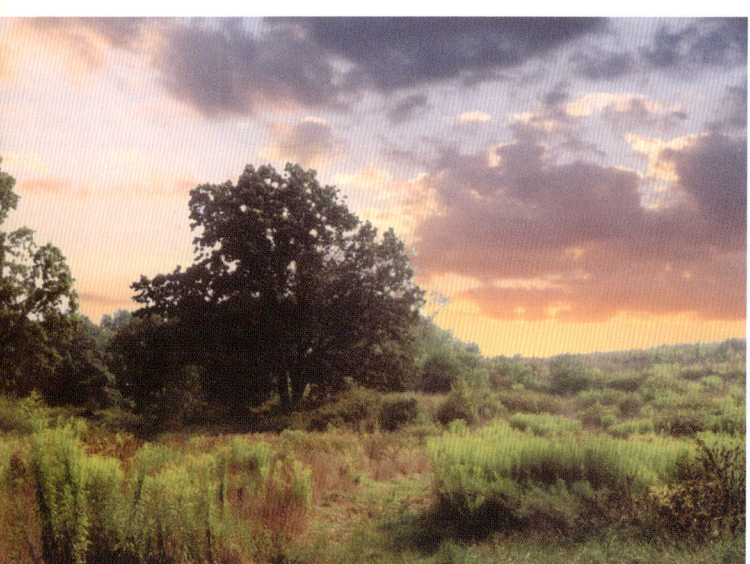
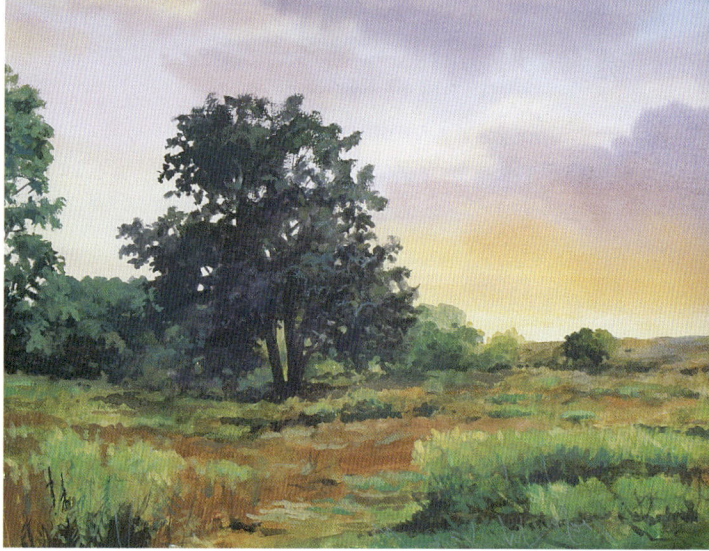

Computer-Altered Photo
The two photos came together rather seamlessly. I copied one sky and pasted it over the other. Once that was done, I adjusted the color balance and value density to come up with the new image. I flipped the landscape photo so that it would work better with the large violet cloud shape. The warmth in the field echoed the sunset, and the trees were dark enough to be silhouetted—as they would be against an evening sky.

Create a New Landscape
I worked only from the ink-jet printout. Just as for *Frozen Stream* (see page 56), I resisted looking at the reference photos for more details. The entire painting was done in watercolor and enhanced with acrylic. There are a few small touches of colored pencil in the trees and field. This painting has a much more exciting sense of color and atmosphere than the original landscape photo does.

Sunset Field » Mixed media on 140-lb. (300gsm) rough paper » 15" x 22" (38cm x 56cm)

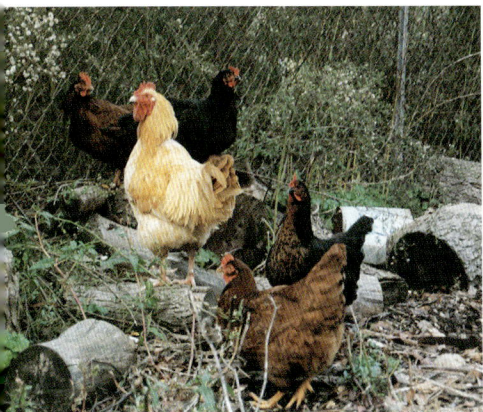
Reference Photo

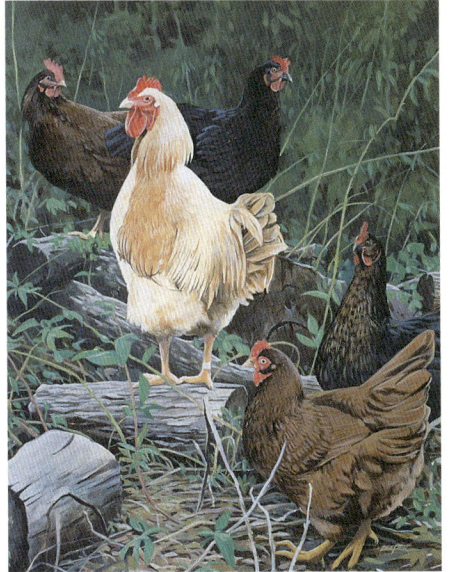

It's Never Too Late to Fix a Painting
I did this painting of my cousin's chickens more than five years ago. When I finished it, I realized I had followed the photo too closely and created a strange composition. I guess you could call it the "three-headed chicken" syndrome! I remember being embarrassed and astounded that I didn't see the flaw until the painting was finished. I put it on a shelf and licked my wounds.

Summer Chickens » Acrylic on 140-lb. (300gsm) hot-pressed paper » 19" x 13" (48cm x 33cm)

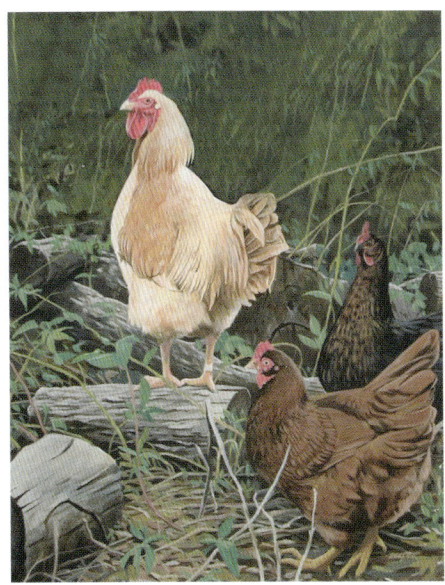
Computer-Altered Composition
Recently, I came across this painting and thought I would fix the flaw. I took a digital photo of it and created a few manipulated versions in Adobe Photoshop. First I rearranged the chickens in the background, and then I tried it with no chickens behind the rooster. I liked the latter version best and printed it on my ink-jet printer.

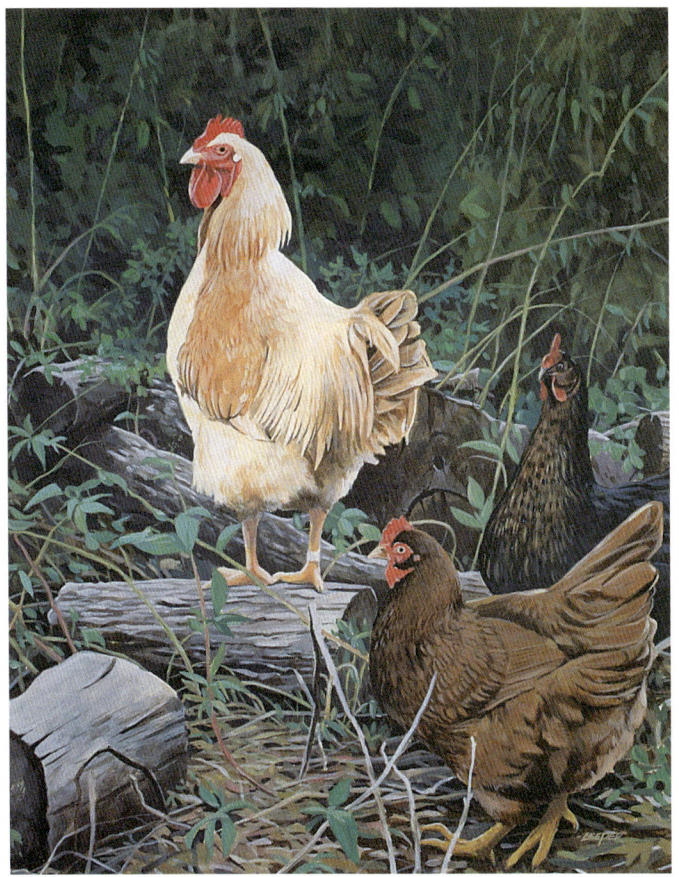
Summer Chickens (Revised) » Acrylic on 140-lb. (300gsm) hot-pressed paper » 19" x 13" (48cm x 33cm)

Revised Painting
In retrospect, it seems like such an easy change that I don't know why I didn't do it five years ago. The composition is much stronger now. There is so much activity with the remaining chickens and foreground that the two removed chickens are not missed. It took about three layers of semi-opaque acrylic to paint them out of the picture. The change was done in about half an hour.

59

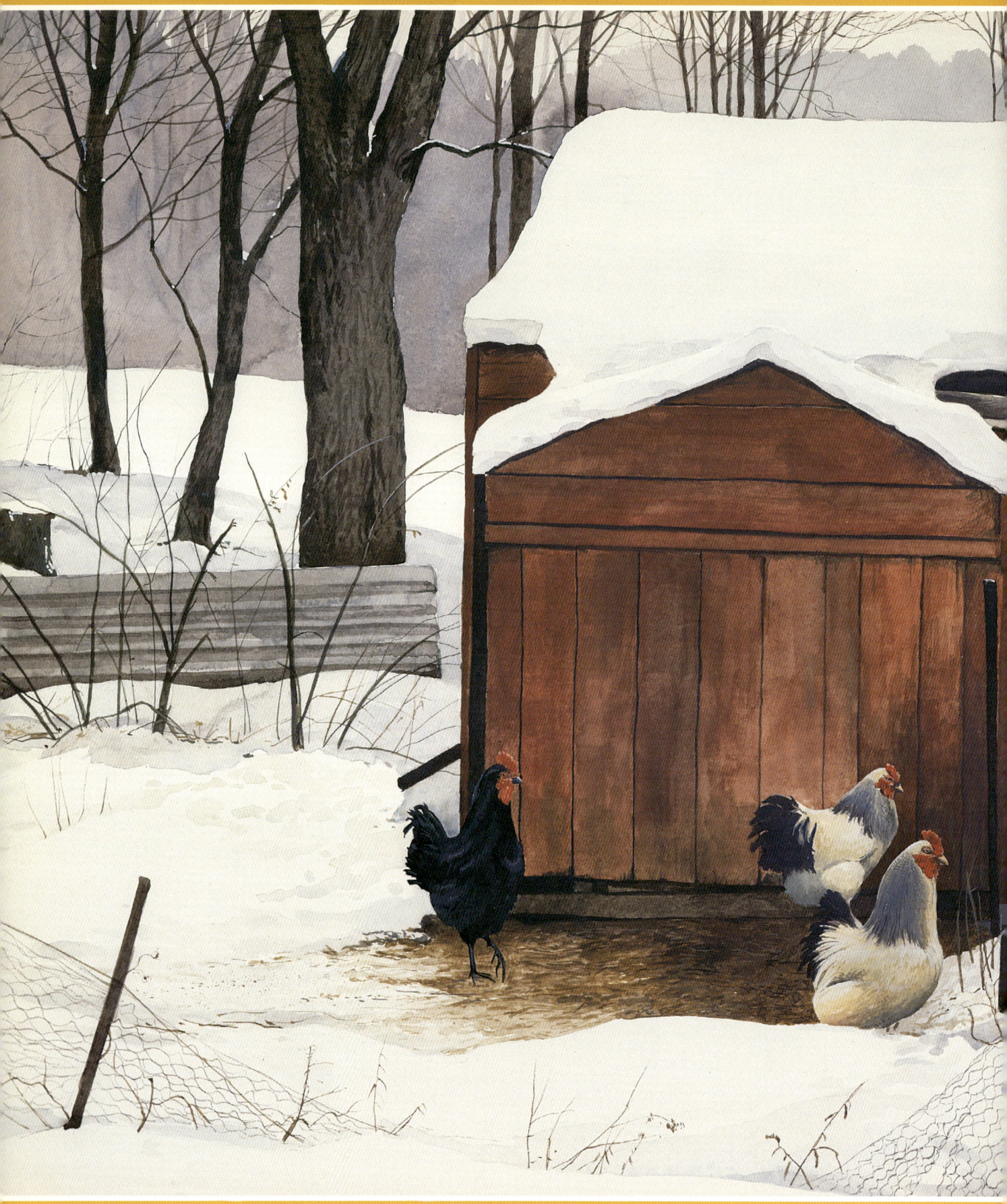

Snow Chickens » Mixed media on 140-lb. (300gsm) hot-pressed paper » 17" x 22" (43cm x 56cm)

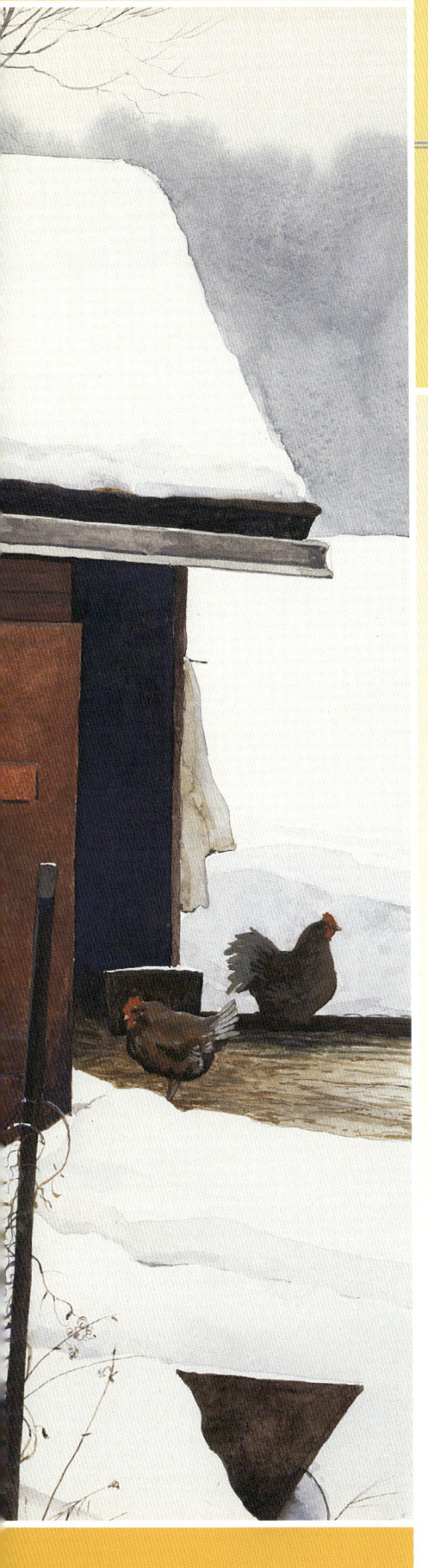

5 »

watermedia techniques

From opaque to transparent and everything in between, watermedia techniques are as varied as the artists who use them. Before starting a painting, my first decision is usually what medium to use. I don't have a formula to help me decide, but often the techniques that are available lead me in one direction or another. If my subject or painting goals involve rich, dark values, I consider using layered acrylics. If a delicate approach is necessary, then transparent watercolor on a hot-pressed sheet might be in order. Once in a while, just a mood or feeling directs the decision. Splashing paint around on a large, textured sheet of paper can be very cathartic. Most often, watermedia paintings are a combination of many of the techniques discussed in this chapter.

technique 1 » watercolor

Lay Down Warm Colors First

When your painting calls for luminous color or warm reflected light, the key is to lay down warm colors first. Unlike with opaque mediums, once a cool color is established in transparent watercolor it is quite difficult to warm it up without creating a tired, muddy painting. For example, shadows on a sunlit yard will look much more luminous if the cool shadows are layered on yellow-green. Violet and blue look more vibrant on top of yellow-orange, and even cool red looks better on top of a yellow-orange base.

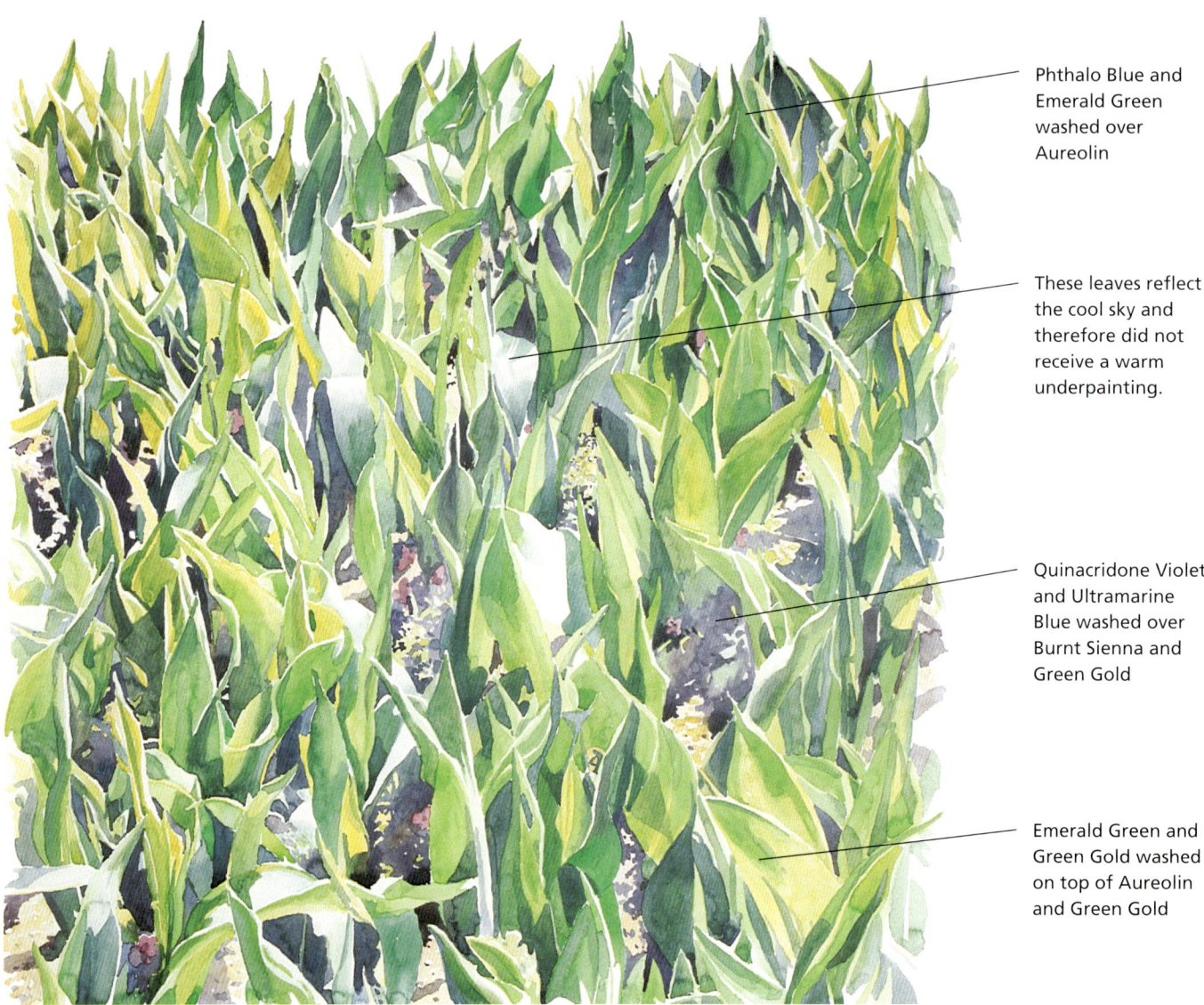

Phthalo Blue and Emerald Green washed over Aureolin

These leaves reflect the cool sky and therefore did not receive a warm underpainting.

Quinacridone Violet and Ultramarine Blue washed over Burnt Sienna and Green Gold

Emerald Green and Green Gold washed on top of Aureolin and Green Gold

Paint Warm Washes First to Create Glowing Foliage
Early washes of warm transparent color such as Aureolin and variegated washes of Emerald Green and Green Gold helped create the range of rich glowing greens in these tulip leaves. With transparent watercolor, it is much easier to make a color cooler than it is to add warmth.

Tulip Chaos » Watercolor on 140-lb. (300gsm) hot-pressed paper » 21" x 21" (53cm x 53cm)

technique 2 » watercolor

Variegate Your Washes

A great technique to create interesting colors and washes is to use variegated washes. The most pleasing combinations usually include a warm color and a cool color. For example, if you are painting a green tree, prepare a green mix, a blue-green mix and a puddle of yellow instead of mixing just one green on your palette. Establish the tree shape with yellow. While that wash is wet, drop in the green mix, and apply the blue-green wash on the shadow side. The colors will blend on your paper and make a much more interesting wash than one painted from a single mixture.

What makes this technique work is that the colors mix on the paper instead of the palette. It is important to have two or three puddles of color ready to go on your palette before you lay down the wash.

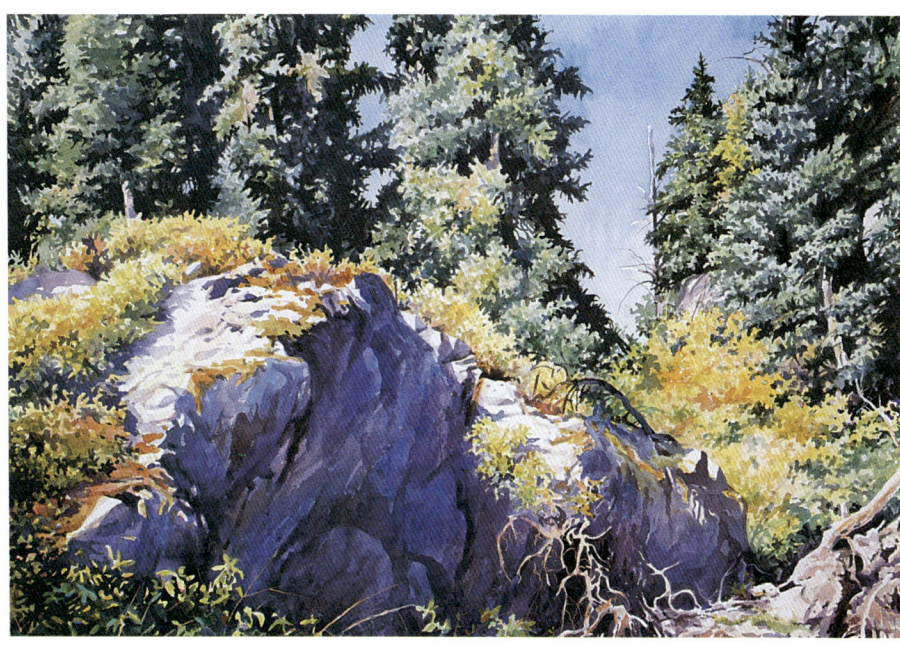

Increase Color Interest With Variegated Washes
This painting utilizes temperature layering and variegated washes to capture the morning light and shadow. In the detail images below, look for the interest and variety provided by variegated washes.

Looking Up » Watercolor on 300-lb. (640gsm) cold-pressed paper » 22" x 30" (56cm x 76cm)

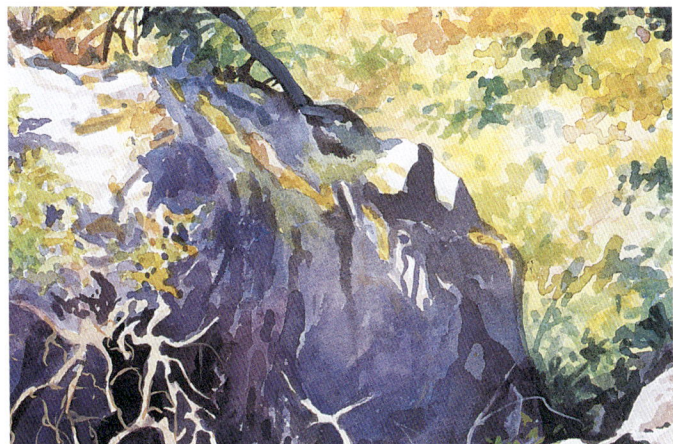

Boulder Detail
The first wash on the shadow side of the boulder is a variegated mixture of pale Burnt Sienna and Winsor Red. While that wash was still wet, I floated washes of Ultramarine Blue, Phthalo Blue, Cobalt Blue and a bit of Alizarin Crimson. The different colors blended together on the paper, leaving an interesting color and wash texture.

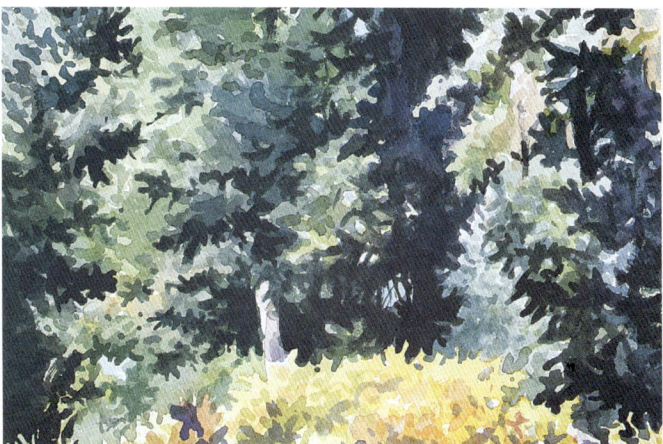

Tree Detail
The trees were built with warm washes of New Gamboge, Aureolin and Cobalt Blue. As more layers were added, cooler washes were superimposed using mixes of Cobalt Blue, Cerulean Blue, Phthalo Blue, Green Gold and Aureolin. The darkest values were done with a dense mixture of Phthalo Blue, Emerald Green, Winsor Red and a touch of Burnt Umber.

mini-demonstration » watercolor

Start Warm for September Flowers

These flowers were cut from our garden late one September. I worked from a photo of a vase on our picnic table. I liked how the sunlit grass created a warm backdrop for the dahlias and sunflower shapes. The backlighting also shined brightly through the glass vase, creating a dazzling highlight at its base. Since the sunlight effect was so prevalent, washing in a base of warm colors was a must. This created a warm-color harmony throughout the painting and made for more interesting color. To see the full finished painting, flip back to page 8.

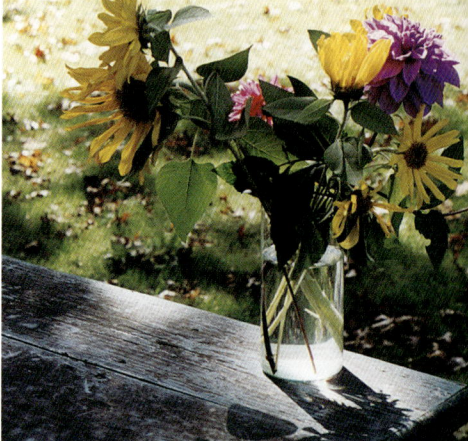

materials

paper
140-lb. (300gsm) cold-pressed

watercolors
Alizarin Crimson • Aureolin • Burnt Sienna • Burnt Umber • Cadmium Orange Light • Cobalt Blue • Emerald Green • Green Gold • New Gamboge • Phthalo Blue • Quinacridone Gold • Winsor Red • Winsor Yellow

brushes
Nos. 16, 12, 10, 8 and 4 synthetic rounds
No. 2 kolinsky sable round
1-inch (25mm) synthetic flat

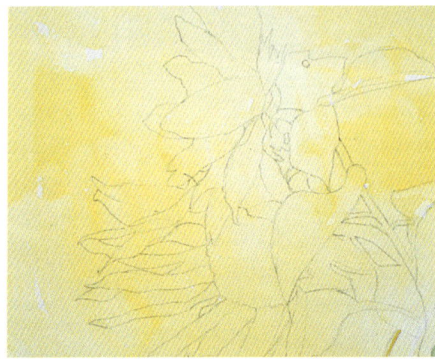

Reference Photo

1 Start With Broad, Warm Washes
Apply a variegated wash of New Gamboge and Aureolin. Since the background had to project warm sunlit grass, I made the wash more intense there. Keep the background simple and loose. Remember that applying too many layers reduces the brilliance of your colors. Let this dry.

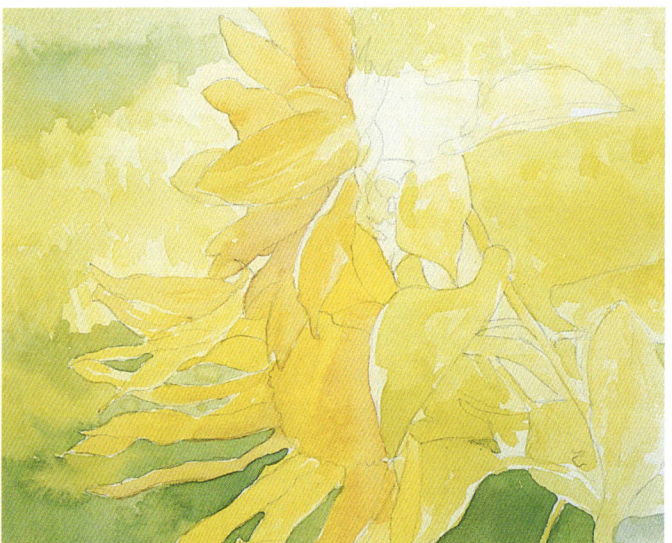

2 Establish Basic Shapes
Re-wet the background, and add variegated wash mixtures of Aureolin, New Gamboge, Green Gold and Cobalt Blue. After the background dries, establish the sunflower petals with washes of New Gamboge and Cadmium Orange Light.

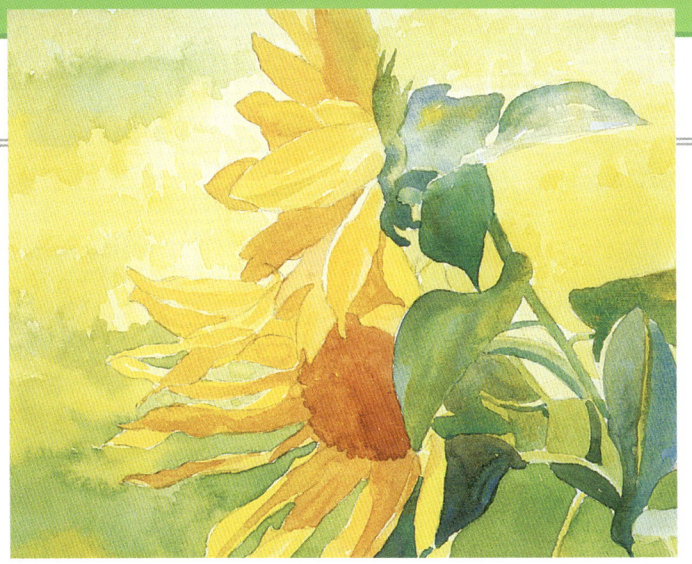 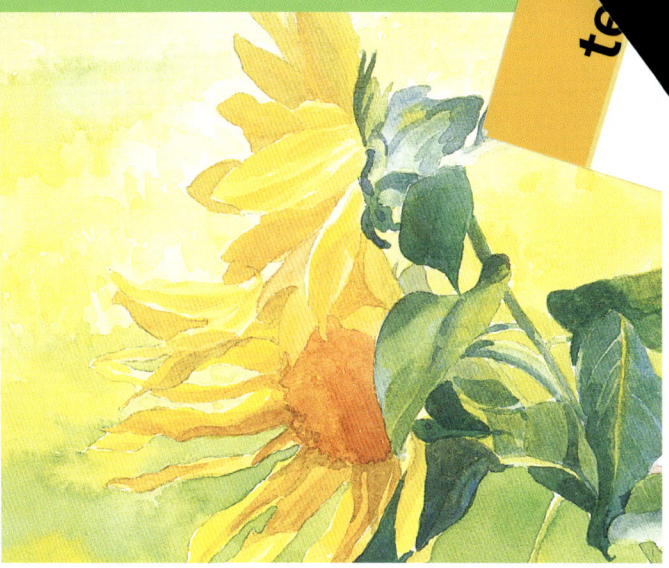

3 Establish Value Pattern

The background will be lighter than the flowers, so apply a pale wash of Alizarin Crimson and Burnt Sienna with a touch of Quinacridone Gold to the petals. Use a mix of Burnt Sienna and Quinacridone Gold for the sunflower's center. Paint the leaves with variegated mixes of Cobalt Blue, Emerald Green and Winsor Yellow. Some leaf surfaces reflect a bit of the sky, so they should be left on the blue side; the leaves that show some backlighting from the warm background should get more yellow. Allow Phthalo Blue to dominate the deepest shadows. Looking at steps two and three, compare the background green at the bottom right. Notice how it settles into its proper value relationship when contrasted with the darkest leaves.

4 Refine the Shapes and Forms

With the same color mixes used in step three, paint subtle washes to refine the flower petals and leaves. Deepen the shadow values and establish the textures of the leaves with some additional washes.

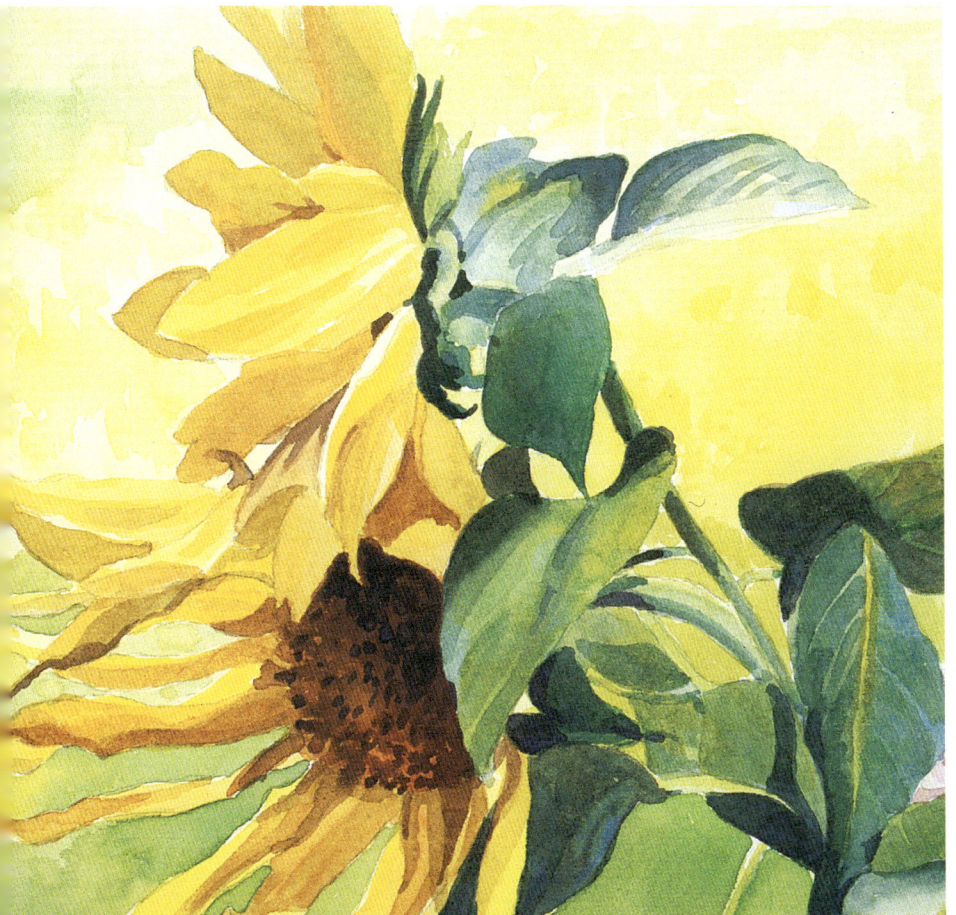

5 Create Contrast With Your Darkest Values

Deepen the leaf shadows again with a mix of Phthalo Blue and a bit of Emerald Green and Winsor Red. Paint the dark center of the sunflower with a mix of Alizarin Crimson and Burnt Umber. Develop some of the darkest petals with a mix of Quinacridone Gold, Burnt Sienna and a bit of Cobalt Blue. This final step is what gives your painting zest. The subject has been rendered with a full range of values, and these values all have a distinct color note.

Technique 3 » acrylics

Paint Dark Values First

Unlike traditional transparent watercolor, acrylics on paper are painted with a combination of transparent, semitransparent and opaque layers. This layering process can be much more extensive than layering in watercolor. As you build layers of color, it is easy to obliterate your drawing and lose edges and shapes essential to your painting.

Painting the darkest values first helps establish the basic design and keeps it there as you paint the subsequent layers. This allows you to paint more freely. The dark values will peek through as you build your medium and light values, so you never have to worry about losing the design of your shapes and forms. Also, seeing this pattern of lights and darks gives you instant feedback as to how well your painting has been designed. It is better to catch a design problem at the beginning than at the end.

These early dark values will get lighter as semiopaque washes are applied. Often, these become the medium-dark values, and the darkest values and shapes have to be reestablished. This process automatically extends the value range and creates many subtle value shifts that give a convincing sense of form.

use image-editing software to see the value pattern

A helpful way to see the value pattern in a photo is to scan it into image-editing software such as Adobe Photoshop. By manipulating the contrast and color balance settings, you can produce a high-contrast image of your reference photo. This will show you the basic pattern of lights and darks. It is a more sensitive version of what a black-and-white copier does to a photo.

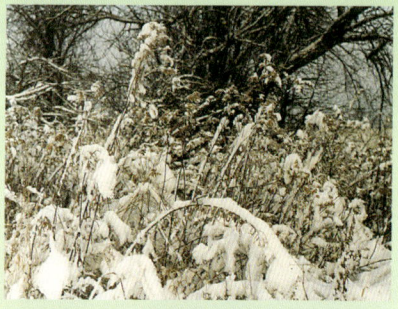

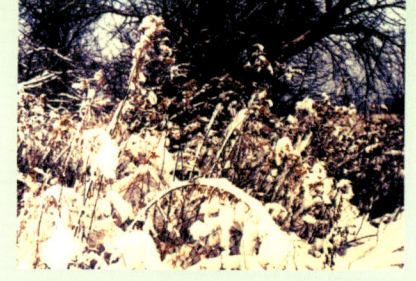

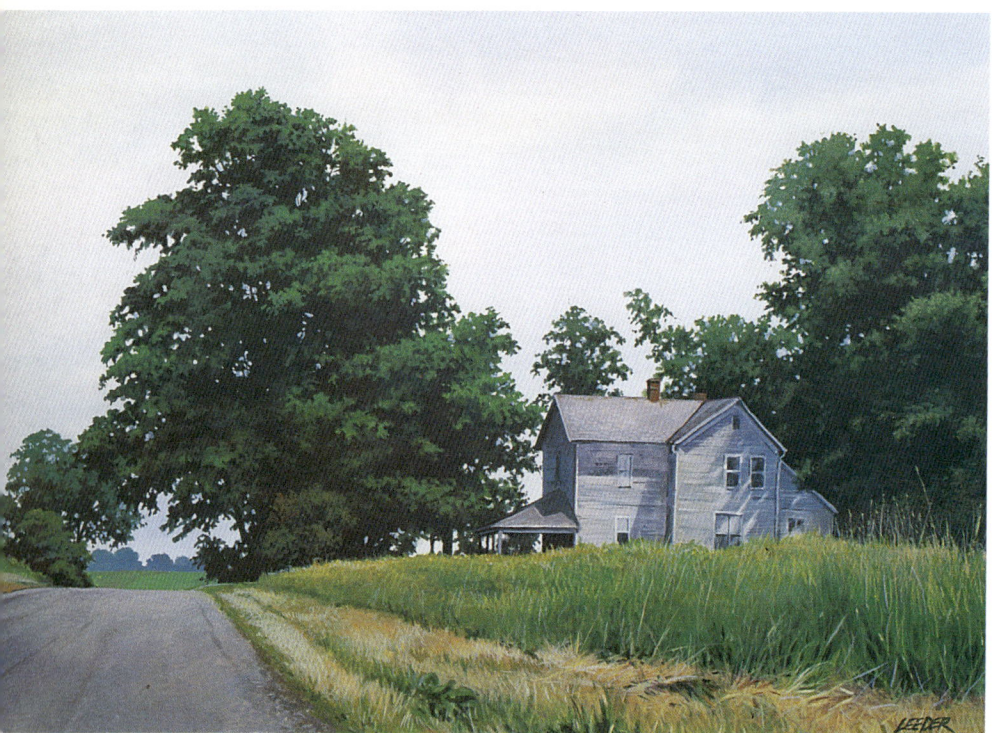

Establish Dark Value Structure First
This old farmhouse in Lisbon, Ohio, has captured my imagination for several years. I have painted it from many angles and in every season. In this painting I did the shadow shapes in the trees, field and house first. I painted the sky wet-into-wet. I worked the rest of the painting dark to light, similar to a traditional oil painting.

Miller Road House—July » Acrylic on 140-lb. (300gsm) cold-pressed paper » 12" x 18" (30cm x 46cm)

mini-demonstration » acrylics

Render Glass With Layered Acrylics

I came across this array of bottles and objects in the foundation drawing room at the university where I teach. I photographed them using a digital camera and worked from an ink-jet printout. For this demonstration we'll layer transparent washes over the darkest values. To see the full finished painting, see pages 8-9.

materials

paper
140-lb. (300gsm) hot-pressed

acrylics
ACRA Crimson • Burnt Sienna • Burnt Umber • Diozaxine Purple • Permanent Green Light • Phthalo Blue • Titanium White • Yellow Orange Azo

brushes
Nos. 10, 6, 4 and 2 synthetic rounds
No. 1 kolinsky sable round
½-inch (12mm) synthetic flat

Reference Photo

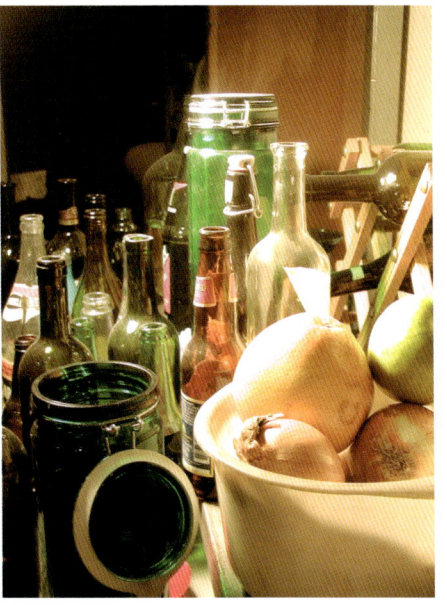

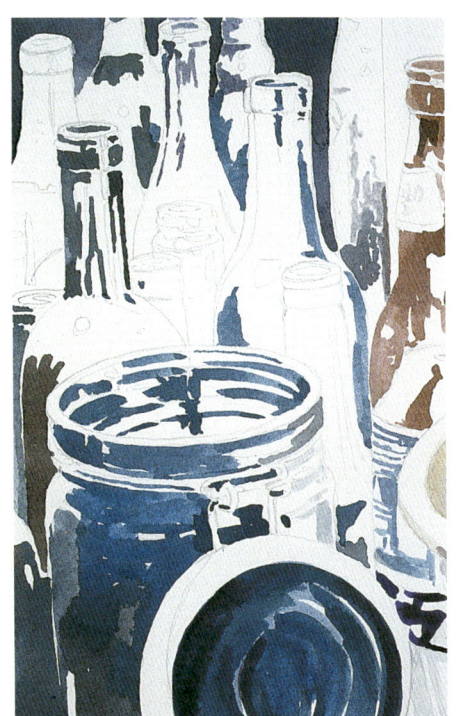

1 Paint the Dark Values and Details
Using a mix of Phthalo Blue, Burnt Umber and Burnt Sienna, paint the dark shapes. I used more Phthalo Blue or Burnt Sienna where necessary to match more closely the local color of the bottle.

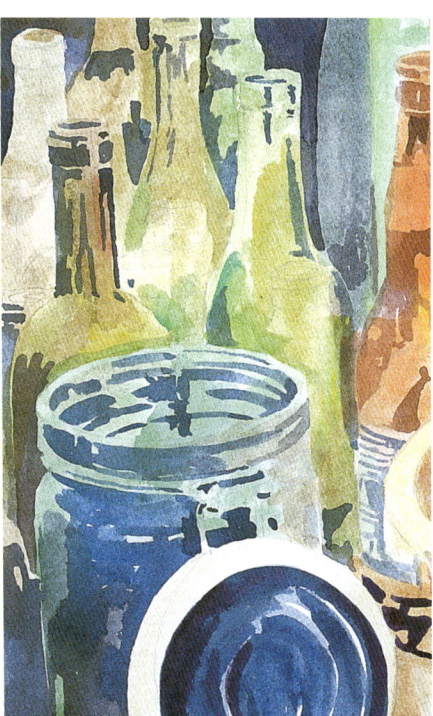

2 Establish Local Color
With the dark underpainting dry, add transparent layers of local color. Use various transparent mixtures of Phthalo Blue, Permanent Green Light, Yellow Orange Azo and Burnt Sienna for the green bottles and the jar. The brown bottle is a transparent mix of Burnt Sienna, ACRA Crimson and a bit of Dioxazine Purple. At this stage the painting should resemble a transparent watercolor.

67

3 Add Transparent and Semi-transparent Layers

After the first transparent layers are dry, add another layer of the same colors. This layer should be a bit more heavily pigmented but still fairly liquid in consistency. Paint the shadow shapes on the bottles using a mixture of Phthalo Blue and Burnt Umber. Using a bit of semiopaque Titanium White, delineate the edges and rims of the bottles.

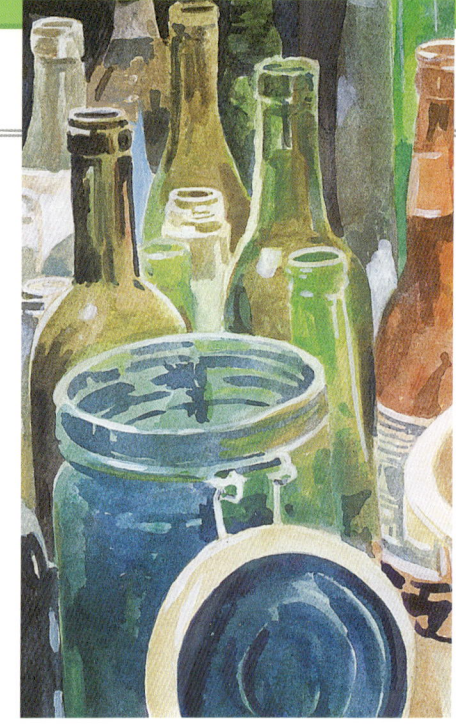

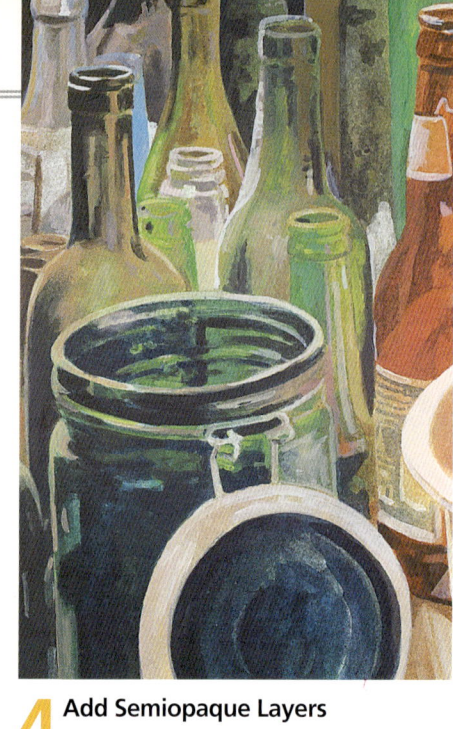

4 Add Semiopaque Layers

This step is where we shift from watercolor to acrylic techniques. Using semiopaque mixtures, brush color over all the areas of the painting. Dab relatively opaque mixtures here and there to build richness and depth. Use the same colors as in the previous steps, with Titanium White added to some lighter mixtures.

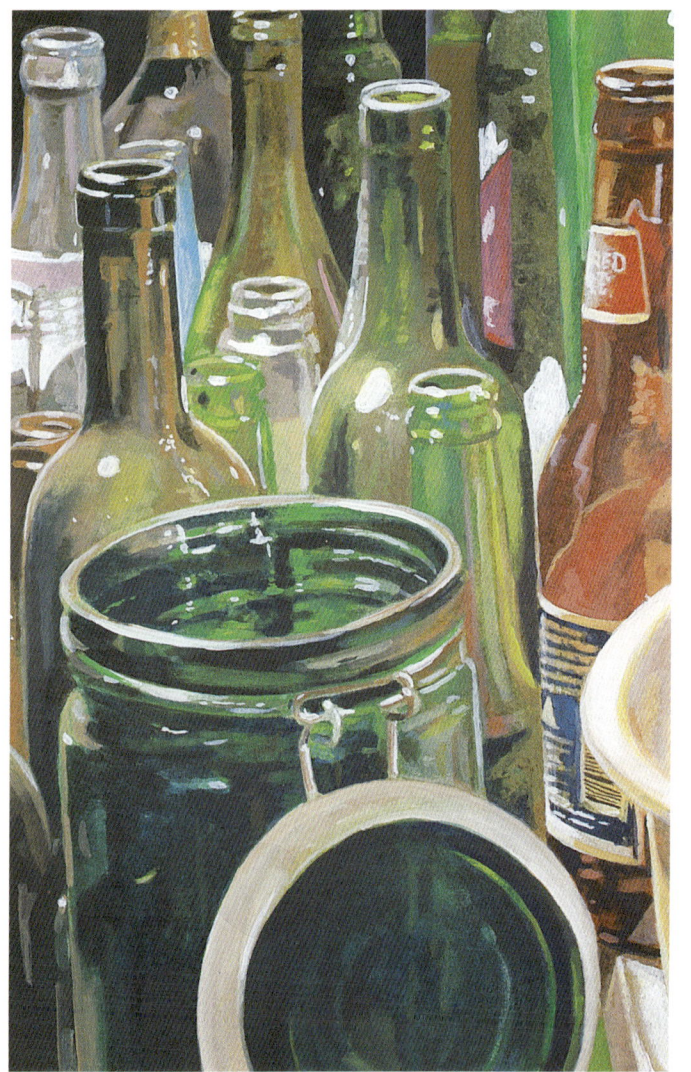

5 Add Final Layers of Opaque and Transparent Color

This layer pulls everything into focus. Add the brightest reflections using opaque Titanium White. Sharpen edges using the same semiopaque and opaque colors as in previous steps. Finally, modify values with transparent and semitransparent washes of the same colors as in previous steps.

technique 4 » watercolor

Use Rich Color Mixes for Drama

Most watercolorists want rich, beautiful color. But painting directly with a large brush plump with intense color can be quite intimidating. The payoff, though, is a painting that would never be thought of as just another wishy-washy watercolor. Here are some tips:

- **Have a plan.** Panic can set in once you put brush to paper and find out you are not sure where you are going with a wash. Planning what gets painted when can help alleviate some of this stress.

- **Create value sketches to understand the value structure of your painting.** If you need to work out more ideas, then a small colored pencil drawing or even a small watercolor rough can help.

- **Create a sound drawing.** Having a solid, complete drawing on your paper will really help. Think of what a paint-by-number painting looks like. You don't have to go to that extreme, but the more shapes and forms you delineate on your drawing the better chance you have to render your subject well.

- **Test colors before you paint.** Keep a scrap piece of the same paper as your painting surface nearby to test color and value. Let the test wash dry to see if it's going to be vibrant enough.

- **Match the brush size to the wash area.** Big washes require big brushes. A wash made up of four strokes looks fresher than one made from forty.

- **Be patient.** Students often tell me how frustrated they get with the idea of planning a painting; they just want to paint. I understand; I'd rather paint too! But what's the goal of the painting? If a realistic interpretation is the goal, then a bit of planning on the front end will greatly increase your chances of success. Having a plan and a solid understanding of your subject even allows you to be more expressive and take some chances with color, value and technique.

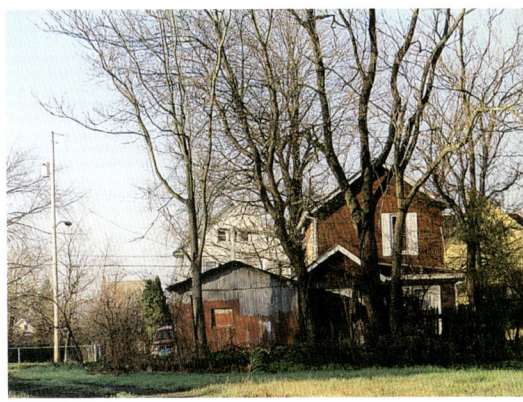

Reference Photo

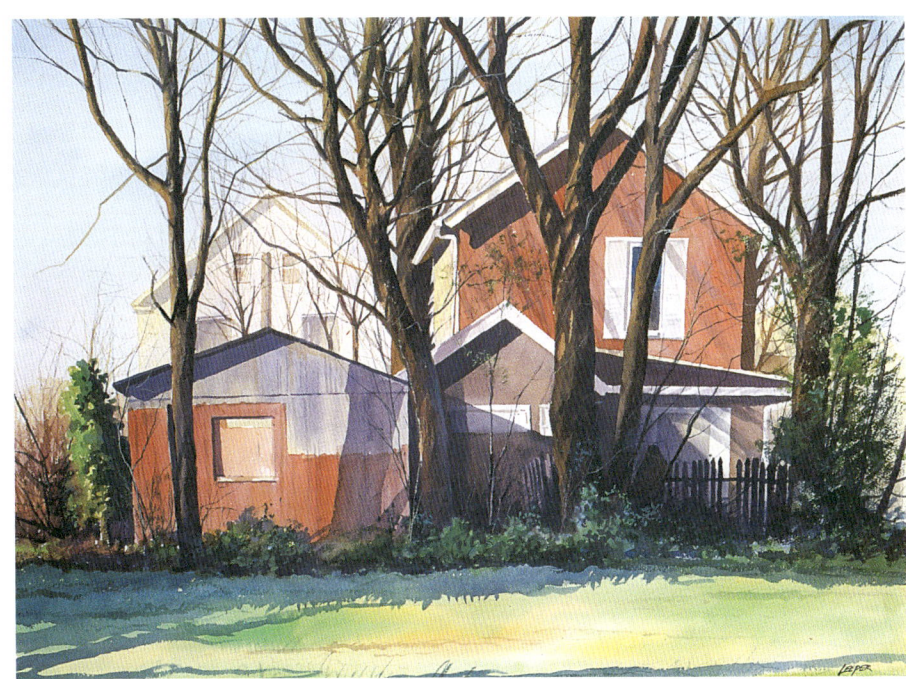

Enliven Your Paintings With Rich Color

I think of this painting as a portrait of a house. This old red house is near the university where I teach, and I often thought about painting it. One morning I snapped a picture, and I used that as my reference for this painting. I debated whether to put the entire house in the painting since that created a rather centered and static composition. Thinking about it as a portrait of a place instead of a landscape, I decided to design it this way. I also wanted to emphasize the rich colors on the trees and the building. To achieve this, I mixed large, heavily pigmented puddles of color on my palette. This also reduced the need for multiple washes, which in turn kept the color fresh and vibrant.

The Red House » Watercolor on 300-lb. (640gsm) cold-pressed paper » 30" x 40" (76cm x 102cm)

technique 5 » watercolor

Use a Variety of Brush Techniques

Just as monotonous colors or values can make for a boring painting, so can one brush technique used repeatedly. When painting with rich, bold color you can work with a variety of brush techniques to add zest and interest to your painting. Keys are choosing the right brush and using the right pigment load for your washes. The variety of washes in a painting might include:

Delicate, transparent passages made with plenty of water in your brush.

Rich yet transparent color. This calls for big puddles and plenty of color.

Linear or calligraphic brushstrokes. These can be made with rounds as well as flat brushes.

Opaque color areas. These call for pure pigment with little water.

Study the watercolor brushwork of John Singer Sargent to see the potential of using a variety of techniques.

mix your watercolors generously

Big color requires big puddles. Don't be afraid to mix more color than you think you need. It is surprising how fast it goes away when you paint a larger area. It helps to have a large palette surface that can accommodate such mixes. Use the lid of the palette or an enamel butcher tray for additional mixing surfaces. If you work with a really large area that needs intense color, consider mixing puddles of color in separate cups. I keep old butter containers handy for such instances.

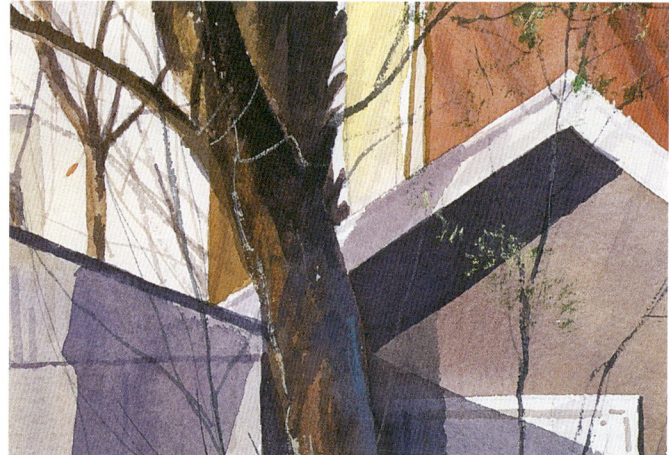

Detail: Match Brushes to Your Painting Goals
Study the variety of washes and brush techniques used here. Large areas were covered using large brushes and large puddles of color—you don't want to run out of color in the middle of a wash. Notice the blue on the tree trunk; it is Cerulean Blue used very opaquely. The green leaves were also put on with dabs of opaque color. The shadows were done in one wash. This is important in achieving luminous color. The shadowed subject should show through, and a shadow made with two or three washes can look too heavy. A variety of linear strokes was used to render the limbs and tree branches. Matching the size of your stroke with the right brush is crucial. A no. 10 and a no. 2 round were used along with a rigger.

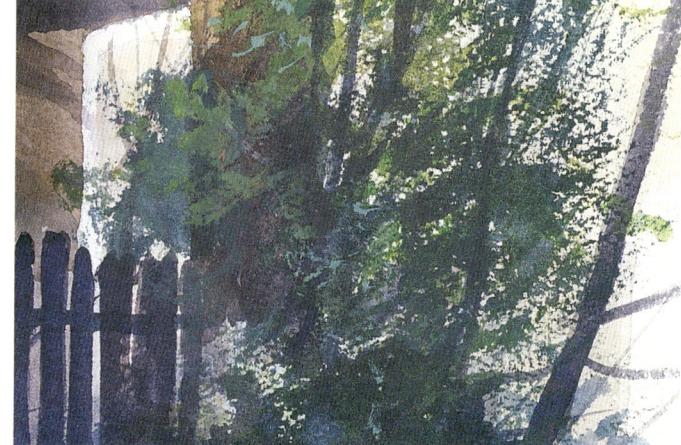

Detail: Use Wet and Dry Techniques
Rich color can be painted with clean transparent washes as well as more-opaque applications. The shrubs in this detail section show an aggressive dry-brush technique. I loaded a no. 8 round with very pigmented color and then dabbed on a paper towel to eliminate excess moisture. I then dragged the side of the brush across the paper. The 300-lb. (640gsm) cold-pressed sheet has plenty of tooth, and I took advantage of this to create the broken texture.

Even though this is a fairly opaque passage, I still used the concept of warmer color first. Notice the warm yellow-green peeking from behind the Phthalo Blue and Burnt Sienna mixture used for the deep green. I also included some touches of opaque Cerulean Blue to add variety. Into this shrub I painted the small trees with a more traditional transparent brushstroke. Because these strokes were wetter than the shrub, they blended with the deep green pigment; this helped give the impression that the trees were growing within and behind the shrub.

technique 6 » acrylics

Blending Technique 1: *Finger Blending*

Acrylics dry fast. If you like hard edges and mark making, this will appeal to you. However, blending color to achieve softer edges or atmospheric color can be a problem.

There are a few techniques to get around this. Color can be pushed and rubbed out with your fingers, color can be blended using traditional watercolor wet-into-wet washes and wash layering, or color can be scumbled using an old brush. These techniques can be used together or separately, depending on the subject or the painting goals.

One of my favorite techniques for blending acrylics is to use my fingers. Finger blending does not work as well on dry paper, so I usually have a layer or two of local color down before I start pushing color around. As layers build up on the surface, the paper gets a bit slicker; color slips and slides on the surface and can be easily manipulated with fingers.

Sometimes you can add paint to the paper with a brush and then blend the paint with your fingers. If a more opaque color is called for, wet your finger, touch a bit of color on your palette, and then spread this color onto your paper. If you have too much paint you can drop some water onto your paper and then blend out the color with your fingers or a brush. Small areas can be blended with the edge of your fingertip; large areas can be blended with a lot of semiopaque paint and two or three fingers.

I really enjoy using this technique on portraits. It reminds me of sculpting in clay as I push and manipulate paint to create a rendering of a three-dimensional form. This technique is part of the overall layering used in most acrylic paintings. It is important to wait for each layer to dry before adding more color. This keeps color fresh and protects the paper.

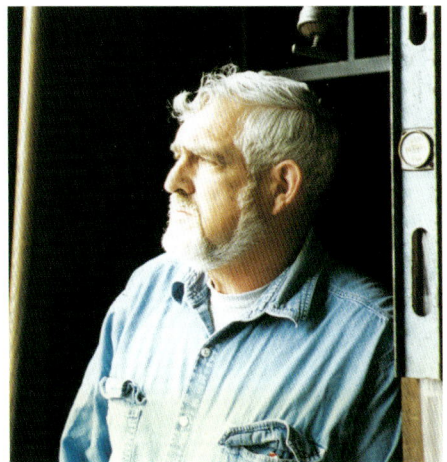

Reference Photo

Use Your Finger for Lifelike Skin Tones

Kenny is a friend whom I have painted several times. I worked from a photo that I had taken of him outside his blacksmith shop. I liked the contrast between his strong profile and the dark background. I painted several layers of color to get the depth of color in the face. I let each layer dry and alternated between brushed washes and finger blending.

Kenny » Acrylic on 140-lb. (300gsm) cold-pressed paper » 22" x 15" (56cm x 38cm)

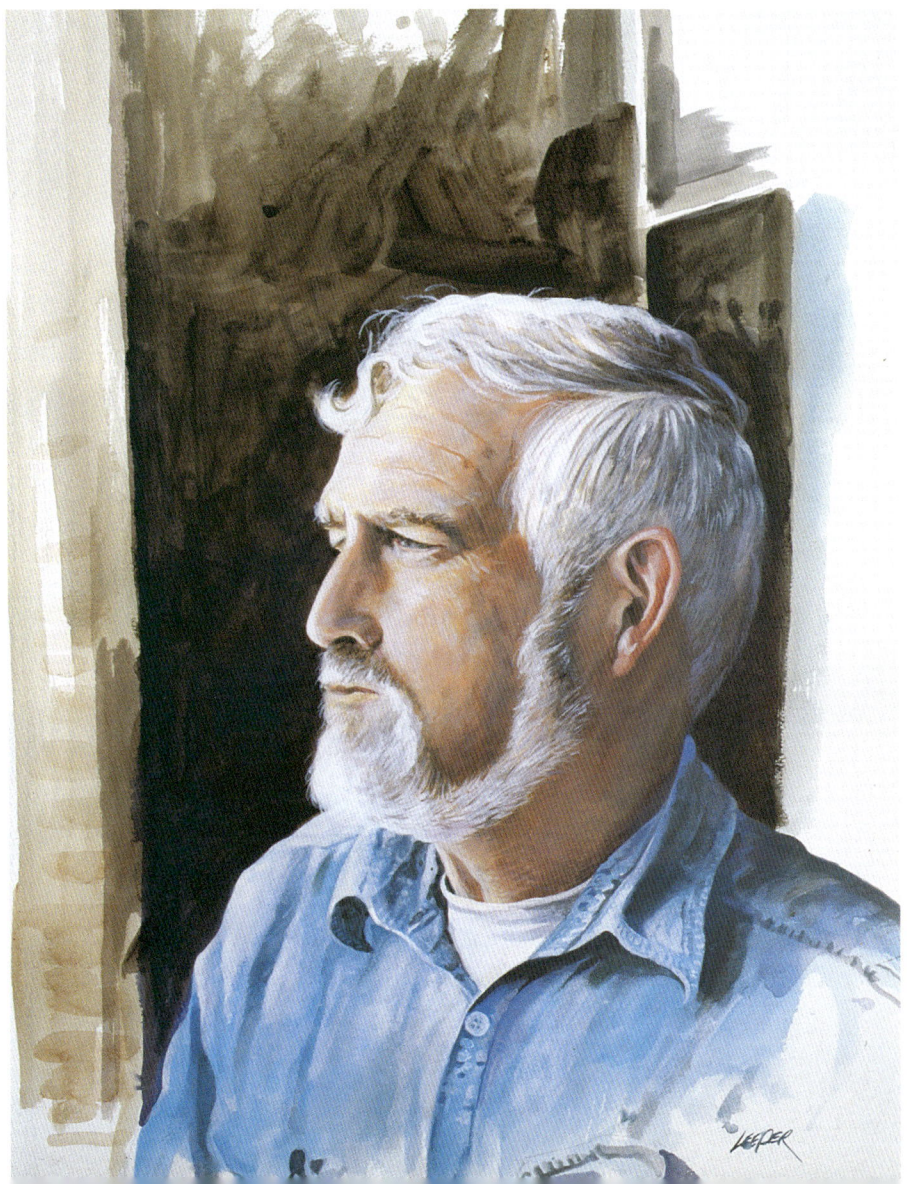

1 Establish a Base of Titanium White

I established transparent washes indicating local color and the darkest values. Once these dried, I brushed on a layer of semiopaque Titanium White and pushed it around with my fingers. I did this a couple times. I allowed each layer to dry before adding any more paint. Letting each layer dry seals the surface of the paper slightly and creates a base on which to build additional layers of color.

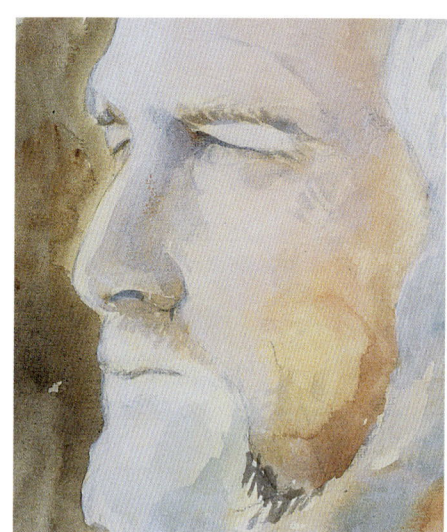
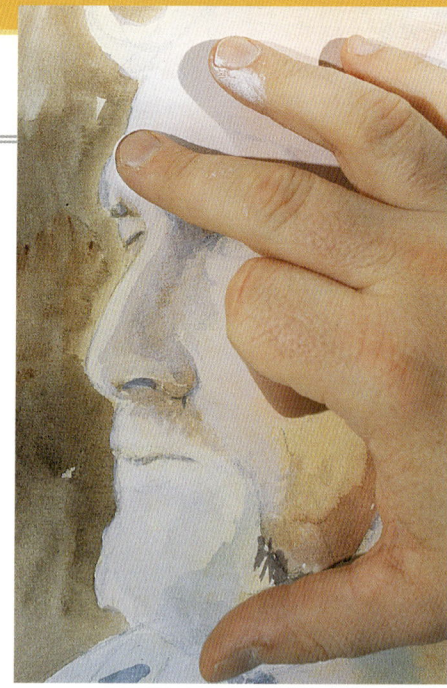

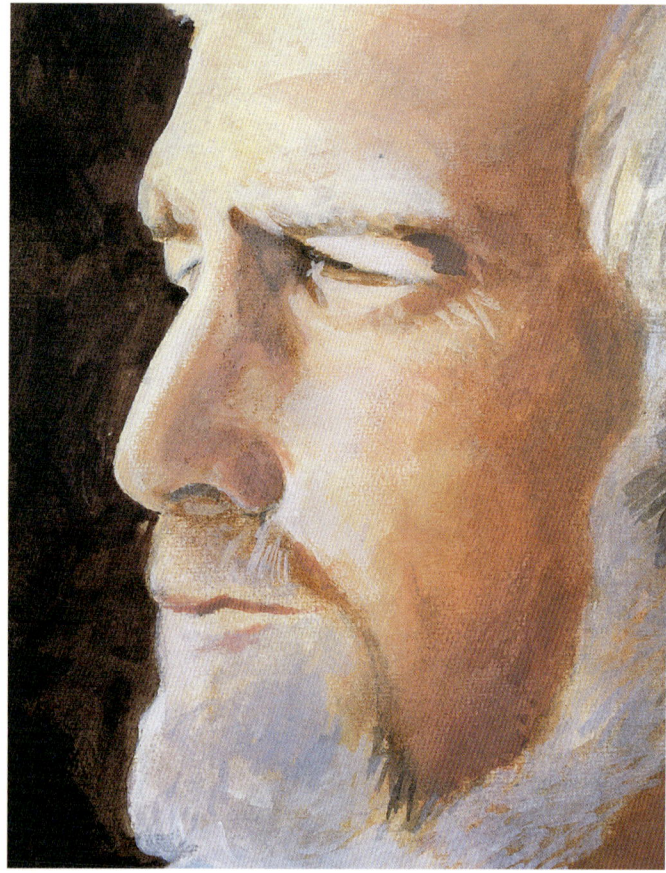

2 Layer Transparent Color

I painted transparent washes on top of a base of white. The colors I used for the flesh tone were various mixtures of Naphthol Red Light, Yellow Ochre, Yellow Medium Azo and ACRA Red. The shadows on the face meant adding Ultramarine Blue and Burnt Sienna to these colors. I put on a couple layers of color and, like before, allowed each layer to dry.

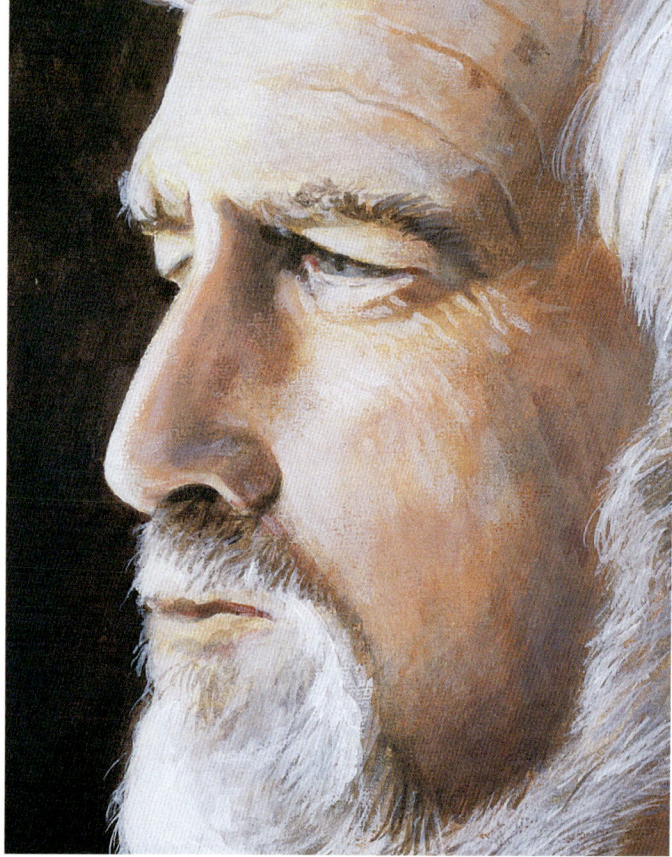

3 Alternate Between Brush and Finger Blending

I added Titanium White and color mixtures and finger-blended. These layers are a bit more opaque. On top of that, I added more transparent and semitransparent color. Sometimes I blended these brushed layers a bit with my fingers; other times I used the brush to leave a harder edge. I added the final touches like hair and wrinkles with a small round.

technique 7 » acrylics

Blending Technique 2: *Wet-into-Wet Layering*

Acrylics can be blended easily using the traditional wet-into-wet watercolor technique. Since acrylics dry so quickly, this is the technique of choice for covering large areas. You can paint much like you would with traditional transparent watercolor, or you can blend more-opaque colors wet-into-wet. You can layer several wet-into-wet washes of color until you get the desired blending or the correct color and value.

A technique that allows a great deal of control and gives you more blending time is to paint into a wet base of white. The idea is to have a thin layer of gesso or Titanium White suspended in the wet-into-wet area. (I prefer gesso since it disperses more evenly. The gesso keeps the subsequent layers of color from spreading, and it provides time to manipulate and blend colors.) The white shouldn't be too heavy or it might overpower your color mixes.

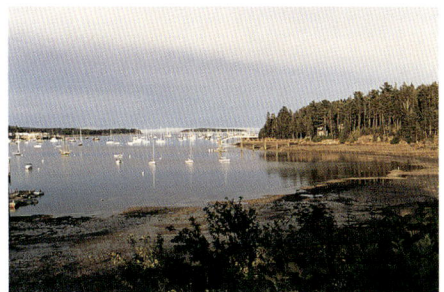
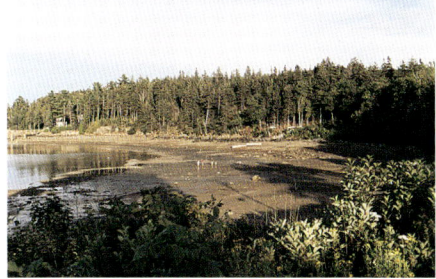

Reference Photos

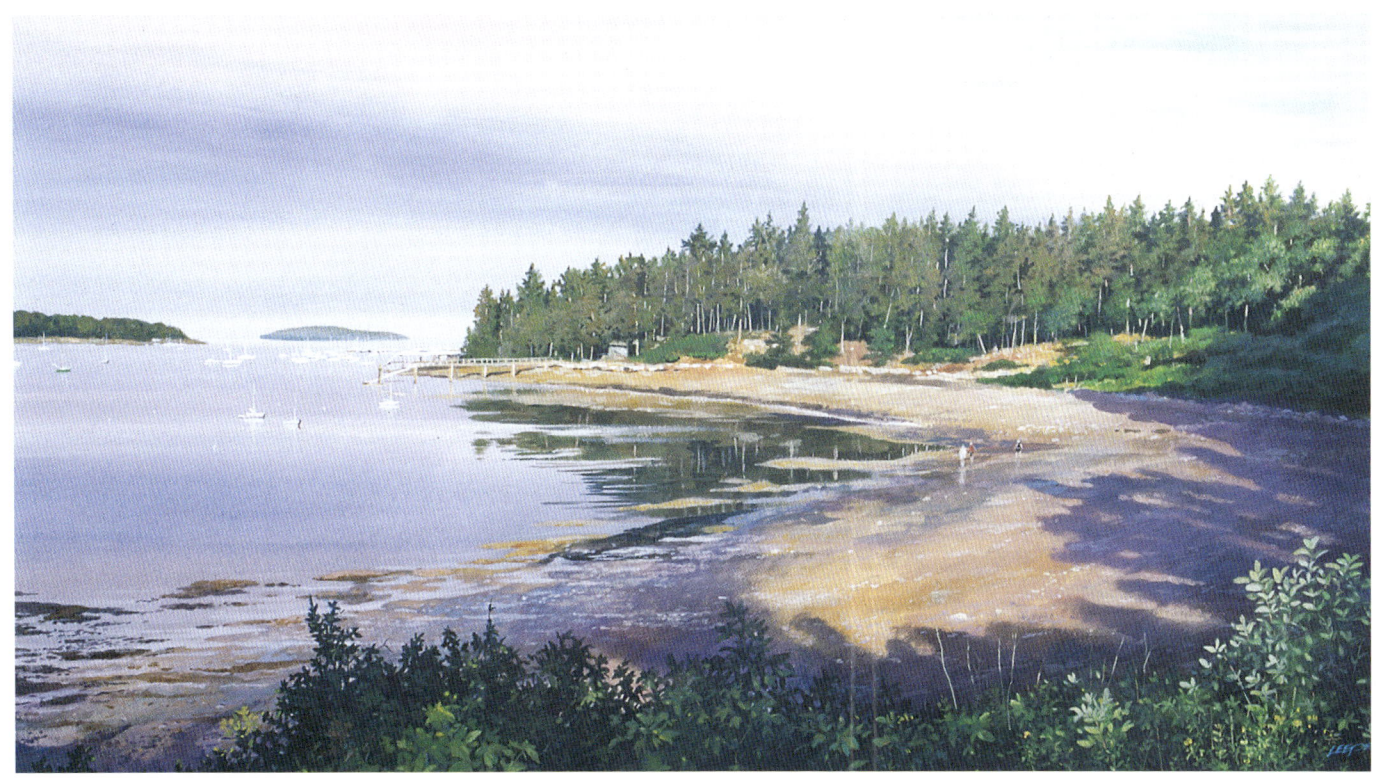

Use Multiple Techniques to Blend Color
This painting is of low tide along the Maine coast. I combined two photos to create the composition. I liked the long shadows and color contrasts between the warm coastline and cool water and shadows. This painting has a little of everything. Scumbled color is used extensively as well as wet-into-wet, finger blending and plenty of layered washes.

Low Tide » Acrylic on 140-lb. (300gsm) cold-pressed paper » 20" x 36" (51cm x 91cm)

1. Start With a Wet-Into-Wet Wash

I painted the darkest values first, then brushed local transparent color on everything except the sky and water. After this dried, I wetted the paper extensively from the sky to the foreground with a 2-inch (51mm) flat. I used a no. 32 round to float a mixture of Ultramarine Blue, Brilliant Blue, Titanium White and a bit of ACRA Crimson. Since my paper was so wet, I kept these color mixes fairly pigmented. To smooth out some darker color areas I used the 2-inch (51mm) flat.

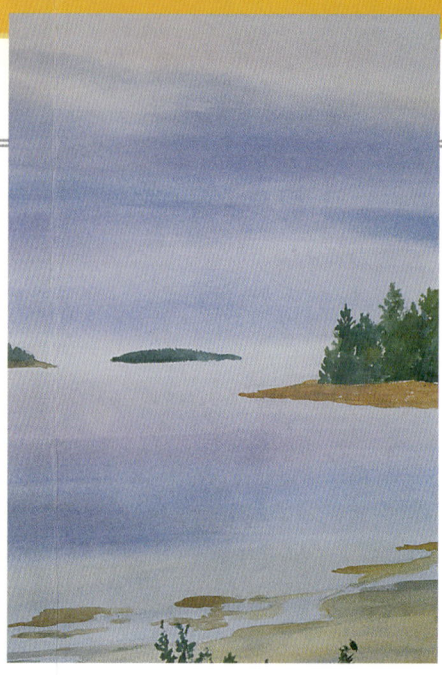

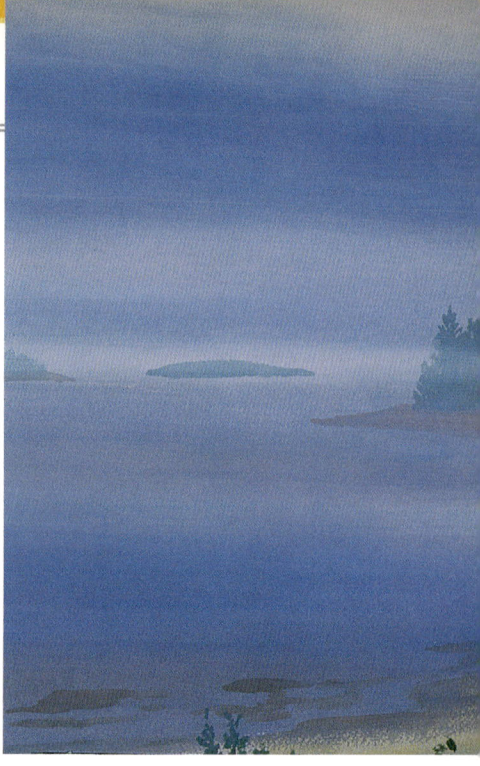

2. Layer Wet-Into-Wet Onto a Base of White

After the first wash had dried completely, I re-wetted the sky and water. Before using any color I brushed a layer of slightly diluted gesso across the wet paper. I used a more opaque application of gesso to indicate a fog bank along the horizon line. The paper was really saturated, so I waited a minute to let it dry slightly. Then I used the same blue mixes as I used in the previous step and repainted the sky and water. The base of gesso kept the second wash of color from being too intense. It also kept the paint from spreading, and I was able to move the paint around and better construct my cloud shapes.

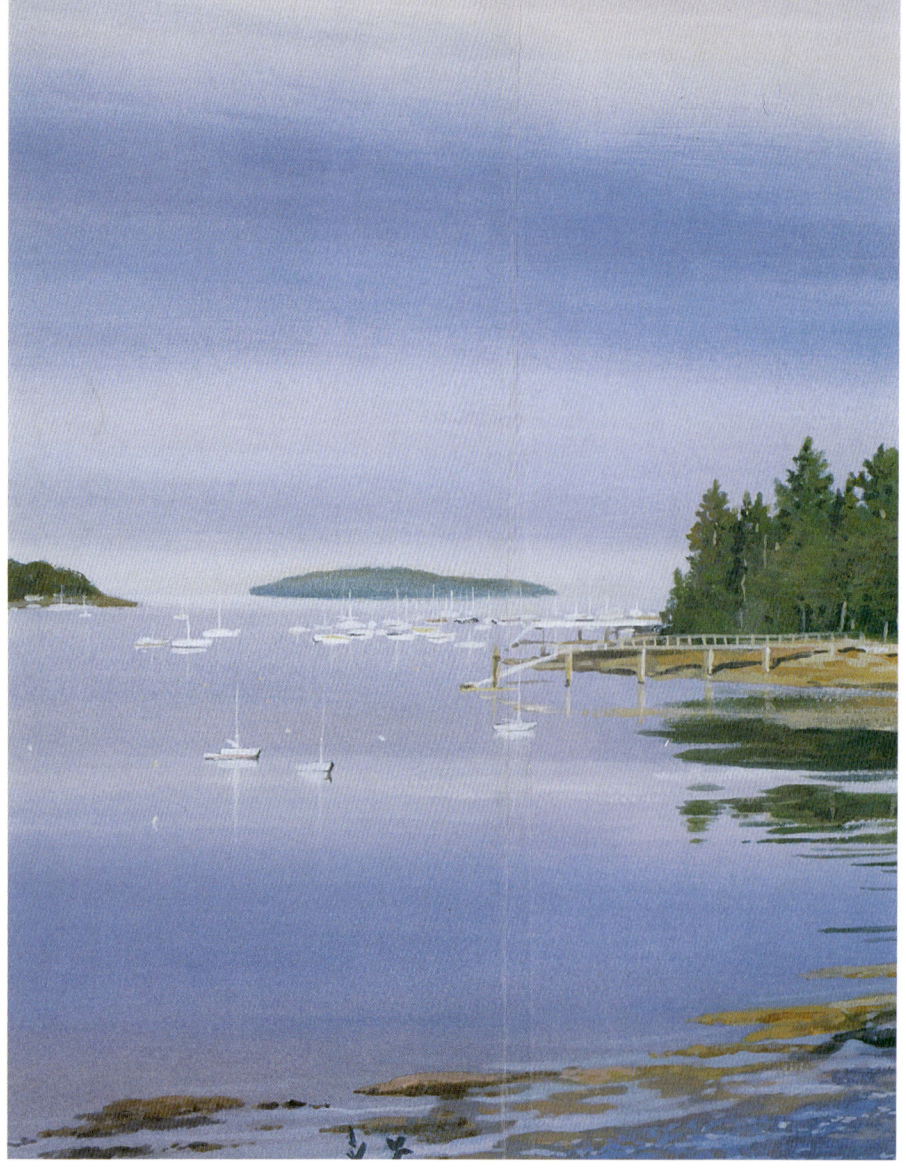

3. Repaint Areas Softened by the Wet-Into-Wet Layers

This detail shows the sky and water after the land masses were in their final stage. I added the boats with opaque Titanium White. I added a few reflections to the water. Notice how the boats give a sense of the scale of the water and sky.

technique 8 » acrylics

Blending Technique 3: *Scumbling*

The term scumbling is most often associated with oil painting, but this technique can be used just as effectively with acrylics. Scumbling isn't difficult. It involves loading a brush with semiopaque to opaque color and scrubbing it onto your paper until all the color is dispersed.

You can use the tip of your brush for more delicate blending, or you can use a scrubbing action. As you might guess from the term scrubbing, this technique is rough on brushes. For this reason, I seldom throw away an old brush. As synthetic brushes get worn out, their hair fibers begin to curl at the ends. Once this happens it is difficult to make a clean brushstroke, so this is when they get retired to scumbling duty.

I have brushes in many shapes and sizes for scumbling. My favorites are a ½-inch (13mm) flat for larger areas and a no. 8 and a no. 4 round for smaller applications. Sable brushes don't work as well because of their soft fibers and the fact that they don't break down the same way synthetics do. Bristle brushes can be used for rougher applications of opaque color.

Early stages of a painting may involve scumbling more-fluid color as an underpainting is built. I like to use several analogous colors to create color interest. This concept is similar to using a variegated wash in watercolor. As color is layered, I blend more-opaque colors with this technique. Scumbling is particularly helpful for putting in a soft-edged highlight. It also works well as a way to impart texture because it can lay down a path of broken color similar to that of watercolor drybrushing.

Let's look at how some of these techniques were used to finesse the details of *Low Tide*.

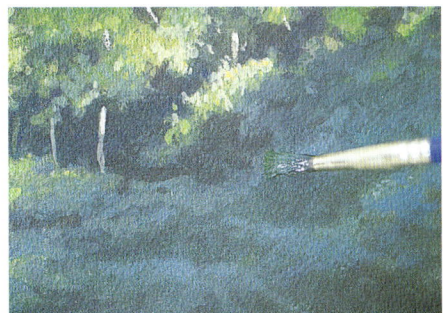

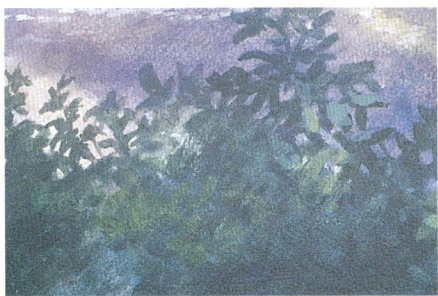

Scumbling for an Underpainting
In these details of *Low Tide*, you can see the underpainting for the shadowed area of background trees and foreground bushes. Atop layers of semitransparent paint, I roughly scrubbed or scumbled fairly opaque color. I used several colors. This blending of color produced a soft, variegated base for the final details.

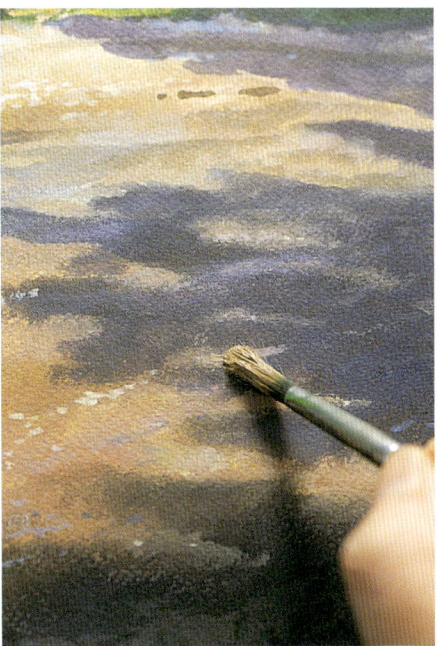

Scumbling to Blend Highlights
I produced much of the dappled sunlight on the beach with scumbled opaque color. This technique is very effective when you have a small area of highlight but don't want a hard edge. I often use this technique in combination with a bit of finger blending.

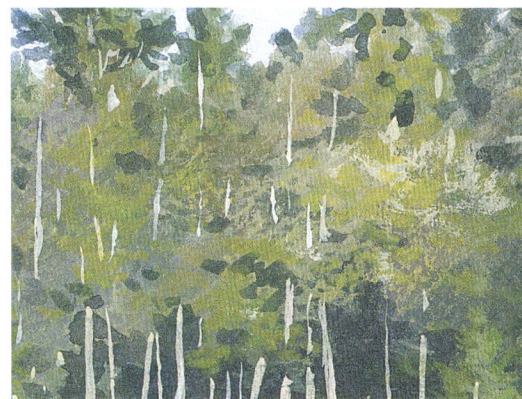

Scumbling to Add Texture
I painted the long strip of pines with scumbled color. This technique not only creates an interesting variegation, it also imparts texture. This detail shows the interesting pattern of scumbled color that makes up the mass of trees. On top of that, I scumbled lighter colors to create a broken texture. I overpainted the shadows with more-fluid touches of a Phthalo Blue and Burnt Sienna mix. I put in the tree trunks with opaque Titanium White.

technique 9 » watermedia

Brushwork Tip 1: *Broken-Color Layering*

An effective technique for rougher textures is something I call broken-color layering. It is a buildup of small, short brushstrokes of transparent color in watercolor and transparent and semitransparent color in acrylic. I like the term broken color since that essentially is what the application of color looks like. It also refers to the rougher textures often rendered with this technique.

Because there is a lot of layering with this technique, watercolors applied this way are at risk of becoming dull and muddy. To avoid this problem, use warm colors first and try for clean, transparent mixes.

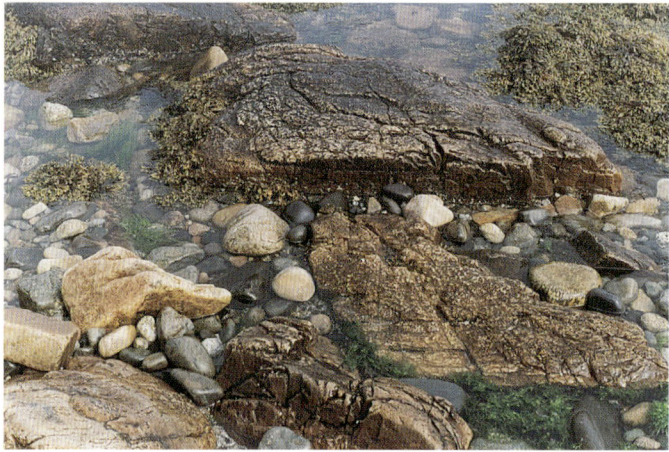
Reference Photo

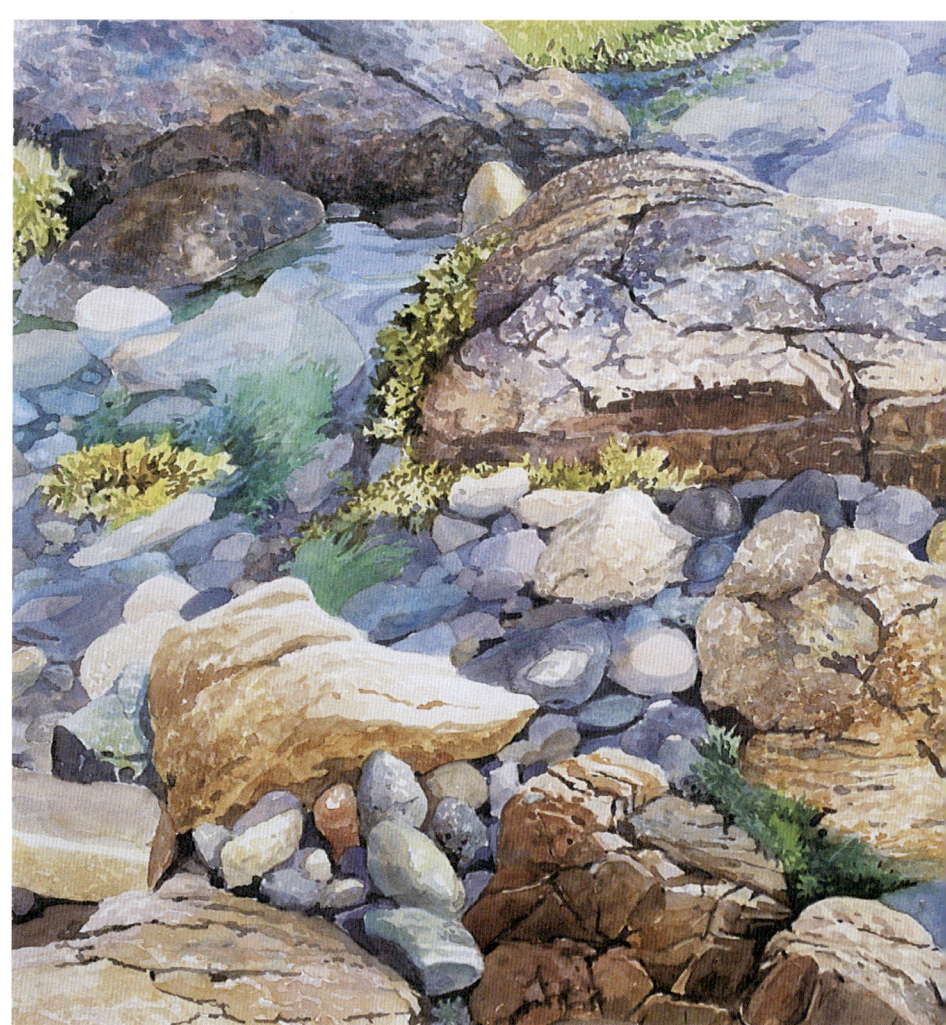

Broken-Color Layering Creates Texture
The challenge in this study was depicting the textures of the pink granite and the seaweed and the illusion of rocks under shallow water. I rendered the rougher textures with broken-color layering. Where the textures were smoother I tried for even, relatively flat washes.

Rocks at Sea Wall » Watercolor on 140-lb. (300gsm) hot-pressed paper » 11" x 15" (28cm x 38cm)

1 Establish a Light-Value Transparent Base

Using light, transparent colors and a no. 8 round, I blocked in all the shapes and forms. Most of the mixes were fairly warm, but I painted shadow areas and a few rocks with cool colors. Notice the variety of washes used—flat for underwater stones and broken for more-textured surfaces.

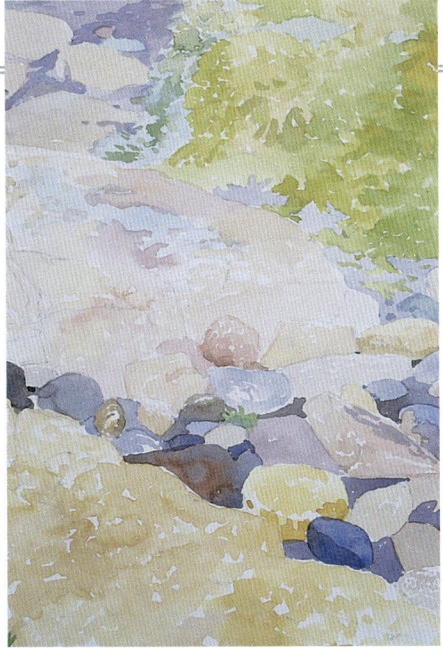
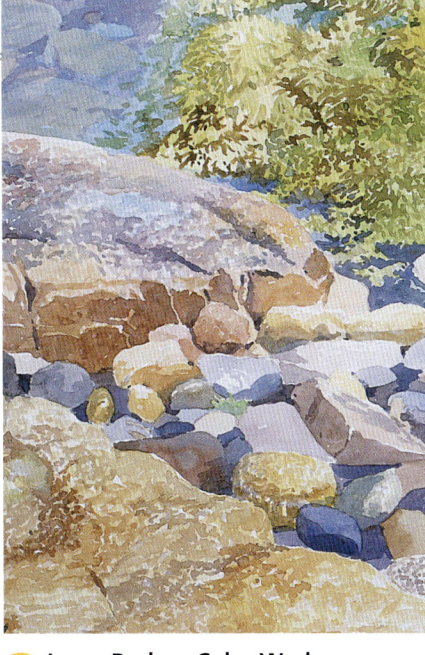

2 Layer Broken-Color Washes

Using a no. 6 round, I built up layers of small brushstrokes on the seaweed and larger granite rocks. I used deeper values as I developed the rock forms and shadow areas. I laid a light wash over the rocks at the upper left. This represents the shallow water that reflects the sky.

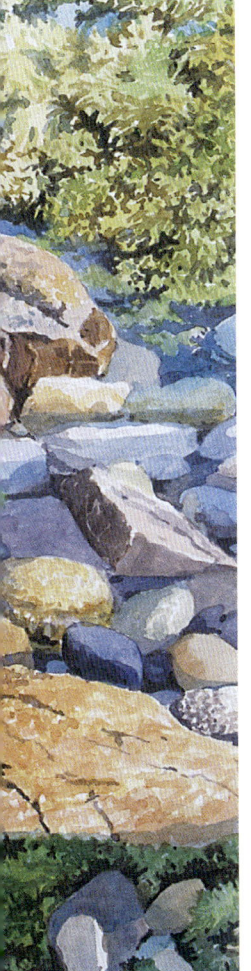
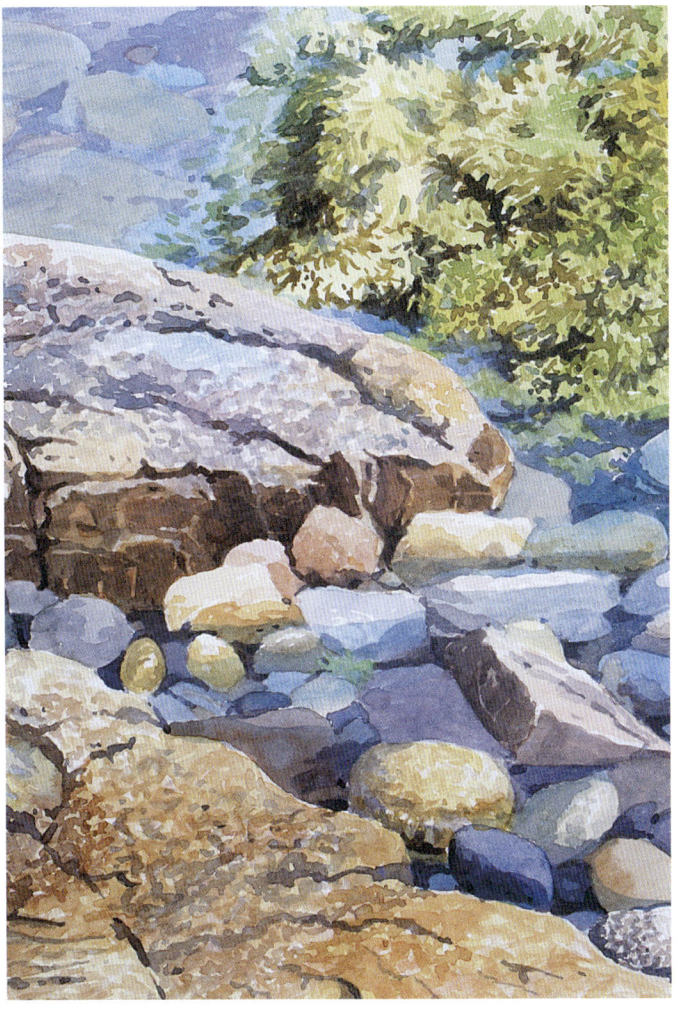

3 Add Final Layers and Darkest Values

The more-textured rocks received another layer or two of broken color. I intensified the shadows and painted a light, slightly variegated wash of various blues over the underwater rocks. Where the blue needed to be richer, I added a couple layers of color. I did the fine brushwork with a no. 2 round.

technique 10 » watermedia

Brushwork Tip 2: *Hatching and Crosshatching*

Hatching and cross-hatching are techniques familiar to anyone who has drawn with pen and ink. Hatching is a series of parallel lines that create tone. Cross-hatching is two or more intersecting sets of parallel lines. In watermedia, these techniques are a great way to build value and mass. They can also be used to convey certain textures like hair or grasses.

Keys to success in using these techniques are controlling the length and width of the marks, controlling the value and layering a variety of colors. I like to use longhaired rounds for my cross-hatching. Sometimes I even use a rigger or script liner to make really fine lines. Early layers are usually done with broader strokes; as layers are added, the lines become finer.

When rendering a form or large mass, you should make the lines blend together, but on close inspection they should retain their crispness. Controlling the value of the strokes is essential. If a layer is too dark or too light it will stand out and not integrate with the other marks. This problem usually is not an issue with transparent color; it becomes a factor when the strokes begin to have a degree of opacity.

Also, be sure to allow each layer to dry as you proceed. Layering with a variety of colors adds interest the same way a variegated wash adds spice to a watercolor. Mixing warm and cool layers is a great way to build a really interesting color area.

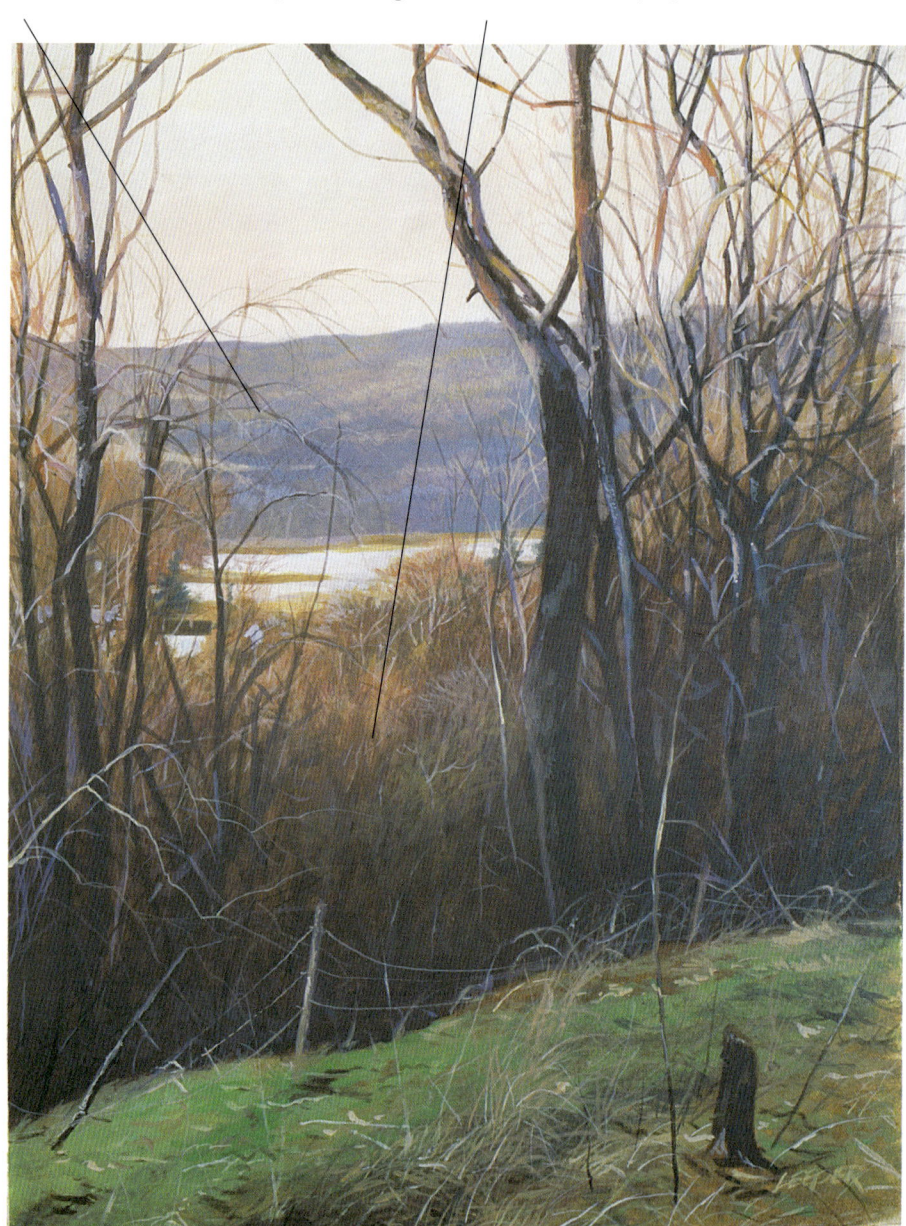

Notice the limited range of value contrasts between the layers of hatching and cross-hatching. Visual interest comes from the mix of warm and cool colors. Before the hatching layers were started, the hillside was covered with a semi-transparent wash of Ultramarine Blue and Napthol Red Light.

The broader transparent hatching lines were put in first and subsequent layers were finer and more opaque.

Build Layers With Cross-Hatching
This view is seen from my family's farm. It is loosely based on a photo. I depicted the warm evening light from memory. Cross-hatching works well in rendering large masses like these trees. The layers of marks vary in size, color and value. This variety adds visual interest to what could be a rather mundane subject.

Hillside Opening » Acrylic on 140-lb. (300gsm) hot-pressed paper »
15" x 11" (38cm x 28cm)

technique 11 » watermedia

Brushwork Tip 3: *Stippling*

Stippling is a term most often associated with pen-and-ink rendering. With pen and ink, stippling is a series of dots bunched together to create a full range of values. In watermedia, a brush is used to make small marks resembling dry-brush strokes. The technique starts with loading the front half of the brush with fairly opaque color. With the brush perpendicular to the painting surface, just the tip of the brush is touched to the paper. This leaves a rough circular mark. Making marks like this over and over can produce a whole range of tones. The key is to use mostly paint with little or no water. Just as with drybrushing, touching the brush on a paper towel before painting helps remove any excess paint. This technique works best with gouache, but it can also be done with acrylics and watercolor.

After painting the tomatoes with broad brushstrokes, I stippled and drybrushed layers of fairly opaque color. Getting all the marks to blend was a challenge. I achieved subtle transitions by controlling the value of each mark and occasionally stippling into wet paint. I also used stippling in the cast shadows.

I created the highlights with several layers of stippled Titanium White. Because they were on top of a few layers of red-orange, they lost some intensity as they dried, and they needed to be repainted. On top of the tomato, I used the stipple technique. On the sides, I used a more conventional stroke to reinforce the roundness of the forms.

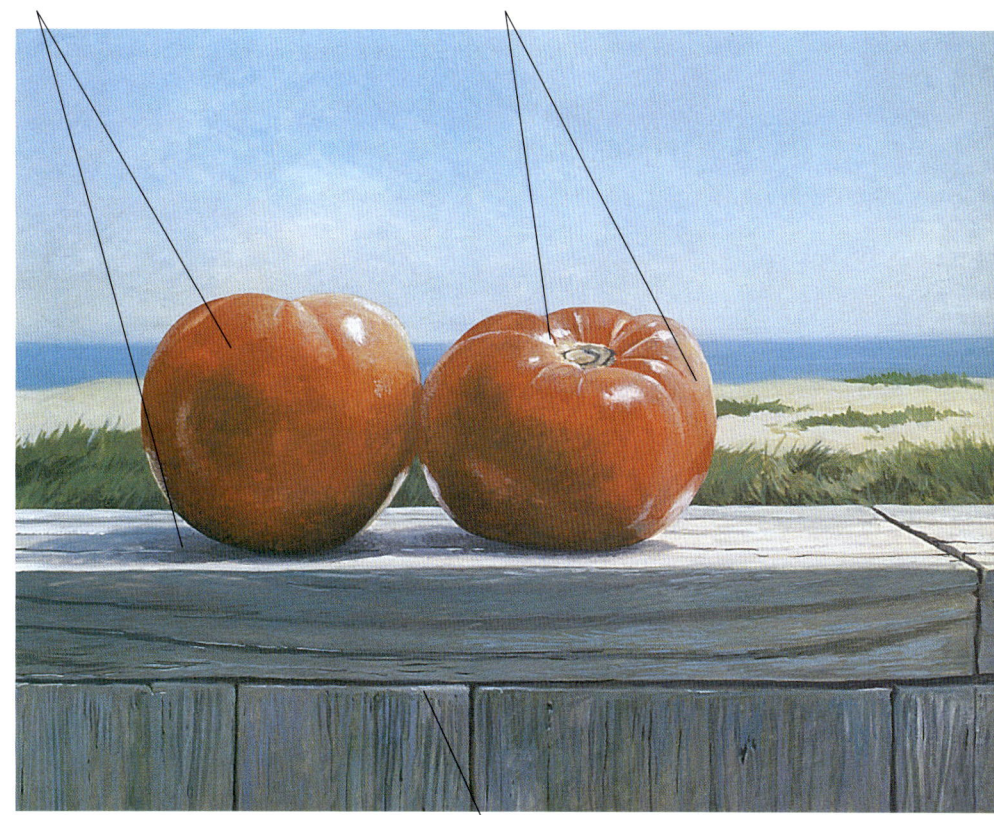

Build Form With Stippling

I painted this while on vacation in North Carolina. A family member had set tomatoes on the deck railing to ripen, and I couldn't resist painting them. I was attracted to the warm and cool color contrasts. This painting was done entirely in gouache and exhibits stippling (on the tomatoes) as well as a good bit of hatching (in the wood).

Vacation Tomatoes » Gouache on 140-lb. (300gsm) hot-pressed paper » 10" x 15" (25cm x 38cm)

I added hatching lines of various lengths, colors and values over several broad washes. The edges of the board were stippled with Titanium White.

mini-demonstration » watercolor and gouache

Combine Watercolor and Gouache for Texture-Filled Realism

This is a study of my late maternal grandfather, Bill Korby. I'm a fan of nineteenth century English watercolors. Their layered mix of small-brush techniques was the inspiration for this painting, which is a mix of conventional watercolor washes, broken-color layering, cross-hatching, drybrushing and stippling.

materials

paper
140-lb. (300gsm) hot-pressed

watercolors
Alizarin Crimson • Aureolin • Burnt Sienna • Burnt Umber • Cadmium Red • Cobalt Blue • Green Gold • Phthalo Blue • Quinacridone Gold • Rose Madder Genuine • Ultramarine Blue • Yellow Ochre

gouache
Alizarin Crimson • Burnt Sienna • Burnt Umber • Cadmium Red • Titanium White • Ultramarine Blue • Yellow Ochre

brushes
Nos. 10, 8, 6 and 4 synthetic rounds
No. 2 kolinsky sable round

1 Loosely Establish Forms With Variegated Washes
After a careful drawing, use loose variegated watercolor washes to block in the background and forms. Apply a very diluted mix of Cadmium Red, Rose Madder Genuine, Aureolin and Yellow Ochre for the skin tones. Paint the darker values with Cobalt Blue and Burnt Sienna with a bit of Alizarin Crimson. Lay in the background with a mix of Quinacridone Gold and Green Gold; allow this to mix in with the hat, shirt and skin tones. This will create a good color relationship between the background and the subject.

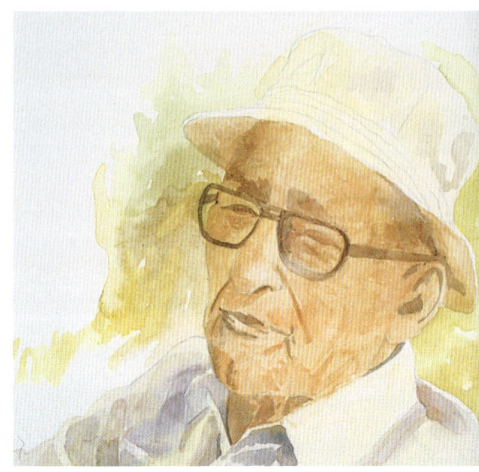

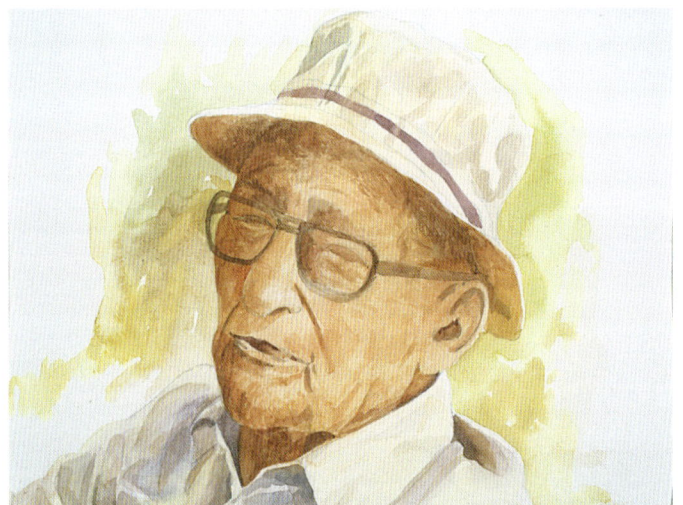

2 Build Value With Broken Color and Cross-Hatching
Apply a layer of transparent broken-color marks and hatching. This is a slow, methodical process. Where the values are darker, allow the marks to build up and blend together. Lighter values should receive very pale applications of color and less layering. The palette of colors remains the same as in the previous step, with Ultramarine Blue, Phthalo Blue and Burnt Umber added for some of the darker values.

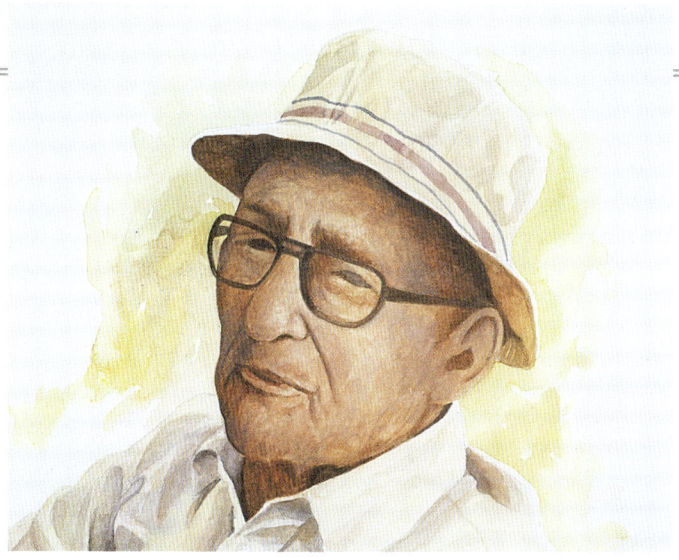
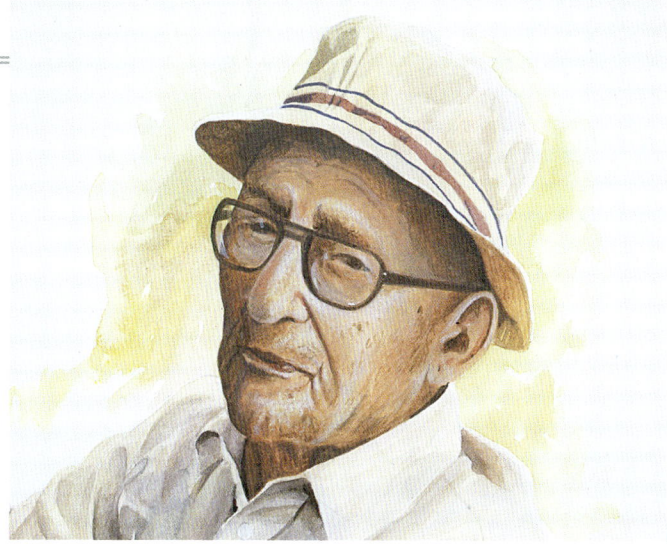

3. Add More Watercolor Layers and Apply First Layer of Gouache

Add some more layers of broken color and hatching. The three-dimensional qualities of the head, hat and shirt are solidly in place; however, the value and color on the head are quite robust and need to be lightened. To do this, brush on a layer of diluted Titanium White gouache. After this dries, add another layer of watercolor to the darker areas.

4. Create Texture With Gouache

Switching over to almost all gouache, build additional layers of color. Slowly develop the highlights with Titanium White using the stipple and dry-brush techniques. The shirt remains mostly watercolor, but add a couple washes of Titanium White gouache to lighten areas around the collar. Reinforce the darker values again with a gouache layer of Ultramarine Blue, Alizarin Crimson, Burnt Umber and Burnt Sienna. These areas include the glasses, eyes, wrinkles and the deep shadows under the hat. So that the wrinkles are not too dark, lightly blend a bit of Cadmium Red and Yellow Ochre with the dark line marks.

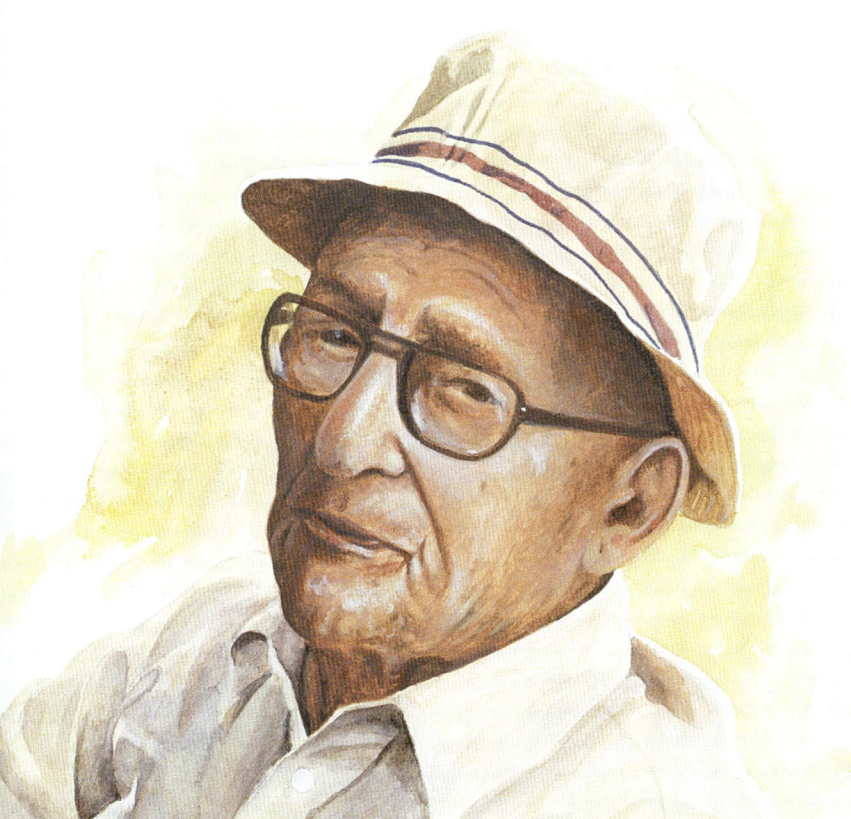

5. Add Final Touches

There are few differences between steps four and five, but the minor changes made are important. Stipple highlights again with Titanium White, and adjust the reflections on the glasses. Soften some brushwork on the cheek and on the edges of a few wrinkles. Finally, adjust values slightly around the mouth. If this portrait were more expressive, these subtle changes would be inconsequential; but for a painting that is created with such a layered and mannered technique, capturing this nuance of texture is essential.

technique 12 » acrylics

Layering Transparent Over Opaque in Acrylics

Acrylics are an incredibly versatile medium. The technique of layering transparent over opaque seems to celebrate this versatility. Early stages of this technique resemble traditional watercolor painting. As layers are built and opaque color is added, these paintings take on distinctive richness and character.

The keys to success in using this technique are keeping a proper pace—not too fast—and letting each layer dry before overpainting. Building the painting progressively with layers gives you control over color and value. It also provides a nice mix of transparent, semitransparent and opaque passages. This mix of paint layers is more interesting visually than if all the layers are densely opaque. For this reason, correcting mistakes with gobs of opaque paint isn't a wise course of action. The correction will probably look rather obvious and out of place.

I have just as many unfinished problem acrylics as I do unfinished problem watercolors. Sometimes it is better to start over than to work a painting to death trying to fix it.

Layer Warm and Cool Colors

With acrylics, layered color is a great way to render a subject as well as add color and value expression. Layering cool over warm or vice versa helps prevent flat, uninteresting local color. The concept is similar to the interest provided by variegated washes in watercolor. As long as the layers have some degree of transparency, the underpainted colors will show through and add a level of visual complexity that is natural as well as expressive.

Use Transparent Washes Over Opaque White

A classic oil painting technique is to paint a small area with pure opaque white, then, after this dries, thinly brush on transparent color. The result is brilliant, glowing color. This technique works equally well for acrylics. The key is not to cover too big an area. I think of this as an accenting technique, so I usually glaze over individual brushstrokes and not flat areas of opaque white. The impact is negated if the area gets too large. If an accent is too bright, allow the transparent color to dry, then paint on more layers.

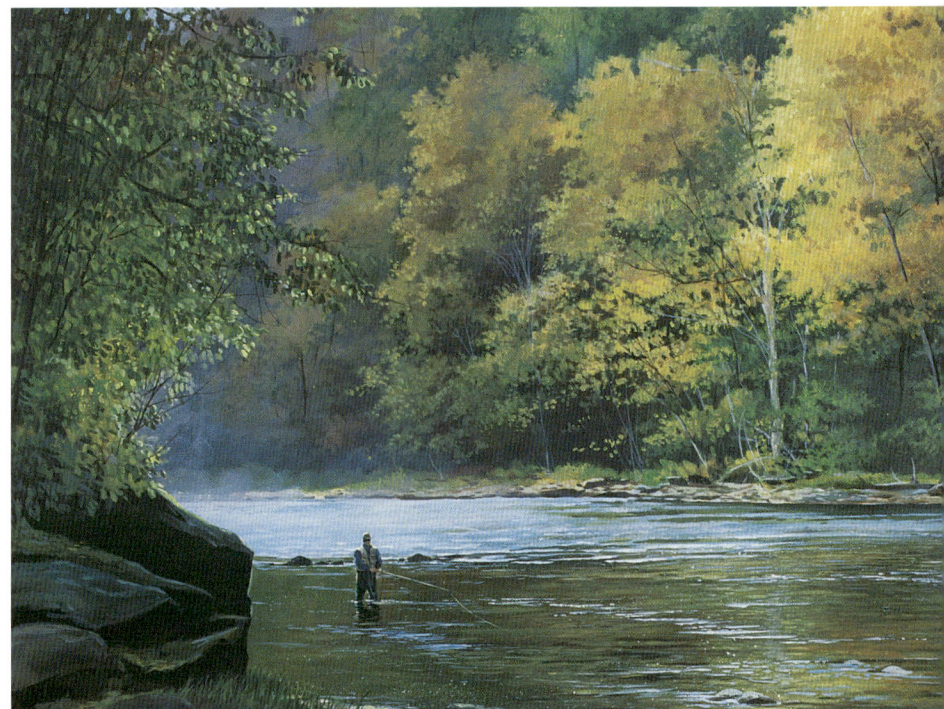

Layering Warm and Cool
This painting is very layered. I rendered the fall foliage with a wide range of warm colors. Over these colors, I brushed transparent and semitransparent layers of blues and purples. I painted the cooler colors and certain areas of the foliage again. I repeated this back-and-forth between warm and cool colors several times. To create a sense of depth, I gave trees that are closer to the viewer more detail, stronger value contrasts and brighter colors. I used warm to cool layers on the water. The lightest areas were put in with touches of opaque Titanium White and lightly washed with transparent Phthalo Blue.

Slippery Rock » Acrylic on 140-lb. (300gsm) hot-pressed paper » 18" x 28" (46cm x 71cm)

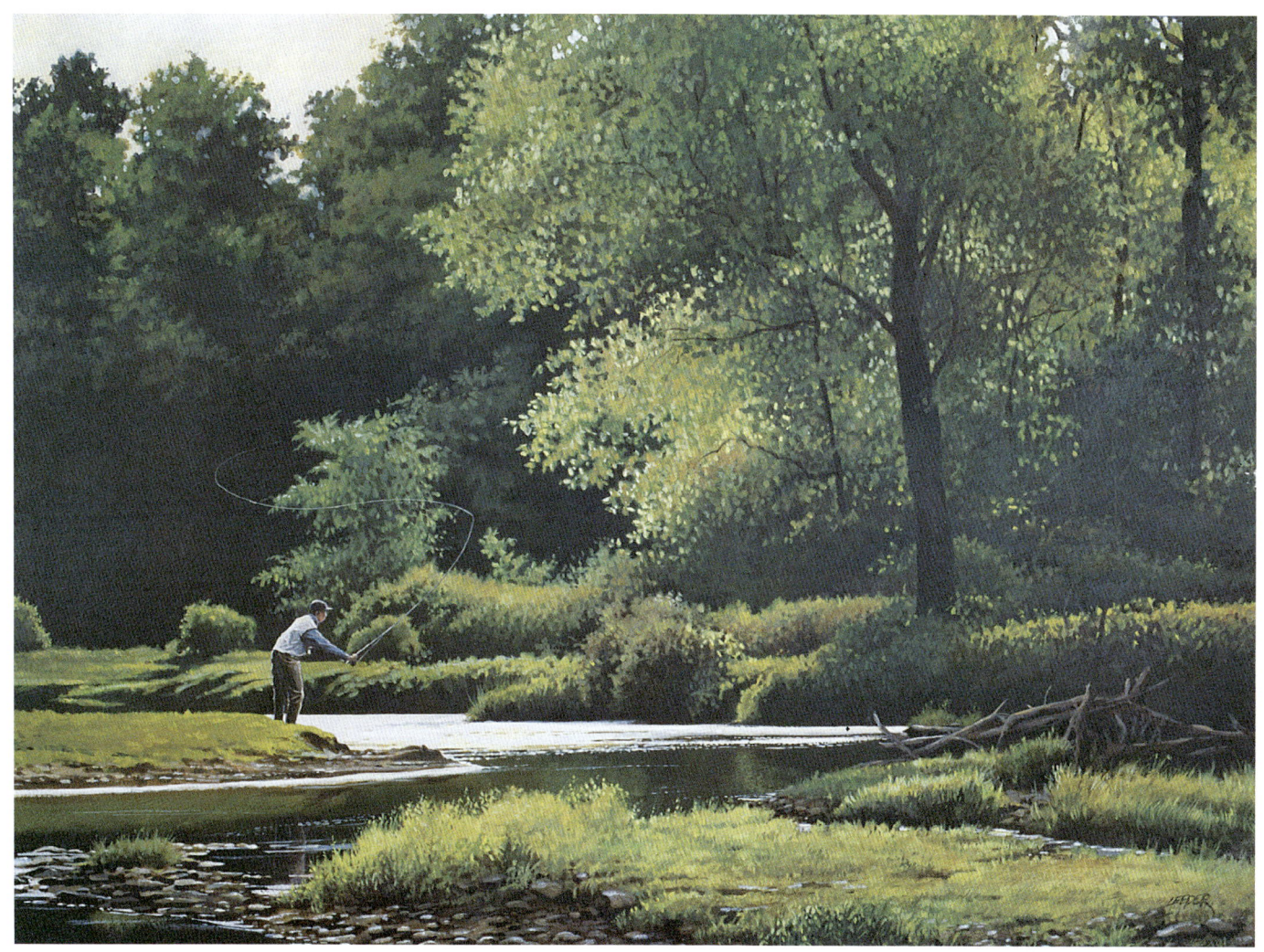

Glazing Over Opaque White for Glowing Color

I painted the background trees and shadowed areas by layering dozens of transparent and semitransparent washes of various mixes of Phthalo Blue, Phthalo Green and Burnt Umber. The only way to get the depth of color needed was to build these layers one at a time. Using a more opaque application of color would have been quicker, but the color wouldn't have had the same vibrancy. I built the large tree on the right with many small brushstrokes representing the foliage. As I built up the brushstrokes and the paint became more opaque, I painted washes of transparent greens and blues. I allowed this to dry and added more foliage.

To create the backlighting effect, I painted some of the leaves with opaque Titanium White. Then I laid delicate transparent washes of Yellow Medium Azo, Yellow Light Hansa and a mix of these yellows with Permanent Green Light. I did this a couple times to get the necessary complexity. I also mixed in with the glazed white leaves some opaque brushstrokes made with the yellow-green mix. This variety of transparent and opaque marks gives the tree realistic accuracy as well as visual interest.

A Delicate Cast » Acrylic on 140-lb. (300gsm) cold-pressed paper » 22" x 30" (56cm x 76cm)

mini-demonstration » acrylics

Paint Dramatic Light Effects With Acrylics

Acrylic is my medium of choice when I'm faced with capturing a dramatic light effect or a subject that calls for deep, rich values. This painting certainly fits both categories. These stepping-stones are along a stream in a township park not far from my home. I used a photo as reference. What really attracted me to this scene, aside from the sunshine streaming through the trees, was the contrast of the warm background against the cool purple and blue of the stepping-stones, gravel bar and stream bank. This painting features many of the techniques discussed in this chapter: layering, finger blending, scumbling and glazing transparent over opaque. Each layer was allowed to dry before new layers were painted; I used a hair dryer to speed this process. The full finished painting is on the cover.

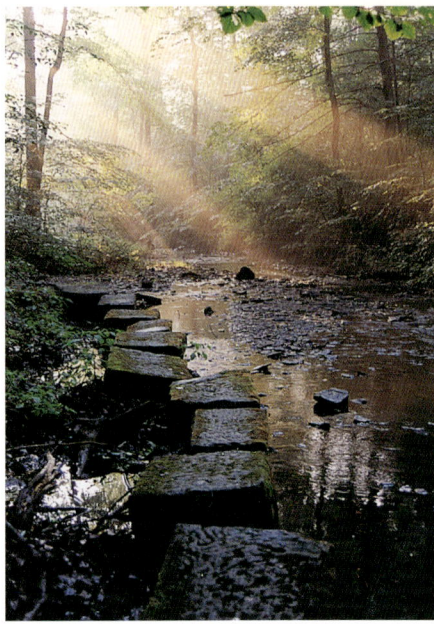

Reference Photo

materials

paper
140-lb. (300gsm) cold-pressed

acrylics
ACRA Crimson • Alizarin Crimson • Brilliant Blue • Burnt Sienna • Burnt Umber • Dioxazine Purple • Naphthol Red Light • Permanent Green Light • Phthalo Blue • Titanium White • Ultramarine Blue • Yellow Medium Azo • Yellow Ochre • Yellow Orange Azo

brushes
Nos. 10, 8, 6, 4 and 2 synthetic rounds
No. 1 kolinsky sable round
Sable rigger
½-inch (13mm) synthetic flat

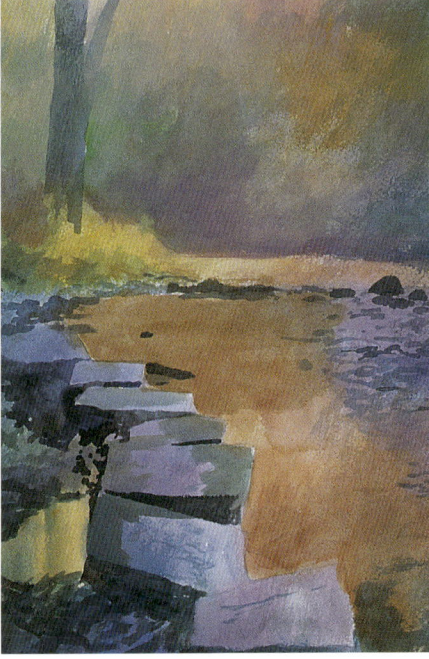

1 Paint Local Color Over Dark-Value Underpainting
On top of a simple drawing, paint the darkest values with a mix of Phthalo Blue and Burnt Umber. Once this dries, add several loose washes of transparent and semitransparent color over the entire painting. For the background, use various mixtures of Yellow Medium Azo, ACRA Crimson, Dioxazine Purple and Phthalo Blue. Paint the stones and gravel bar with a mix of Phthalo Blue, Dioxazine Purple and a bit of Burnt Sienna. Paint the water with a variegated mix of Yellow Ochre, Yellow Medium Azo, Naphthol Red Light, ACRA Crimson and Burnt Sienna. Let dry.

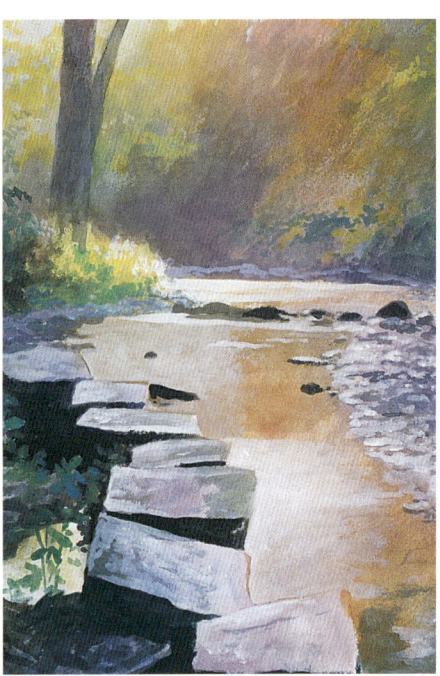

2 Adjust Values With Lighter Colors
Paint a semiopaque Titanium White wash in the sunlit area of the background. Paint brighter background areas with a semitransparent mix of Yellow Medium Azo and Titanium White as well as a mix of ACRA Crimson, Dioxazine Purple and Titanium White. Since these colors are so strong, they should be fairly diluted. Give the water, the stepping-stones and the gravel bar a semitransparent layer of Titanium White, and develop the stream bank.

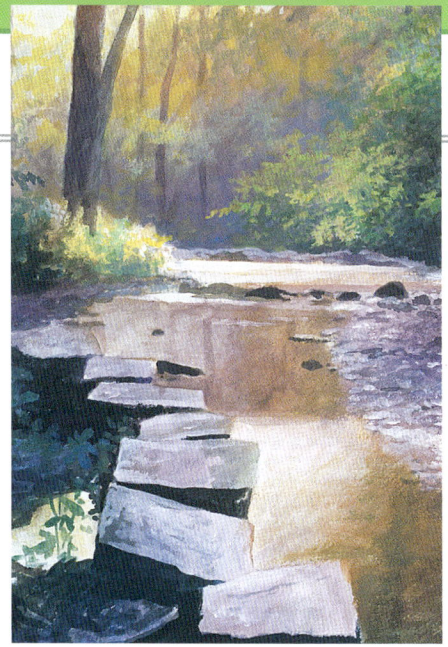

3 Add Transparent Layers and the First Tree Details

Add transparent washes of Dioxazine Purple and Phthalo Blue to the stepping-stones, gravel bar, middle ground water and large tree. Develop the background by adding a few smaller trees and foliage details. Use opaque and semiopaque mixes of Yellow Medium Azo and Permanent Green Light for the lighter leaves and Permanent Green Light, Phthalo Blue, Burnt Sienna and Ultramarine Blue for the darker, shadowed sections. Scumble spots of color on the background with Yellow Orange Azo, Yellow Ochre and Brilliant Blue.

Paint the foreground water with a fluid semiopaque layer of Yellow Orange Azo, Brilliant Blue, Burnt Sienna, Permanent Green Light and Dioxazine Purple. Do not mix all these colors together; pick them up from various two- and three-color mixes on your palette and blend them on the paper using the scumble technique.

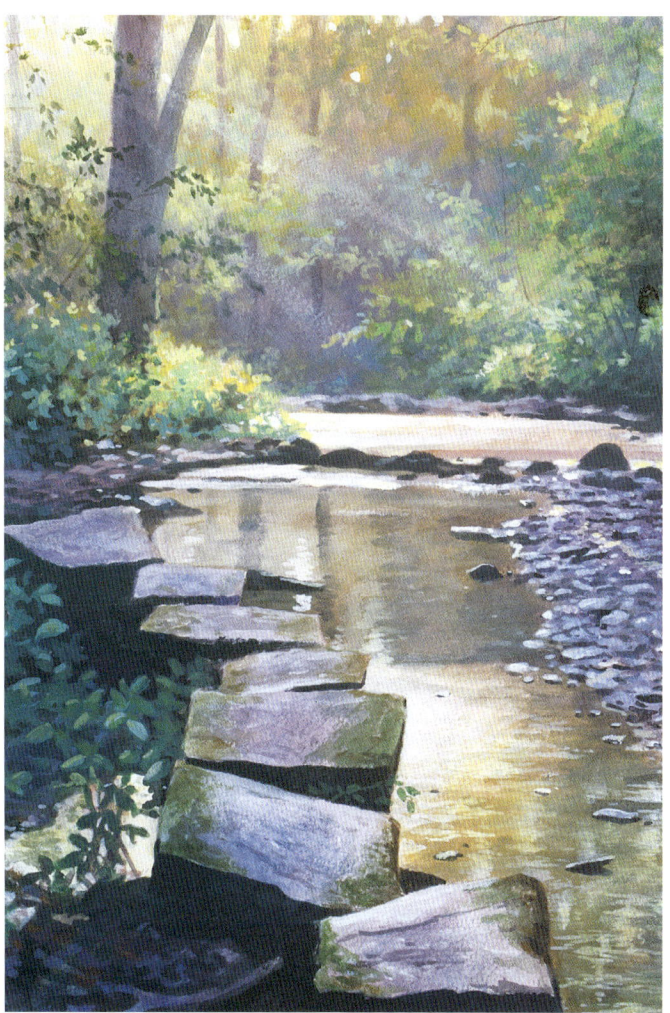

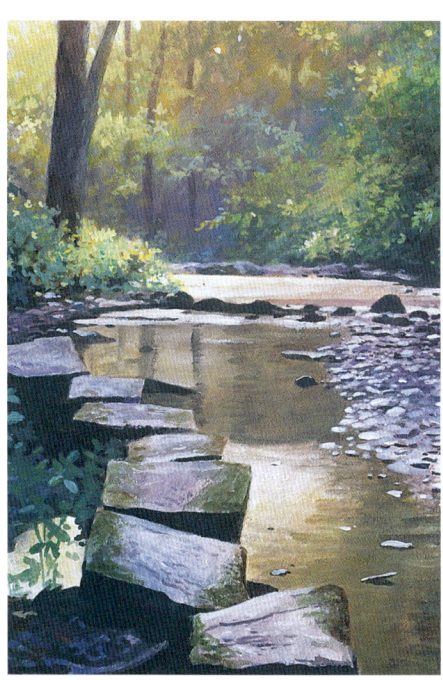

4 Add More Details and Opaque White Accents

Develop the details in the background, stream bank and gravel bar with fairly opaque color using mixes of the same colors from the previous steps. Give the sunlit area of the background another layer of Titanium White with a bit of Yellow Medium Azo and Yellow Orange Azo. Finger blend this area after it is brushed on. Accent the gravel bar and stepping-stones with opaque Titanium White.

5 Add Final Details and Transparent Layers

Go over the white accents from the previous step with a light transparent wash of Alizarin Crimson, Phthalo Blue and Dioxazine Purple. For the sunlight streaming through the trees, apply soupy Titanium White brushstrokes and finger blend. Then add final details—mostly darker accents—using a mix of Phthalo Blue, Burnt Umber and Naphthol Red Light. Add light reflections to the foreground water with semiopaque Titanium White and a bit of Yellow Medium Azo, Yellow Orange Azo and Brilliant Blue.

technique 13 » watercolor

Paint Wet-Into-Wet for Rich Color and Form

Painting wet-into-wet is an integral part of most watercolorists' repertoire. Besides the obvious atmospheric effects so common to the technique, it can be used to build rich color and value as well as convincing three-dimensional forms.

One advantage often overlooked is that wet-into-wet techniques offer the artist time. Because wet-into-wet color dries slowly, the artist has time to build color and value and to manipulate the wash. If the subject calls for a more subtle technique, layering wet-into-wet washes can be very effective. Wet-into-wet painting is also a great way to build a solid base of color and value for depicting forms. The soft blending of colors contrasts nicely with subsequent washes that leave hard edges. This mix of soft and hard edges adds visual interest to a painting.

Create Bold Color With a Direct Technique

When rich color and deep value are called for, painting directly wet-into-wet will ensure the brightest and most vibrant color. Wet the area with clean water. Remember that color will flow until it reaches dry paper. Be sure that hard edge is acceptable. If not, make the wet area larger and paint within one-half inch (one centimeter) or so of the hard edge, or feather the wash out to the edge of the dry paper. After painting the first wash of color into the wet area, recharge your brush with color and very little water. The pigment laden color will not spread as much and actually may need a bit of coaxing with a brush to fill the wet shape.

If the color still isn't rich enough, apply more. The key is to give second

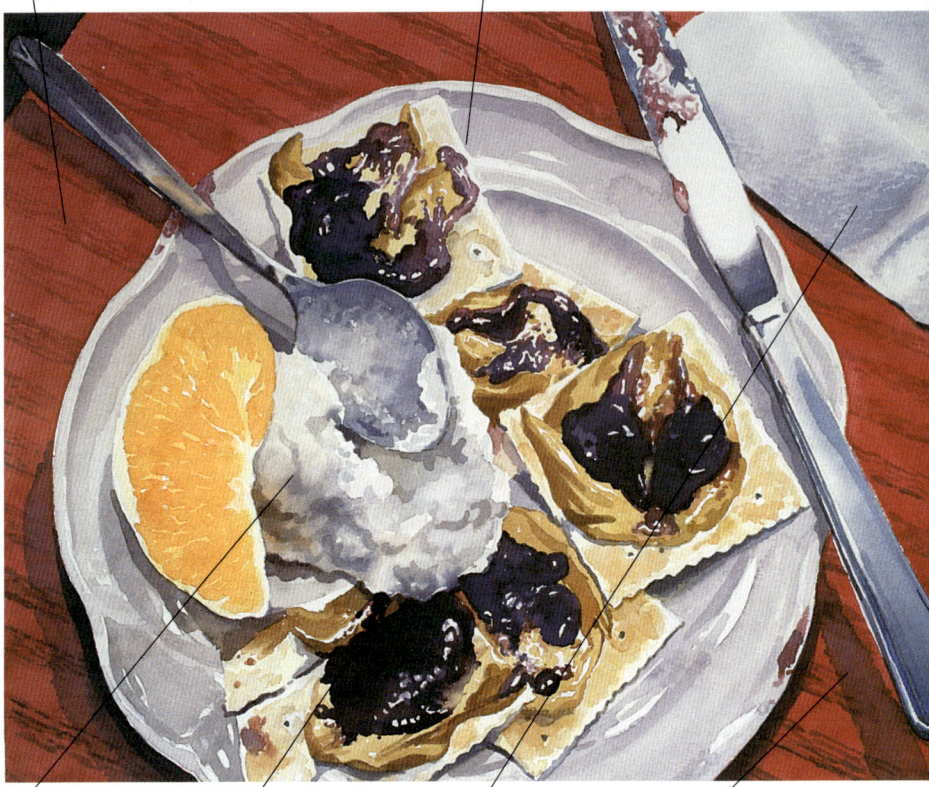

I painted the red cloth with two wet-into-wet layers of intense color.

To get even color and value, I wet each section of the plate with clean water, then painted from a large puddle of color.

I painted the entire shape first with a wet-into-wet wash. Curds—yuck!—were added later.

I painted jelly directly with a wet-into-wet wash and intense color.

I painted subtle napkin texture on top of a dried wet-into-wet wash.

Shadow edges bleed because of heavy pigment in the red underpainting.

Combine Rich Color and Wet-Into-Wet Technique

I stress to my university watercolor students that they should look to their own lives and environments to find painting subjects. Personal associations with subjects usually make for better and more meaningful paintings. A fun assignment that helps them do this is called "paint what you eat." This assignment also explores painting textures in watercolor. They are instructed to do a series of paintings that explore their diets. This painting was done as a whimsical example to get them thinking about rendering food. I wanted to combine foods and objects that had a variety of textures and colors. I put the setup on the floor and painted it from life. The drawing and painting took about five hours. The idea of cottage cheese sitting under hot lights for five hours was pretty repulsive, and I was quite happy to be finished. This painting is a good example of various wet techniques.

Bad Lunch Idea » Watercolor on 140-lb. (300gsm) hot-pressed paper » 11" x 15" (28cm x 38cm)

and third applications of color very little water. If they are too wet, the excess water will disperse the pigment and leave a "blossom" or "bloom" as this is sometimes called. Working this way slows the sometimes hectic pace of watercolor painting. You can push color around or add and subtract without things getting muddy or tired-looking. Essentially, this is still the first wash on the paper, and it retains that "first wash" freshness.

Layer Wet Into Wet

Another technique is to build color through wet-into-wet layers. Allow the first wet-into-wet wash to dry completely; use a hair dryer if there is any doubt. Apply clean water to the same area and float in more color. Depending on how much pigment is used, this can be done several times. Obviously, fewer layers ensure a brighter painting. This technique is suited for subjects that do not have rich color or value. The main reason is that washing color over a dry but pigment-laden wash will sometimes activate the dry pigment and cause unwanted bleeding between the two layers.

Mix Soft and Hard Edges

An all-wet technique doesn't fit every subject. Sometimes it is better to layer harder-edged brushstrokes on top of a base of wet-into-wet color. Actually, this occurs in practically every watercolor painting. This variety of soft and hard edges is desirable in creating a painting that is realistic but also visually exciting. To get the most out of this technique it is important to plan ahead. Make sure that the base of wet-into-wet color will be the correct hue and sufficient in value. If you are planning additional hard-edged washes to define shapes and forms, limiting the wet-into-wet layers will help you avoid dull or muddy color. Finally, if you add brushstrokes to a dried wet-into-wet wash that has a lot of pigment in it, make sure to use a light touch so as not to disrupt and dissolve these pigments.

value check

- **Mix colors before wetting the paper.** This will allow you to move quickly and without interruption.
- **Control how much water is in your color mixes when you paint into a wet wash.** Too much water will leave a bloom.
- **Try 300-lb. (640gsm) paper with wet techniques.** Washes will tend to dry more slowly, and you will have more time to manipulate color.

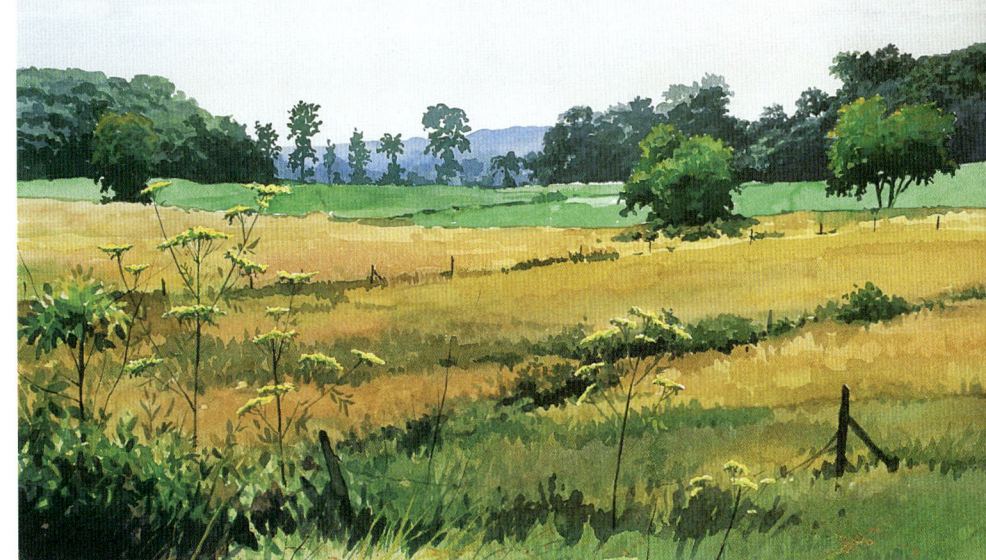

Mix Wet and Dry Techniques

I created the fields with two wet-into-wet layers. The second wash was fairly rich, and the small marks painted on top of this wash were done with a loaded wet brush and a light touch. This kept the edges sharp and avoided disrupting the dried washes. The wet-into-wet washes were a variegated mix of warm and cool greens.

I was pleased with the variety of edges in this painting. The wet-into-wet washes tied the painting together, and the mix of wet-on-dry marks of various values gave it some spark and energy.

Fields at Noon » Watercolor on 140-lb. (300gsm) cold-pressed paper » 11" x 22" (28cm x 56cm)

mini-demonstration » watercolor

Use Wet-Into-Wet Techniques for Dynamic Color and Value

This is a portion of a still life that was set up and photographed in my studio. Working from the photo, I used a combination of wet-into-wet and wet-on-dry layers. This combination created realistic forms and textures as well as a full range of values and color intensities.

materials

paper
140-lb. (300gsm) cold-pressed

watercolors
Alizarin Crimson • Aureolin • Burnt Sienna • Burnt Umber • Cadmium Red • Cobalt Blue • New Gamboge • Phthalo Blue • Quinacridone Gold • Quinacridone Violet • Rose Madder Genuine • Ultramarine Blue • Winsor Red

brushes
Nos. 4, 6, 8 and 10 synthetic rounds
No. 2 kolinsky sable round
¼-inch (6mm) synthetic flat

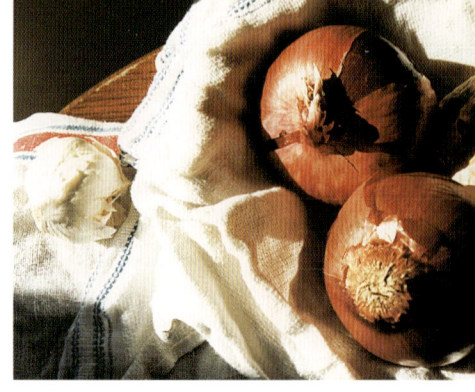

Reference Photo

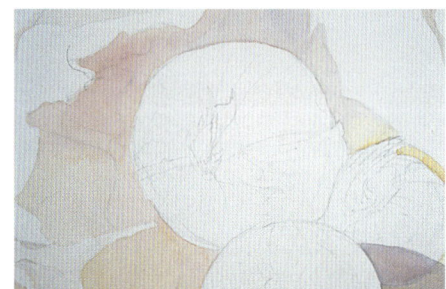

1 Establish a Warm Underpainting
After doing a detailed drawing, establish the shadows on the cloth with a warm, variegated, wet-into-wet wash of New Gamboge, Rose Madder Genuine and Cobalt Blue. Consider reflected color and cast shadows as you carefully place shades of red, orange and violet. Let this dry.

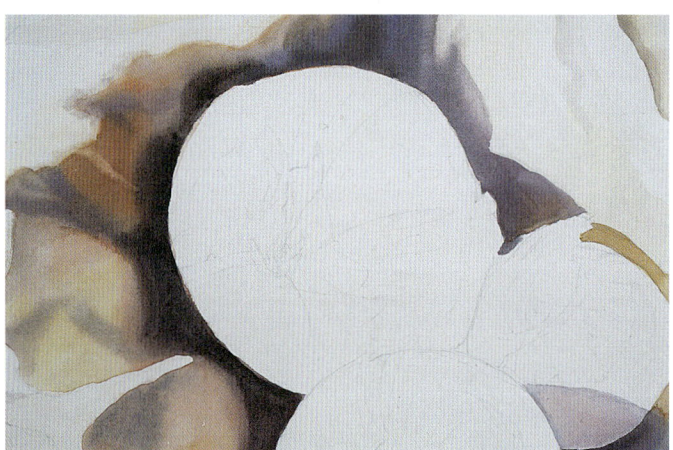

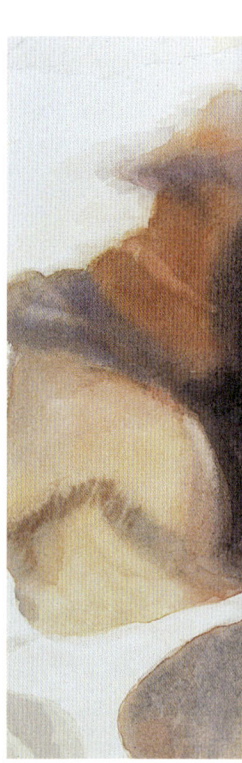

2 Add a Rich Wet-Into-Wet Layer to the Cloth
Re-wet the cloth area with clean water, then paint several consecutive washes on the wet area. First cover the whole area with a warm wash of Aureolin, Rose Madder Genuine and Quinacridone Gold. On top of this, on the shadow to the right of the yellow onion, paint a rich mix of Quinacridone Gold and Burnt Sienna. Add violet shades next with a variegated mix of Cobalt Blue, Ultramarine Blue, Quinacridone Violet and Alizarin Crimson. Add the dark shadow last with a dense wash of Phthalo Blue, Alizarin Crimson and Burnt Umber.

Soften the edges with a slightly damp ¼-inch (6mm) flat. (This brush is rather stiff; I like it for lifting color and softening edges.) Inside the shadow, lift some color with a slightly damp no. 8 round.

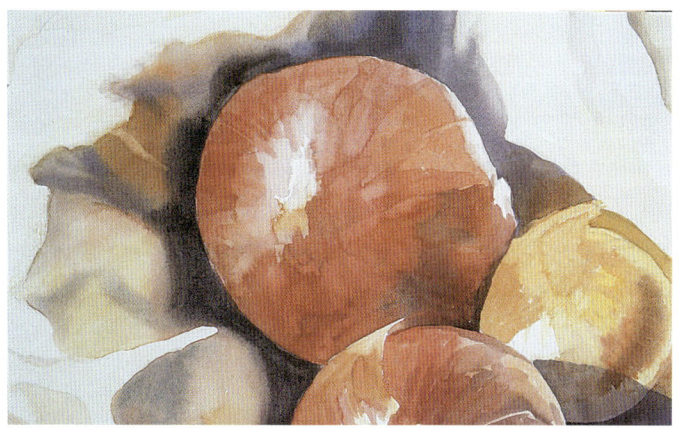 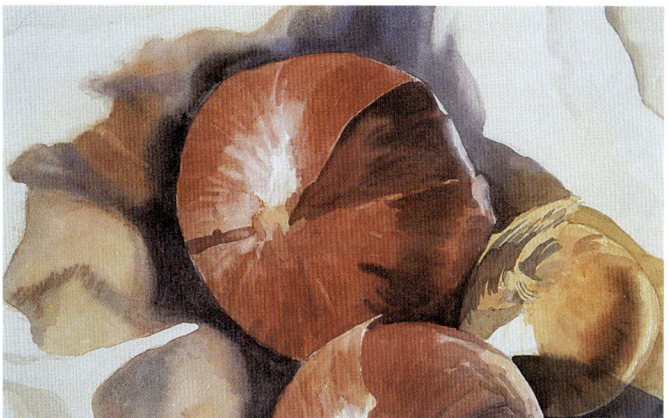

3 Establish the Local Color of the Onions

Don't wet the onions before adding color; this way you can create a few edges as you go along. Paint the red onions with a variegated mix of Cadmium Red, Winsor Red, Alizarin Crimson and Burnt Sienna. Give some areas of the onion more Burnt Sienna and others more red. Add the darker values wet-into-wet with a mix of Ultramarine Blue and Alizarin Crimson with a bit of Burnt Umber to gray the mix. Since the paper was dry, it should be easy to avoid the highlight areas and establish some edges that will later represent the onion's texture. Paint the yellow onion using a variegated wash of Aureolin, Quinacridone Gold, Rose Madder Genuine, Burnt Sienna and Cobalt Blue.

4 Enrich Color and Define Edges

Using the same red mixes, paint another wash on the red onion; make this wash less fluid than the first for richer color. Add the darker shadows wet-into-wet with a dense mix of Ultramarine Blue, Alizarin Crimson and Burnt Umber so the color will stay in place when brushed onto the wet paper. Let this layer dry.

Using a mix of Alizarin Crimson, Burnt Sienna and Cobalt Blue, paint the exposed second layer of onion. Using the same mix on the palette, paint the dark shadows in the second skin area. Give the yellow onion another wash to enrich its color. Paint the warm shadow wet-into-wet with a mix of Quinacridone Gold, Burnt Sienna, Ultramarine Blue and a bit of Alizarin Crimson. Develop the yellow onion's folded stalk with a blue-gray shape made from Cobalt Blue, Alizarin Crimson and bit of Burnt Sienna. Add Ultramarine Blue to this mix for the dark cast shadow.

With the onions now developed, parts of the surrounding shadows on the cloth need to be a bit darker. Brush across the left side of the shadow a very light wash of Winsor Red, Aureolin and Cobalt Blue.

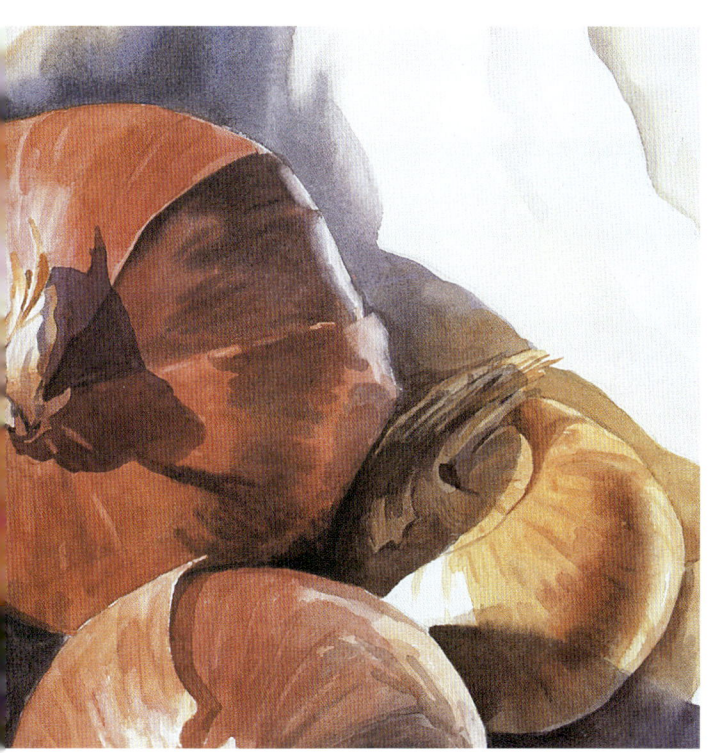

5 Add Final Details and Shadows

Add details around the stalks of the onion, being careful to paint around the white highlights. Paint the cast shadows last. These are critical in depicting the roundness of the form and, since they are so dark, in bringing together the overall design of the painting. Paint them using a mix of Rose Madder Genuine, Ultramarine Blue and a touch of Aureolin to gray them slightly. Add a few dark accents along the base of the onions and shadows with a mix of Phthalo Blue, Alizarin Crimson and Burnt Umber.

technique 14 » acrylics and watercolor

Add Acrylics Over Watercolor

Occasionally I add a few acrylic color accents or washes to a watercolor. Most often, these are demo or plein air paintings that, because of the limited painting time, might need further development. If a watercolor misses the mark or calls for some major changes, then I will work over the entire painting with acrylics. Either way, the two mediums work well together.

Accent With Acrylics

Accenting a watercolor with acrylics is an easy way to inject some much-needed color or visual energy. Most times these accents are done with opaque color. If a larger section needs to be changed in value or color you can add some semitransparent washes, but usually these kinds of changes can be accomplished with watercolor. The advantage goes to acrylic in this situation if the addition of watercolor washes will noticeably dull the area. Using semitransparent acrylics will darken the value but retain the color.

When opaque accents are added they usually harmonize well with the rest of the painting. However, if too much opaque or semiopaque color is added, then you probably should repaint the entire painting with acrylics.

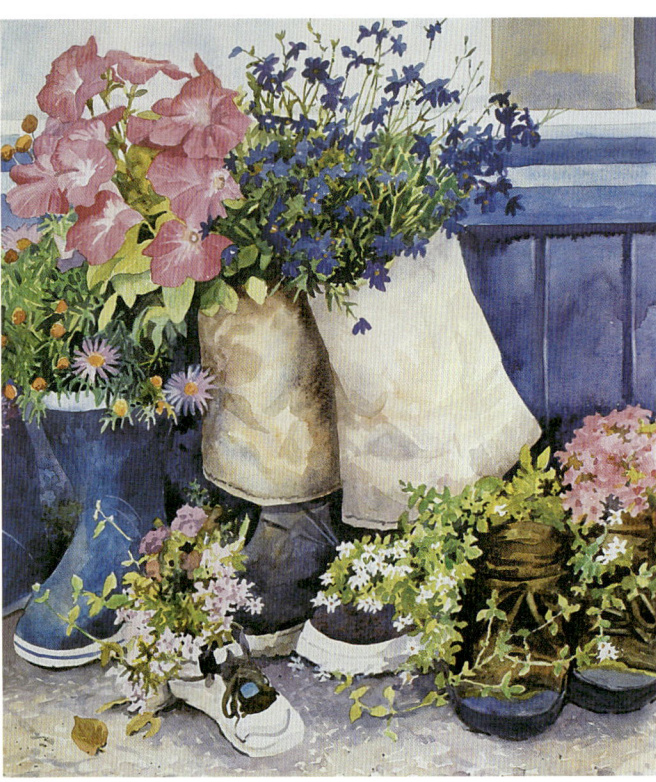

Original Watercolor
This painting was originally painted in watercolor. It was satisfactory but didn't look like my work. I felt it needed richer colors and more-precise details. Adding these in watercolor would have muddied the colors.

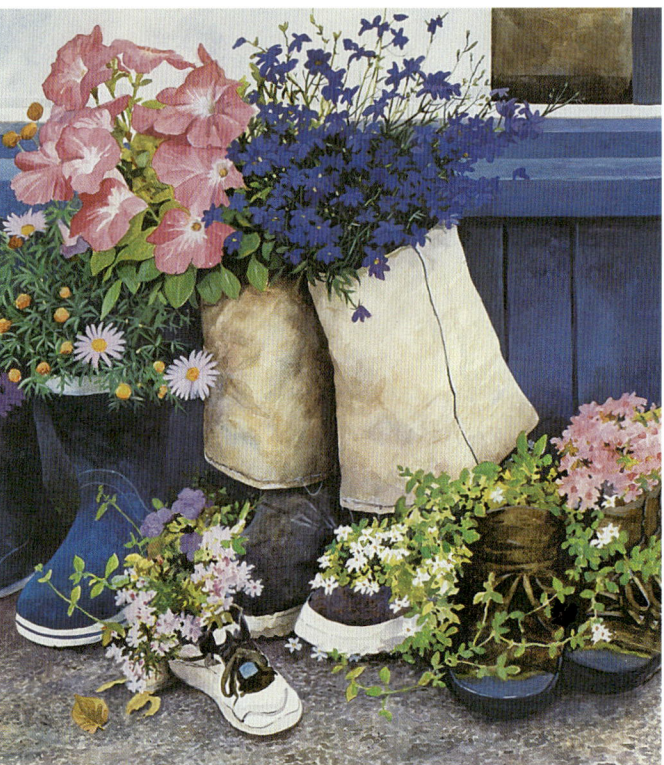

Improved With Acrylic Accents
Using acrylics, I was able to modify the painting without losing the freshness of the original watercolor. With opaque acrylic color I sharpened and enriched the flowers and greenery as well as deepened the darkest values.

Shoe Garden » Watercolor and acrylic on 140-lb. (300gsm) hot-pressed paper » 18" x 24" (46cm x 61cm)

Make Bold Changes

Sometimes a watercolor just doesn't work. For whatever reason, you are not satisfied with the results. If you like working transparently, then the painting will need to be redone. But another option is to work over the painting with acrylics. The original watercolor then becomes an underpainting.

Before adding acrylics, try to identify what needs to be changed. Having a game plan will make this process go much more smoothly. The key is not moving too fast. Build the painting in transparent and semi-transparent layers, just as you would a pure acrylic painting. Add opaque color last. There may be areas that work; you can leave them untouched.

Usually the right values area ha subtly change reflected from the surface of painting. At this point, an otherwise fine transparent watercolor wash may look isolated when surrounded by acrylics and, therefore, will need to be repainted.

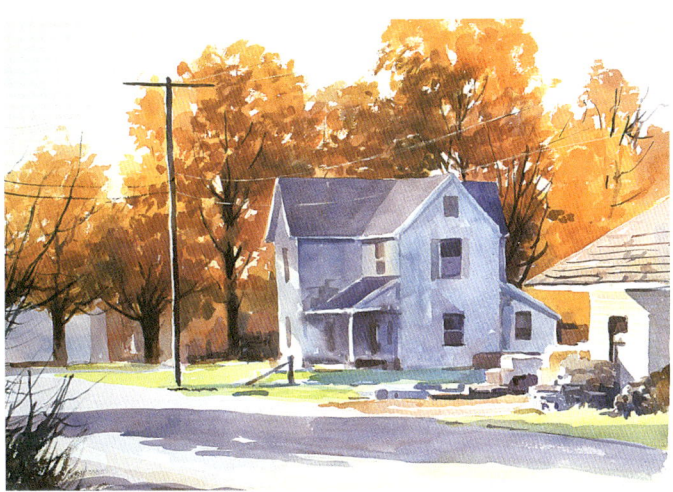

Original Watercolor
The original watercolor was done as a two-hour demo. I thought it wasn't my best effort. I liked the lighting effect and the color was rich, but the value distribution was flat and the technique was too broad. It seemed rather generic.

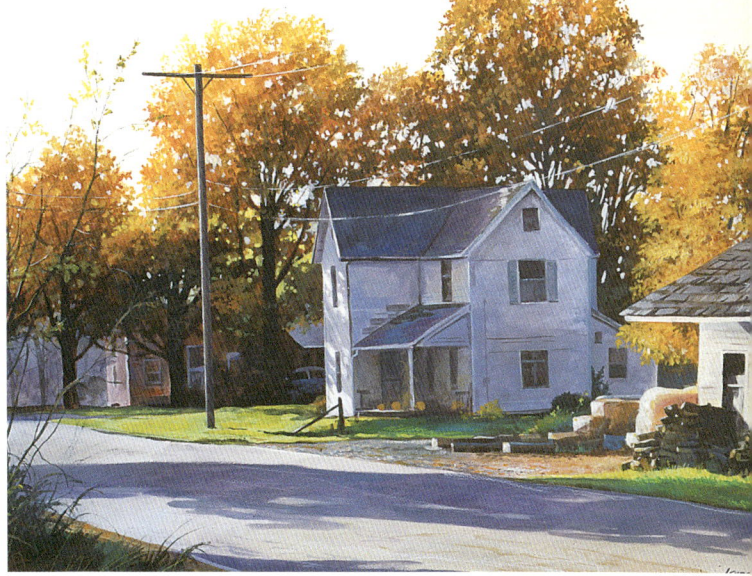

Entirely Revised With Acrylics
Back in the studio, I reworked the entire painting except the sky. I adjusted the values and color with semitransparent layers. I also refined the elements and added a lot more detail—for example, I used opaque color to create the brighter accents like the sunlit areas and the sky holes. As I worked, I took the opportunity to develop all the elements further by adding subtle value shifts and smaller details. Some people may like the watercolor version better, but unless the artist is satisfied the painting is not complete.

Franklin Square » Watercolor and acrylic on 140-lb. (300gsm) cold-pressed paper » 22" x 30" (56cm x 76cm)

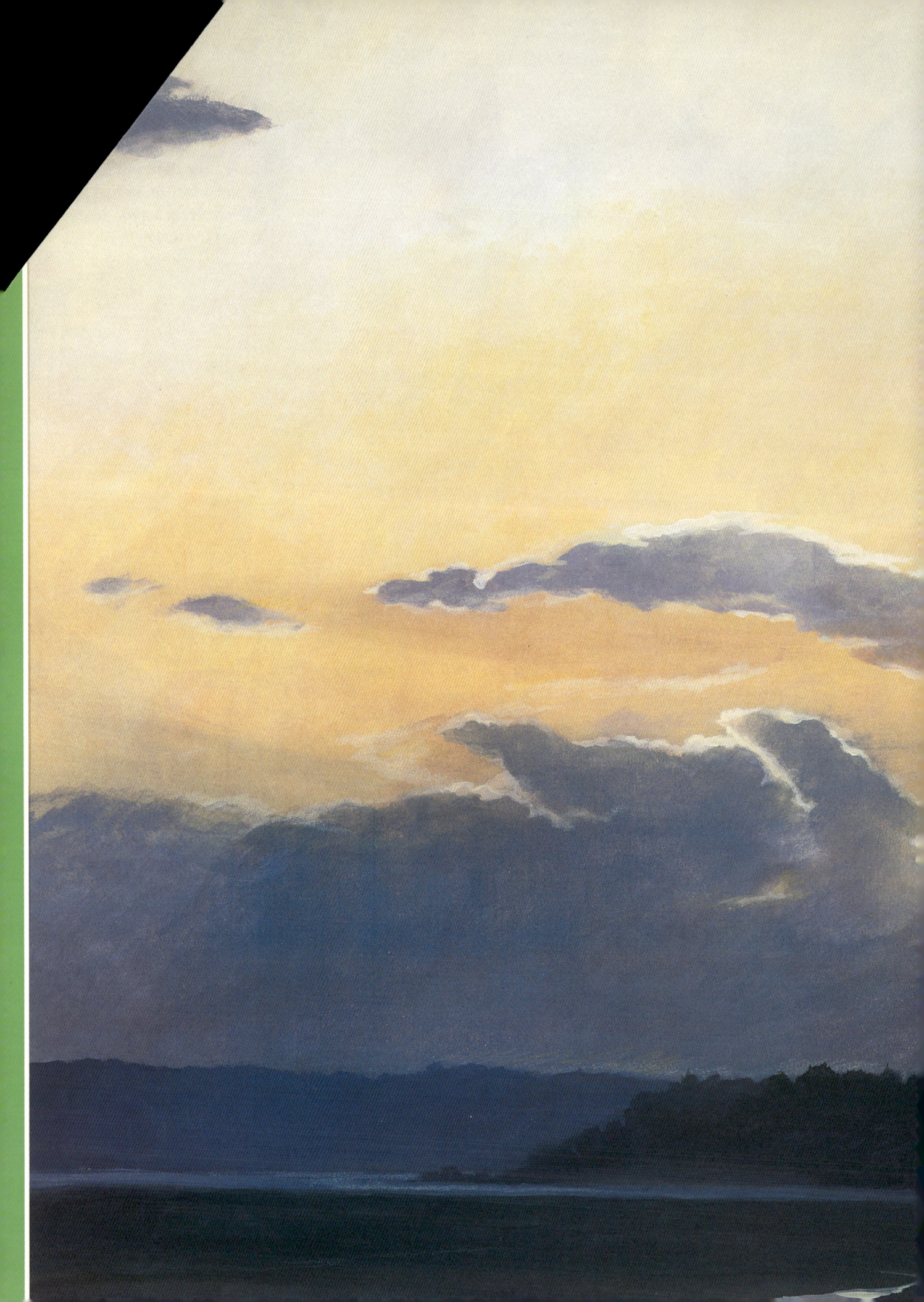

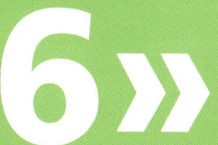

mixed media techniques

The first time I painted acrylics over a lifeless watercolor was one of my most memorable artistic moments. That one painting, done over ten years ago, opened my eyes to the possibilities of mixed media. Today, I readily combine watermedia with dry media such as colored pencil and pastels. Being an illustrator as well as a fine artist, I have found mixed media to be a critical component in my illustrations. Mixed media's versatility can range from expressive color accents of pastel on top of a watercolor to gouache refinements of an acrylic. Mixed-media techniques offer something for every artistic personality.

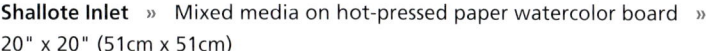

Shallote Inlet » Mixed media on hot-pressed paper watercolor board » 20" x 20" (51cm x 51cm)

technique 15 » pastel and colored pencil

Enhance Watermedia Paintings With Dry Media

Have you ever done a painting that is "almost there"? A painting that seems to be working but lacks something? Next time that happens, try adding a few accents of dry media (pastels and colored pencils). These accents can add color and texture to your painting as well as injecting a bit of expression and personality. You can also plan your painting with dry media in mind—saving the color accents and textures for the pastels or colored pencils. The key to accents is to add only a few so that they retain their ability to complement but not overwhelm the form or shape.

Dry media can be applied to a watermedia painting in two ways: as highlights or lowlights. Highlights are bright and bold accents that really stand out. These are applied with a bit of pressure to create a distinct mark. They are usually done with contrasting colors, which attract attention. Use highlights cautiously—too many can overwhelm the form they are meant to accentuate.

Lowlights are just the opposite. The pastel or colored pencil is applied by gently moving it across the paper so that just the highest point of the paper's texture receives color. This creates a broken-color mark. These marks are great for adding a subtle bit of color in a shadow area or when slight amounts of color and texture are needed to accent a form. Color choices are softer and usually analogous to the area they cover.

Highlights and lowlights can be effectively done with complementary colors. For example, a green area can be enhanced with a touch of bright red or a subtle blush of pink.

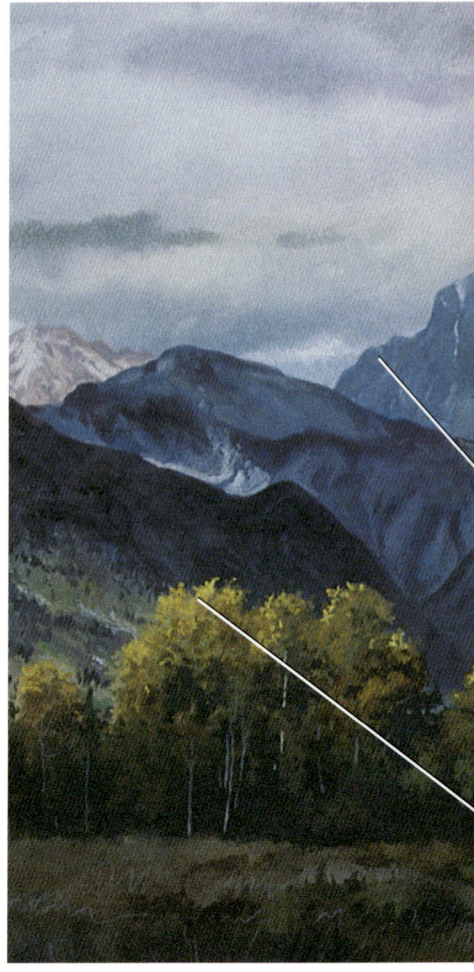

Use Discretion When Adding Dry Accents

This painting was done in acrylics and has a few highlights and lowlights added with pastels and colored pencils. Since the mountains and plain are low-key, the highlighted trees really stand out. Just a few marks were needed to create the illusion of sunstruck foliage.

Teton Vista » Mixed media on 140-lb. (300gsm) cold-pressed paper » 13" x 30" (33cm x 76cm)

watercolor paper makes a great surface for pastels

Pastels need a paper with tooth to hold the dry pigment. Cold-pressed and rough watercolor papers certainly meet this requirement. Try a variety of sheets. Fabriano Artistico cold-pressed paper imparts a consistent pattern to dry media. I also like Arches and Lanaquarelle cold-pressed sheets. Rough papers help produce a more pronounced and expressive mark.

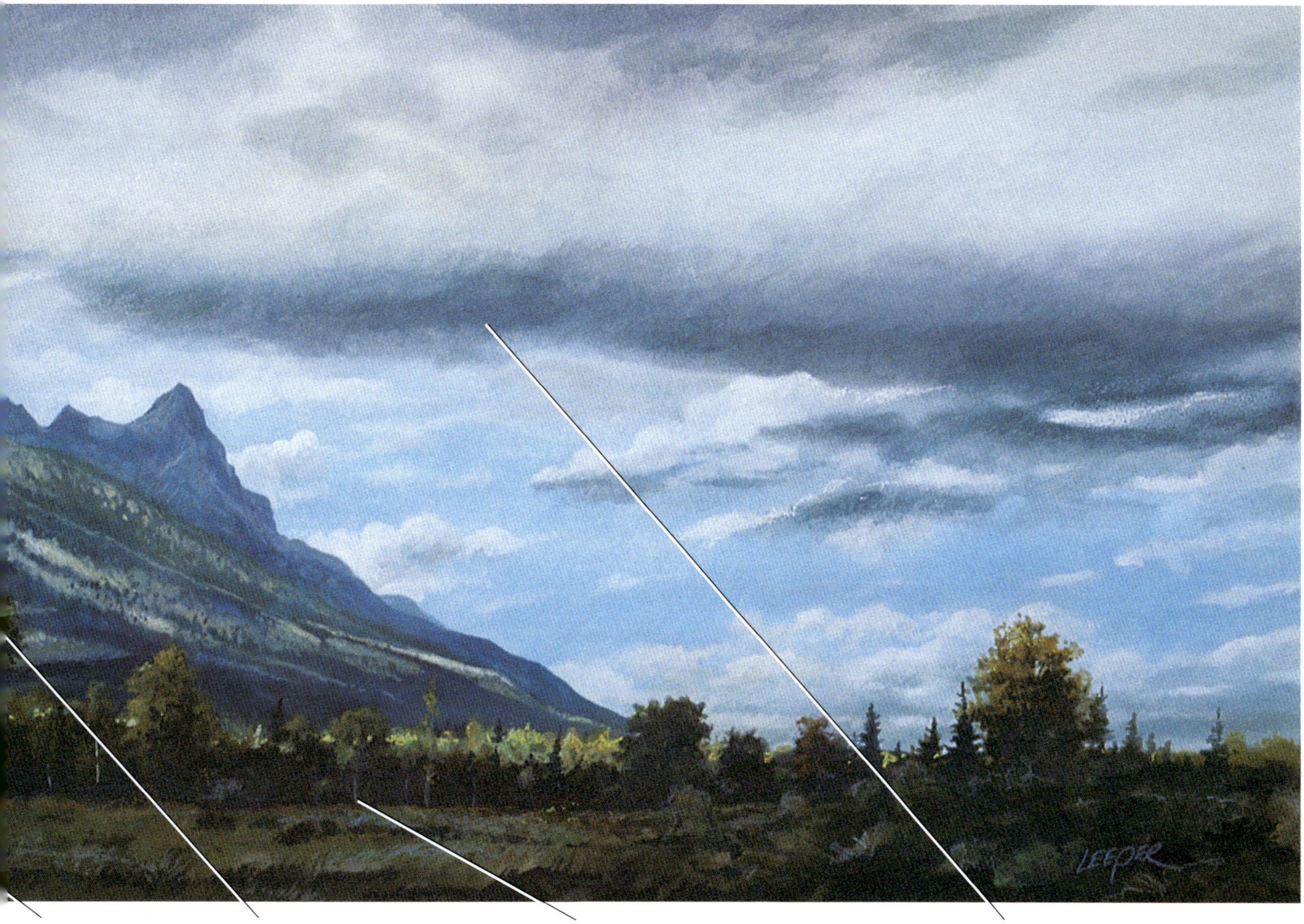

Sunlit foliage rendered with pastel.

Over ten layers of thin acrylic color used to render mountains.

Jade Green colored pencil adds soft texture and color (lowlights).

Clouds developed with finger blending and scumbling.

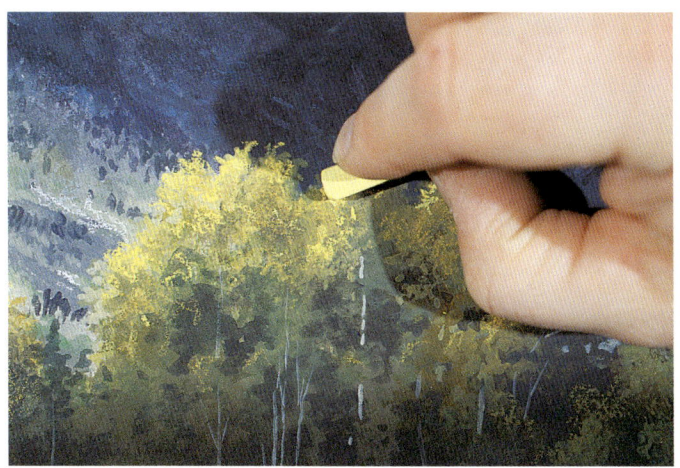

Use a Variety of Marks to Add Highlights

I prefer the harder Nupastels for adding accents. They make a distinctive mark, and the rectangular dimension of the sticks allows for a variety of thick and thin lines. This variety can add a great deal of interest to a subject. To achieve this variety when applying the pastels, rotate them to use different edges and corners. Also, vary the amount of pressure as you make marks.

Develop Texture and Color With Pastels and Colored Pencils

This painting depicts the old spring house on our family farm. Because of the textures of the brick and rock, this piece was a natural candidate for adding dry media. With this in mind I also chose a rough watercolor paper. I did most of the painting in acrylics, and I rendered the final accents and textures with pastels and colored pencils. I painted the barn swallows to add some life to the old building.

Spring House » Mixed media on 140-lb. (300gsm) rough paper » 22" x 30" (56cm x 76cm)

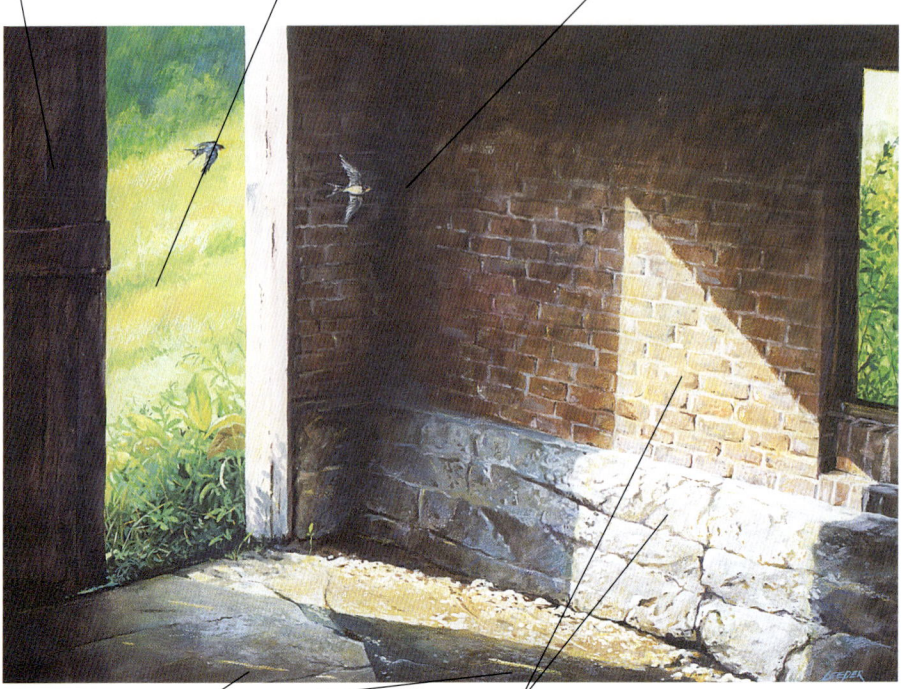

Wood details were done with Spanish Orange colored pencil.

White, Canary Yellow and Spring Green colored pencil marks add texture and color.

Several acrylic layers of Phthalo Blue, Lamp Black and Burnt Umber created the rich, dark shadows.

Shafts of light were added with yellow and white pastel.

Mortar, bricks and stones were accented with white, yellow and orange pastel.

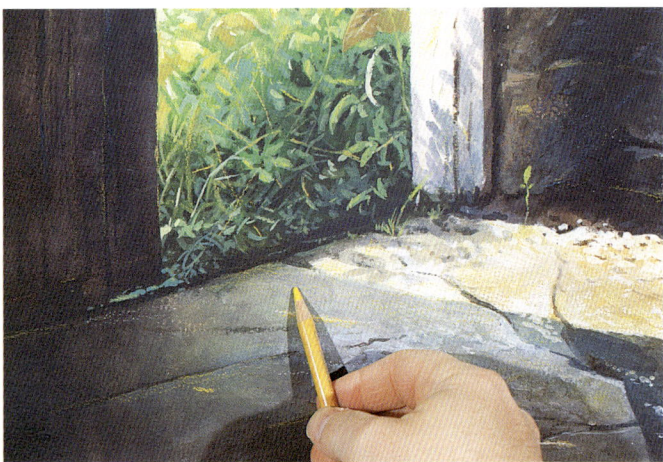
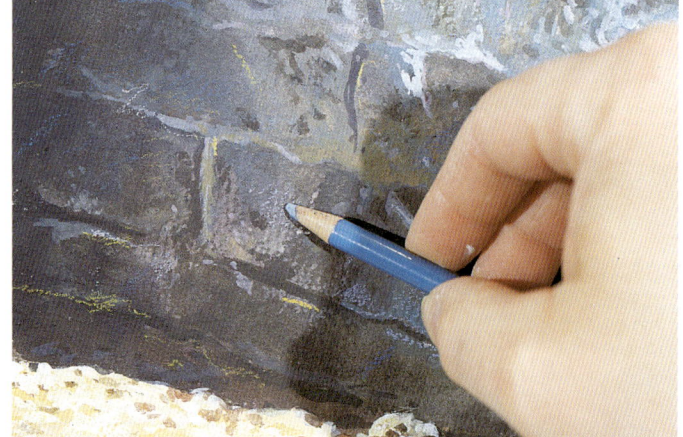

Add Subtle Texture and Color With Lowlights

Using Prismacolor pencils, I added a bit of texture and color to the floor and wall. I used a light touch so that the pencil only grazed the highest points on the paper's surface. The same technique can be used with pastels when you want subtle, broken color.

technique 16 » pastel

Revive a Painting With Pastels

We've all done our share of mediocre paintings. Instead of throwing them on a shelf, try reviving them with a bold application of pastel. The economy of marks is the key to effective accents with dry media. Sometimes, however, accents aren't enough, and it makes sense (and is a lot of fun) to rework a painting with pastels. This technique makes pastels the dominant medium; the painting will take on a "pastel" look. You can try this with a watercolor or acrylic piece.

Sometimes it makes sense to layer a watercolor with acrylics before adding dry media. This helps reduce the contrast of multiple brushstrokes and can also deepen the value of the painting so that the pastel will "pop" off the paper. This idea is not that unusual since many pastel artists will underpaint with acrylics or watercolor as a matter of course. You don't have to ruin a watercolor before trying this technique; you can paint with the intention of finalizing the painting with pastels.

Whenever I do paintings like this, they are looser and more expressive than my usual work. Each time I use this technique, I thoroughly enjoy it and vow that I am going to do more paintings like this. I encourage you to try this technique whenever you feel like painting in a new direction or creating work that is more expressive.

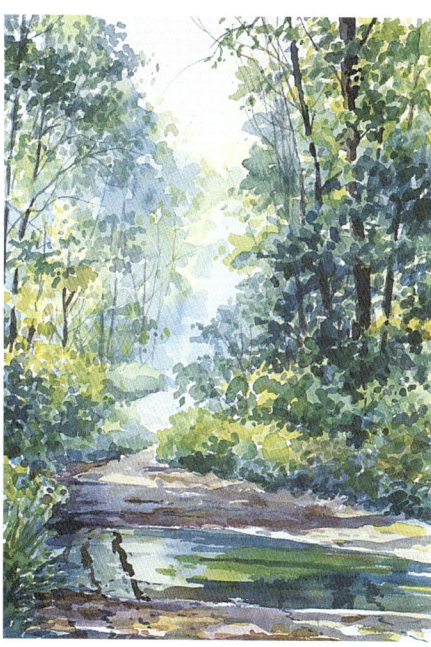

Original Plein Air Watercolor

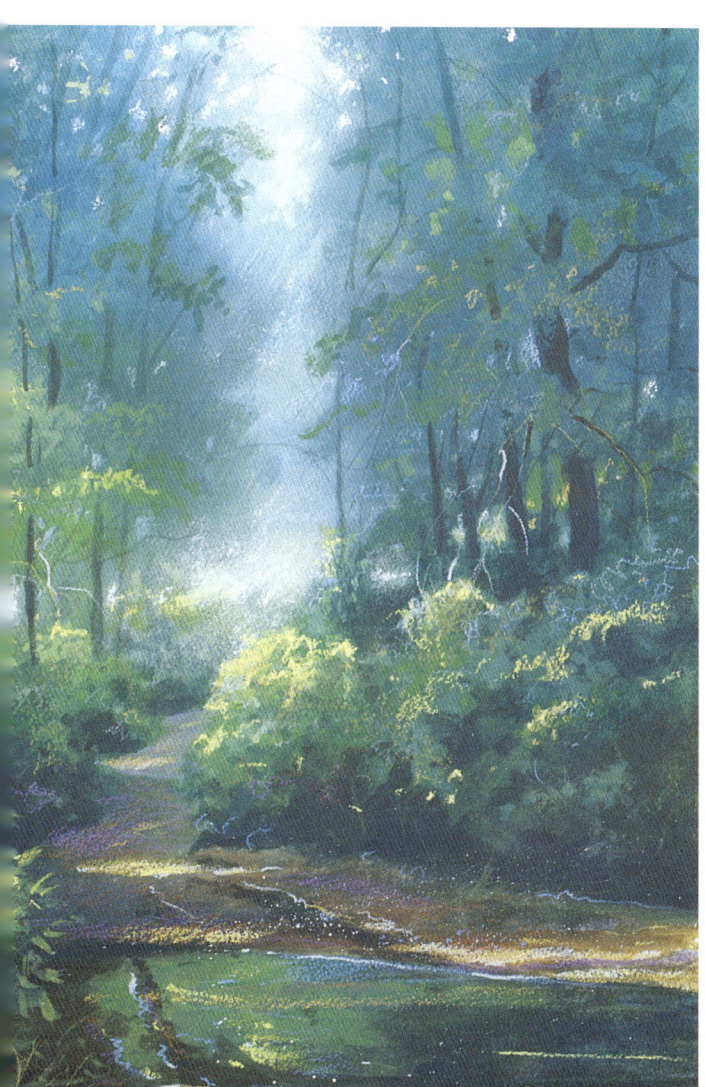

Combine Mediums for Dramatic Color and Value

Originally, this painting was done en plein air in watercolor. Later, I decided to add acrylics and pastel. The watercolor captured the morning light fairly well. While reworking it, I thought of other mornings when I have walked this road—the light was filtered through fog, and the air was filled with a bit of mystery.

I covered much of the watercolor brushwork with several semitransparent and semiopaque applications of acrylic color. Once these layers were dry, I added the pastel, using analogous green and blue-green first. I progressively introduced contrasting colors and put in the bright yellow and white accents last.

Summer Morning—Paden's Road » Mixed media on 140-lb. (300gsm) cold-pressed paper » 15" x 11" (38cm x 28cm)

technique 17 » gouache

Accents With Gouache

Gouache is essentially opaque watercolor. In the eighteenth and nineteenth centuries it was referred to as "body color" and was used with great effect by artists such as John Singer Sargent and Winslow Homer. Body color is an appropriate name since the paint does have body. When it is diluted it retains pigment intensity and opacity. This paint consistency makes for crisp, clean brushstrokes.

Gouache, like dry media, can accent a watercolor or acrylic. Like pastels, gouache accents are often light in value. If you want a dark value, it makes sense to add more layers of dark color using your original medium.

These gouache accents are often added with small brushes and represent highlight areas, details and linear textures. This technique is very popular with illustrators and wildlife artists for adding final details and textures to a watercolor or acrylic painting. I like to use it this way when painting fur or feathers and when creating fine linear elements like winter trees and grasses. Keeping the paint mixtures the consistency of heavy cream ensures that the brushstrokes retain their edges and opacity.

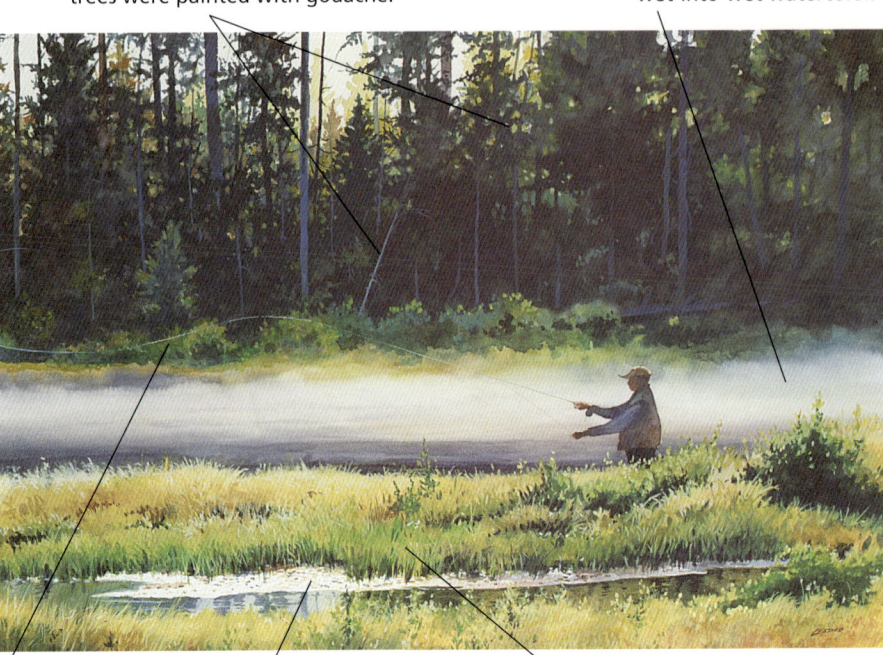

The spots of backlit foliage and bare trees were painted with gouache.

Mist was created with wet-into-wet watercolor.

The fly line was painted with a rigger and white gouache.

White gouache was used to create highlights.

Gouache brushstrokes were layered on rich, warm watercolor washes to create the grass textures.

Accentuate Forms and Textures With Gouache

I energized this watercolor with small touches and accents of gouache. I rendered highlight areas with gouache, and I also used gouache to create textures in the grass and background.

Snake River Flyfisherman » Mixed media on 140-lb. (300gsm) cold-pressed paper » 18" x 27" (46cm x 69cm)

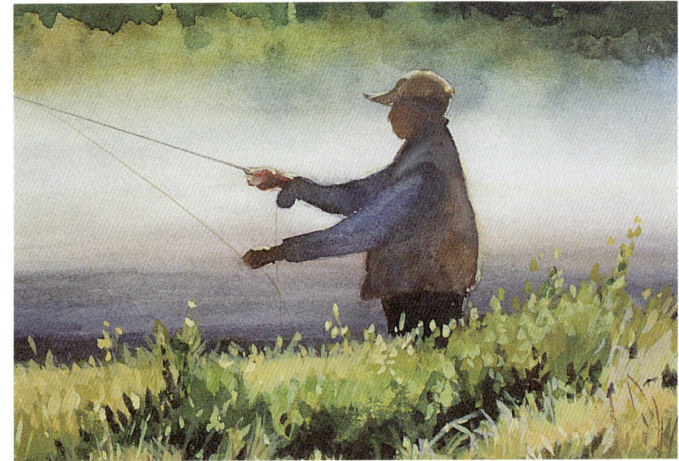

Use Gouache for Light Effects

Notice the distinct brushstrokes of gouache used to render the rim lighting on the figure and the light-value leaves and grasses in the foreground.

technique 18 » mixed media

Try Mixed Media to the Max

Occasionally, a painting will call for you to employ watercolor, acrylic, gouache, colored pencil and pastel. I call these my "everything but the kitchen sink" paintings.

A painting that combines this many mediums usually evolves out of necessity rather than anything premeditated. However, since each medium offers characteristics that fulfill particular painting issues, you can plan a painting that capitalizes on each medium's strength.

At first glance, it might seem that this type of painting would lack fresh color and appear overworked. Avoid this by building your painting from transparent to opaque and from wet to dry. Complete early washes with watercolor, and then add acrylics. Usually acrylics are the main medium in these types of paintings. Use gouache to paint certain details, then add textures and accents with colored pencil and/or pastel.

Each medium should be added carefully with the idea that it will not be overpainted with a previously used medium. Add gouache only after the need to use acrylics has passed, and use dry media last, after all applications of watermedia are done. By layering this way, you can keep the painting looking fresh and exploit the best properties of each medium.

The only major problem that might arise with this type of painting occurs when adding dry media on a heavy buildup of acrylic. In this situation, the paint film will be too slick to hold pastel or pencil marks. However, unless major corrections have caused a thick, opaque layer of paint to be applied, this problem shouldn't occur too often.

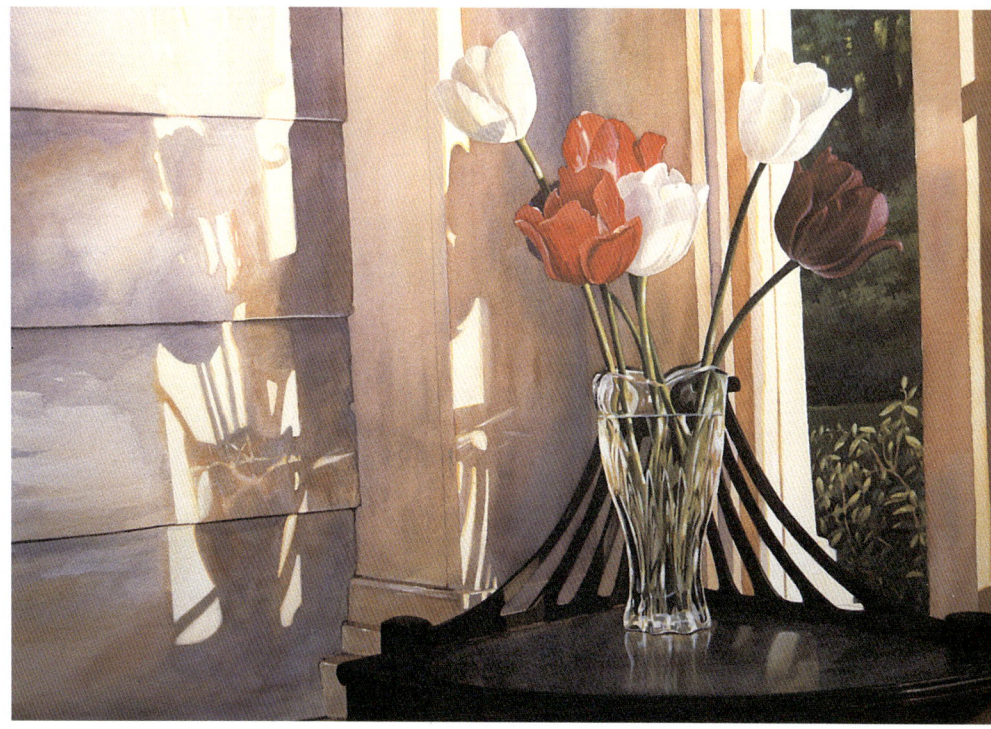

Explore the Versatility of Mixing Several Mediums

I always feel a bit sad when the spring and summer flowers are almost finished blooming. This is when I am most inspired to paint them. I guess I'm trying to extend the time that we can enjoy their beauty. As the title indicates, these were the last tulips that we retrieved from our garden.

The painting was done from a photo of a setup made on our front porch and has in it a bit of every medium I use. I did the colorful shadows and most of the underpainting with watercolor. I developed the background, table and vase of flowers with acrylics. I enhanced light-value details with gouache and added a few final textures on the flowers and background with colored pencil and pastel.

Last Tulips of Spring » Mixed media on 300-lb. (640gsm) cold-pressed paper » 30" x 40" (76cm x 102cm)

mini-demonstration » mixed media

Combine Mediums for a Detailed Rendering

These Belgian horses belong to our friends Mark and Terrie. I was struck by the horses' beauty, strength and size as they were waiting to be hitched to a wagon. The painting is comprised of layers of watercolor, gouache and colored pencil. Hot-pressed paper works well with this type of detailed painting since it has little surface texture to interfere with the delicate brushwork.

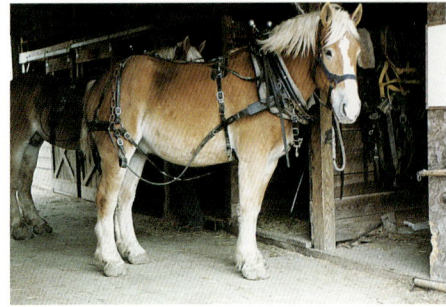

materials

paper
140-lb. (300gsm) hot-pressed, 13" x 17" (33cm x 43cm)

watercolors
Alizarin Crimson • Burnt Sienna • Burnt Umber • Cobalt Blue • Phthalo Blue • Quinacridone Gold • Ultramarine Blue • Winsor Red

gouache
Burnt Sienna • Burnt Umber • Cadmium Red • Cadmium Yellow • Cerulean Blue • Gold Ochre • Ivory Black • Phthalo Blue • Quinacridone Red • Titanium White • Ultramarine Blue • Yellow Ochre

colored pencils
Blue Slate • Burnt Ochre • Orange • Parma Violet • Sand • Spanish Orange • White

brushes
Nos. 16, 12, 10, 8 and 4 synthetic rounds
Nos. 1 and 2 kolinsky sable rounds
½-inch (13mm) synthetic flat

Reference Photo

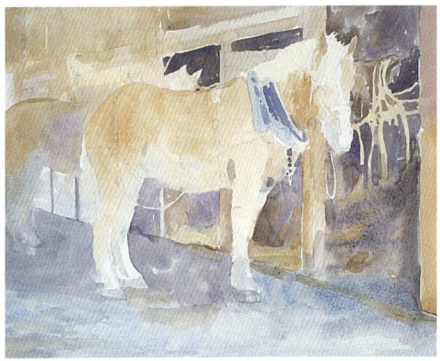

1 Establish Local Color
Wash in local color with variegated watercolor mixes: For the stable and horse, use Burnt Sienna, Burnt Umber, Quinacridone Gold, Winsor Red, Alizarin Crimson and Ultramarine Blue; for the concrete floor, use Cobalt Blue, Ultramarine Blue and Burnt Sienna.

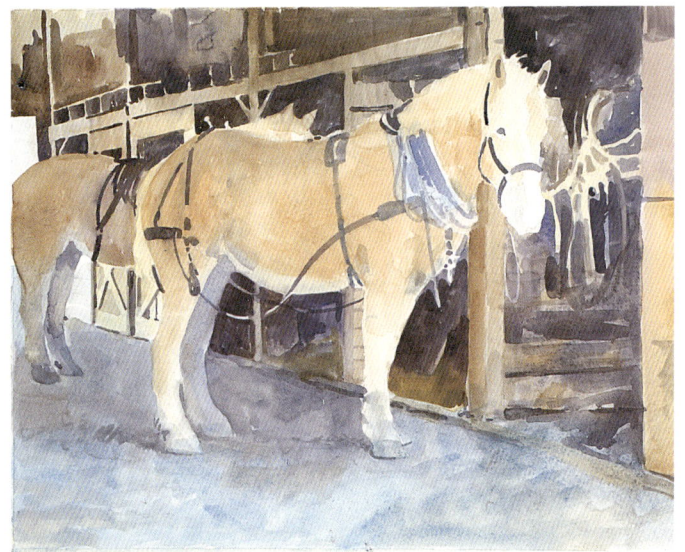

2 Reinforce Shapes and Value Structure
Continue using watercolors. Paint the shadow areas and the rigging and harnesses on the horses with a dark mix of Burnt Umber, Ultramarine Blue and Winsor Red. Develop the horses further with a wash of Burnt Sienna, Quinacridone Gold and a bit of Cobalt Blue. Paint the floor shadows and horse legs with a variegated mix of Ultramarine Blue, Cobalt Blue and a bit of Alizarin Crimson and Burnt Sienna.

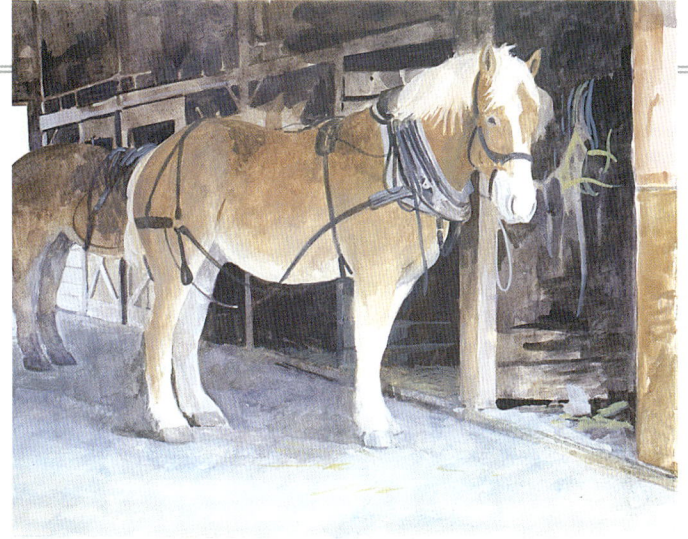

3 Intensify the Painting With Gouache

Now switch to gouache. With thin, purplish mixes of Ultramarine Blue, Quinacridone Red and a bit of Burnt Umber, paint over most of the stable to help counterbalance the earth tones. Reinforce the dark shapes with a mix of Burnt Umber, Ultramarine Blue and a bit of Ivory Black. Use Titanium White with a bit of Cerulean Blue for the part of the stable that reflects outside light.

For the horses, develop their lightest areas with Titanium White and a bit of Yellow Ochre, and work the rest of their bodies with mixes of Gold Ochre, Burnt Sienna, Yellow Ochre, Burnt Umber and Titanium White. Add Ultramarine Blue to this mix for the background horse. Thinly cover the concrete floor with Titanium White and a bit of Yellow Ochre in small, short strokes.

4 Establish Edges and Deepen Color and Values

Add a thicker layer of the same gouache colors used in step three to all the forms. Refine the edges of forms and shapes, using your smallest rounds for more control. Deepen the darkest values with a rich mix of Phthalo Blue, Burnt Umber and Cadmium Red. Establish the harnesses in the background with Cerulean Blue, Burnt Umber and Titanium White. Paint the harnesses and rigging on the horses with Ivory Black, Ultramarine Blue, Cerulean Blue and Titanium White. Layer more Titanium White on the floor. Deepen floor shadows with a thin mix of Ultramarine Blue and Ivory Black.

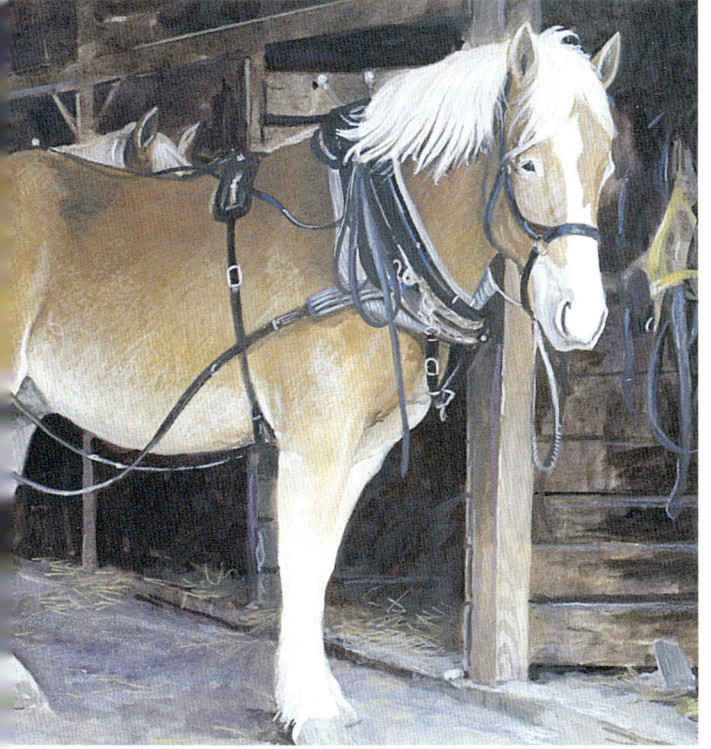

5 Finish With All Mediums

Using a watercolor mix of Phthalo Blue, Alizarin Crimson and Burnt Umber, wash over the darkest parts of the stable. This wash shouldn't be very watery since its purpose is to glaze over the gouache without disturbing the underlying paint. This glaze will deepen the value and lower the contrast of the individual brushstrokes put down in previous layers. Switch to gouache. Using Titanium White and a bit of Cerulean Blue or Yellow Ochre as needed, paint the harnesses' buckles and metal hardware and the mane, tail and leg details. Using delicate strokes of Cadmium Yellow and Yellow Ochre, paint the straw in the stables and on the floor.

Add light strokes of colored pencil for color and texture interest. Add White to the concrete floor. Use Blue Slate and Parma Violet on the floor shadow areas and stable. Accent the harnesses and rigging with the same colors, and add Sand and White for highlights. Use Sand and White on the mane, tail and legs. Finally, use Orange, Spanish Orange, Burnt Ochre and Sand on the horses.

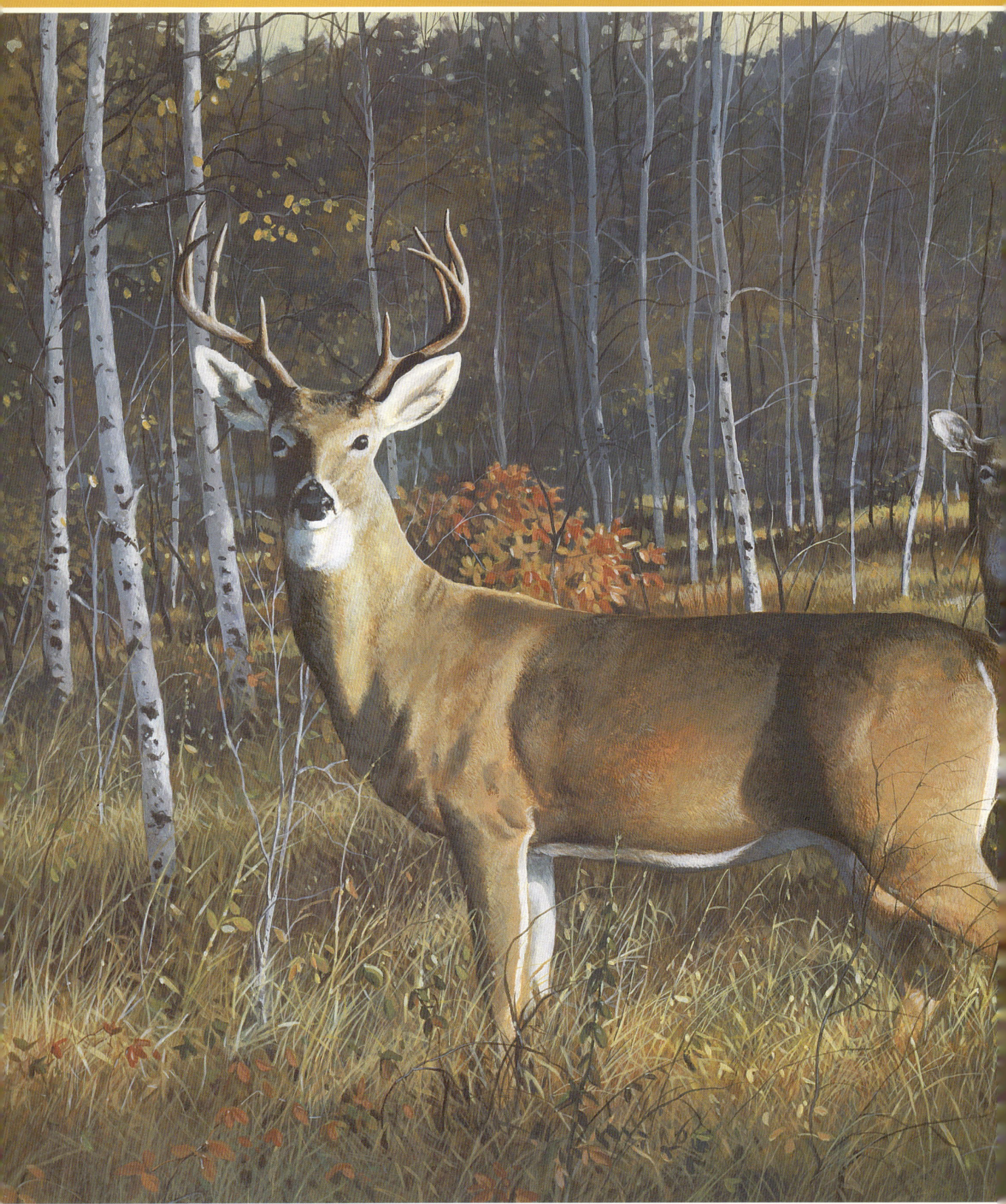

River Bottom Whitetails » Acrylic on hot-pressed board » 18" x 24" (46cm x 61cm)

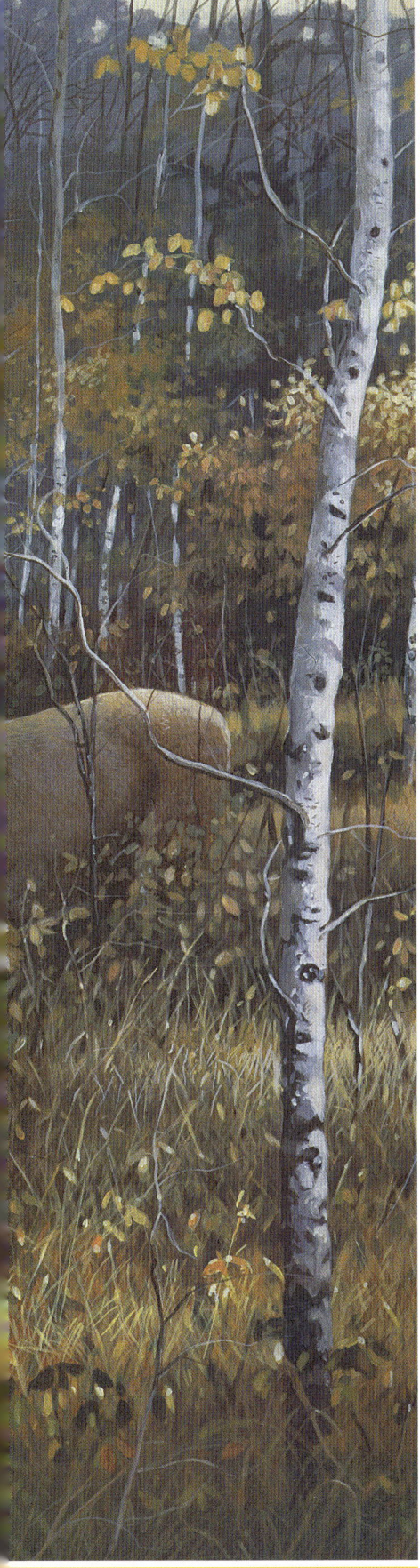

7

step-by-step demonstrations

Three complete demonstrations explore using watercolor, acrylic and mixed media for stunning results. Practice your skills by painting a sun-drenched vegetable still life, a resting figure under an elaborate quilt and a fog-filled harbor scene.

demonstration » watercolor

Fresh From the Garden

These sweet potatoes and tomatoes came from our garden. They filled an antique metal pot, which sat on a sunlit kitchen counter. I took a few pictures and created a sketch from one of the photos.

When painting a strongly lit subject in transparent watercolor, it is important to work warm to cool and to save your white paper. You can always make things cooler and reduce the size of your white highlights, but it is much harder to add warmth and highlights without resorting to opaque color.

paint value shapes instead of objects

Early in the painting, paint large areas of similar value and color instead of concentrating on painting each object separately. This will help give your painting solidity and color harmony.

materials

paper
140-lb. (300gsm) cold-pressed, 15" x 19" (38cm x 48cm)

watercolors
Alizarin Crimson • Aureolin • Burnt Sienna • Burnt Umber • Cadmium Red • Cerulean Blue • Cobalt Blue • Green Gold • New Gamboge • Phthalo Blue • Quinacridone Gold • Quinacridone Red • Rose Madder Genuine • Ultramarine Blue • Winsor Red • Winsor Violet (Dioxazine)

brushes
Nos. 16, 10, 8, 6 and 4 synthetic rounds
No. 2 kolinsky sable round
¼-inch (6mm) synthetic flat

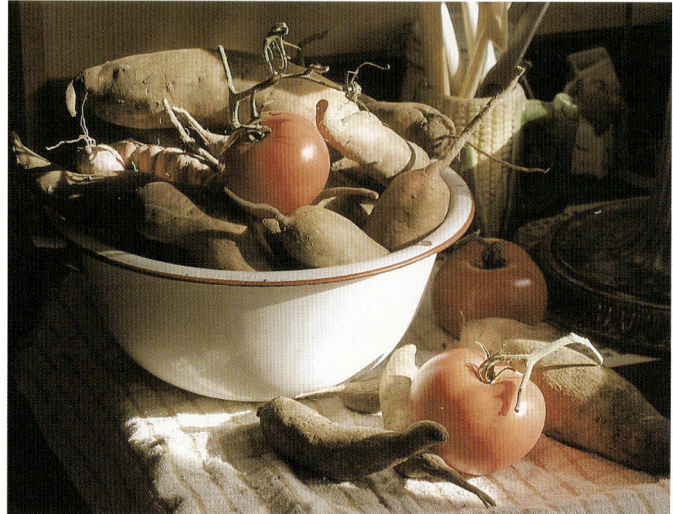

Reference Photo

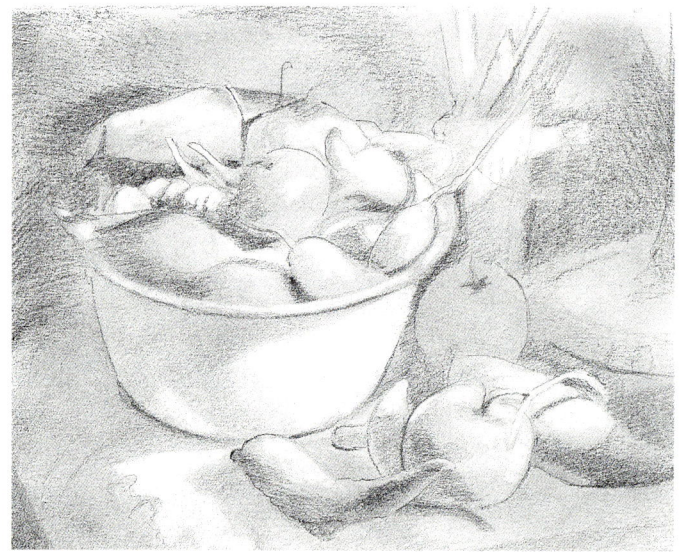

Value Sketch

104

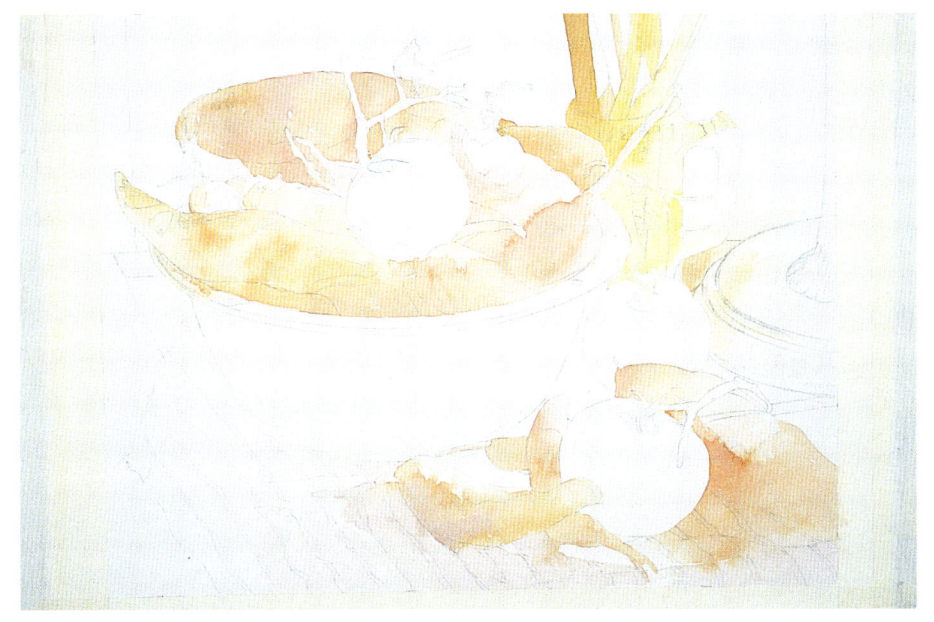

1 Establish the Warm Underpainting

Using a very sharp no. 2 pencil, make a light, careful drawing. Each tomato and potato has distinct character and shape; this is what gives the painting its visual interest. Sharpen the pencil several times to ensure a clean, distinct line. Erase lightly with a kneaded eraser as necessary.

Since the subject is sunlit, warm variegated washes are a natural beginning. Mix large puddles of color on your palette with your largest round. This underpainting is made up of Quinacridone Gold, Winsor Red, Rose Madder Genuine, Cadmium Red and Aureolin. Begin by washing in some Aureolin. Into this wet wash add the other colors. Alternate the colors until everything you want painted is covered.

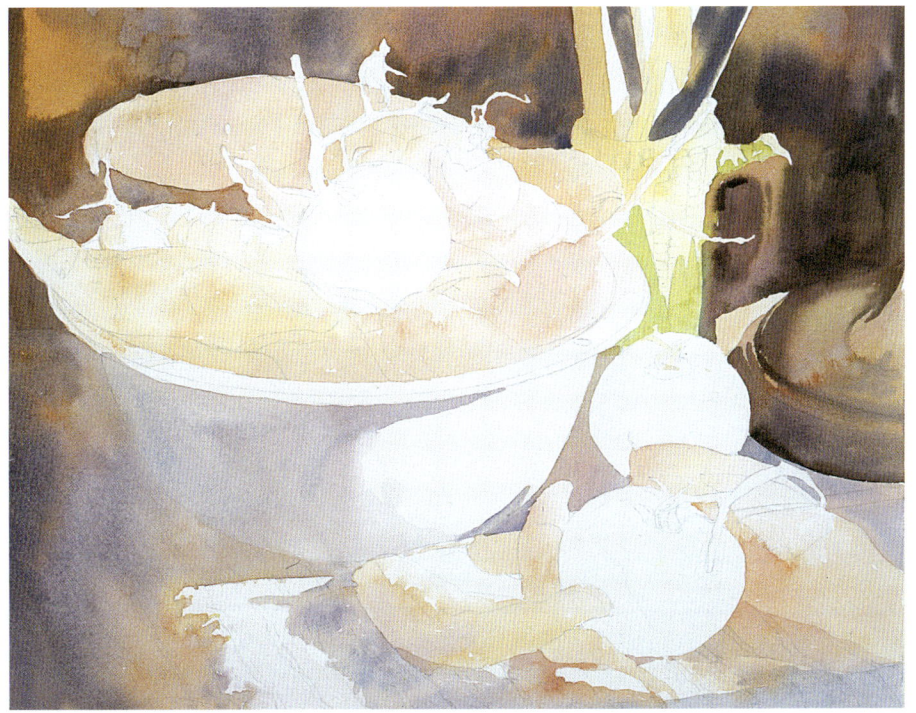

2 Paint the Background and Establish the Shadow Areas

Recharge the warm-color puddles on your palette. Additionally, create a few dark puddles with mixes of Ultramarine Blue, Alizarin Crimson, Winsor Violet (Dioxazine) and Burnt Sienna. The dark puddles range from blue-black to blue-violet to deep reddish brown. Also, create a few light shadow colors by mixing light-value puddles of pure Cobalt Blue and Winsor Violet (Dioxazine).

Establish a very wet base of the colors from step one. As the background blends into the shadows on the pot and counter, add Cobalt Blue and Winsor Violet (Dioxazine). Then paint the dark values wet-into-wet.

3 Begin Rendering Forms and Textures

With the big washes established, concentrate on the individual forms and surfaces. Paint the tomatoes using a variegated mix of Winsor Red, Cadmium Red and Quinacridone Red. Paint the majolica corn mug with a variegated mix of Aureolin, New Gamboge, Green Gold and Ultramarine Blue. Paint the lines in the dish towel with Burnt Sienna, adding a bit of Cobalt Blue for the darker lines.

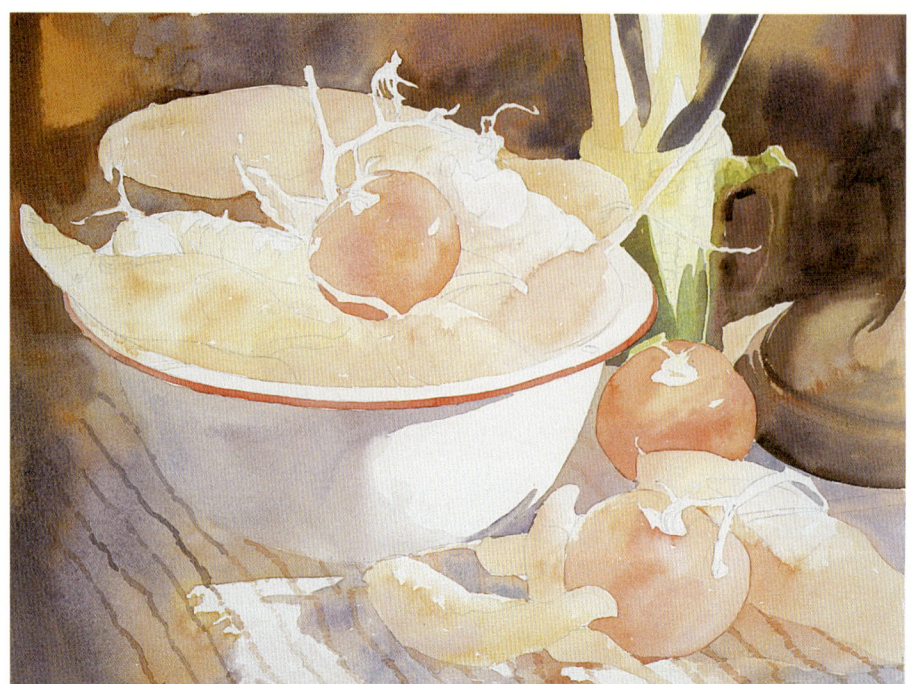

4 Deepen the Values

Darken the shadow areas around the dish towel with a mix of Ultramarine Blue, Alizarin Crimson and Burnt Sienna. After this dries completely, brush a transparent wash of Cobalt Blue and Winsor Violet (Dioxazine) over the shadow areas of the cloth. Add some of the dark shadow mix to this wash wet into wet along the pot edge. Notice how much lighter the shadow on the pot looks. Remember, a value is only dark or light in relation to its neighbor.

Deepen the value on some of the potatoes using a variegated mix of Burnt Sienna, Quinacridone Gold and Cobalt Blue. The potato on the bottom right picks up reflected light from the tomato. To render this effect, paint intense Cadmium Red wet into wet into the variegated mix of gold, sienna and blue. Add Ultramarine Blue to the mix to paint the potato's darkest shadows. Paint the stripe on the pot with Winsor Red.

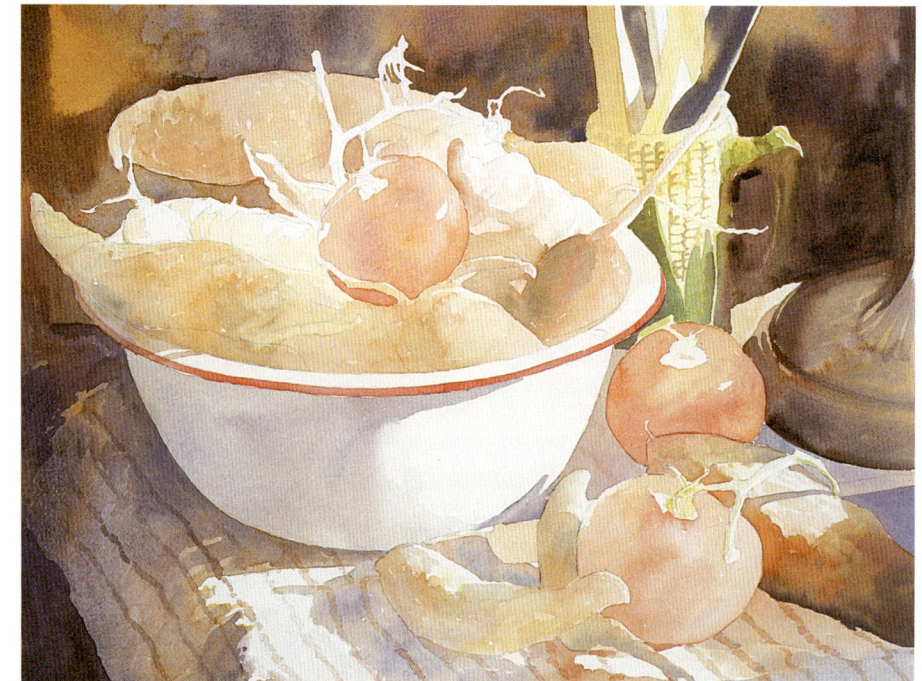

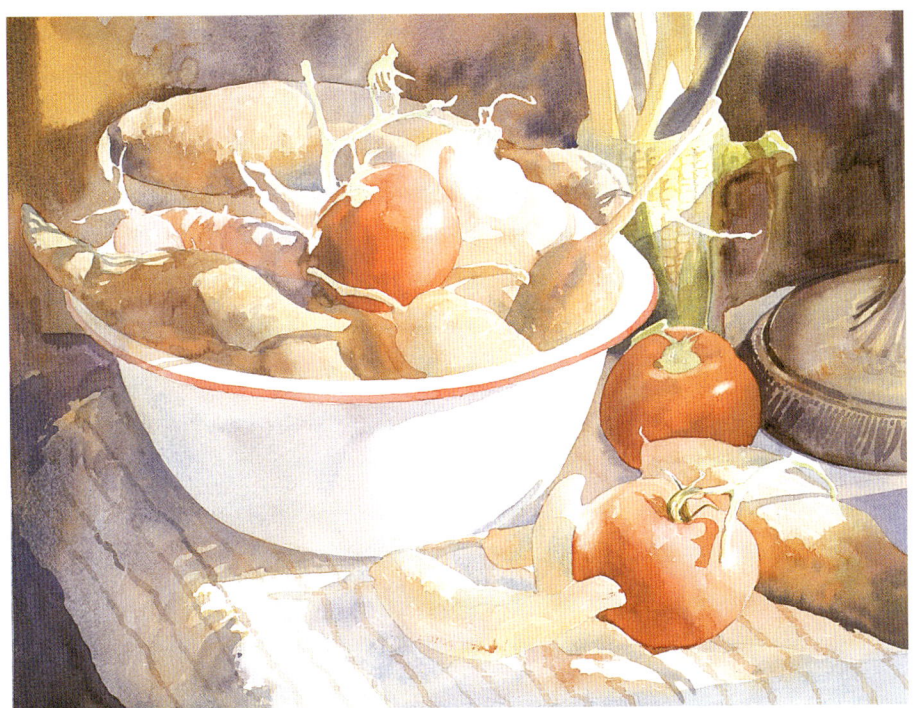

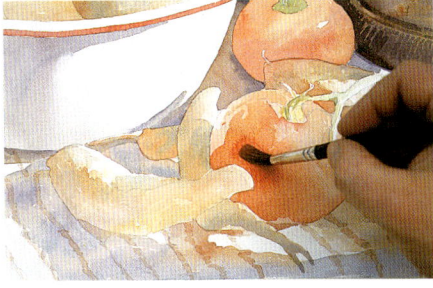

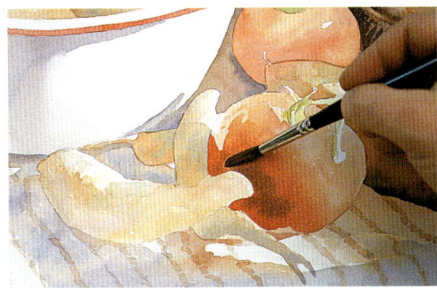

5 Define Forms by Painting Shadows

Since the subject is strongly lit, the shadows define the three-dimensional qualities of the forms. Using a variegated mix of Cobalt Blue, Burnt Sienna, Winsor Red and Quinacridone Gold, further define the potatoes and mug by painting the shadow areas. Paint the tomato stems with a mix of Aureolin, Green Gold and a bit of Cobalt Blue.

Use the same variegated mixture used in the previous step and develop the shadow areas on the other potatoes. At this stage, complete the tomatoes with one final wet-into-wet wash.

Detail: Establish Final Color and Value of the Tomatoes

Prepare intense puddles of color on your palette: a mix of Cadmium Red and Quinacridone Red for the deep red; a mix of Ultramarine Blue, Alizarin Crimson and a bit of Burnt Sienna for the shadow color. Apply a deep red wash on the shadow side of the tomato. Rinse your brush and wipe the excess water on a paper towel. Use the damp brush to soften the edge of the intense red wash and drag it toward the lit side of the tomato. Pick up some of the dark shadow mix and lightly paint that into the red wash. It will spread wet into wet, creating a soft-edged shadow.

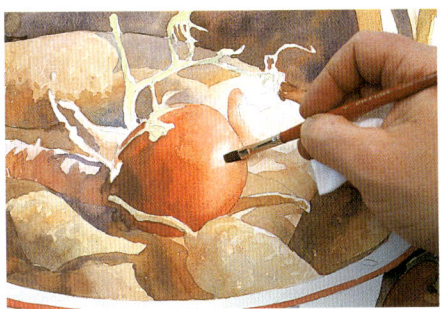
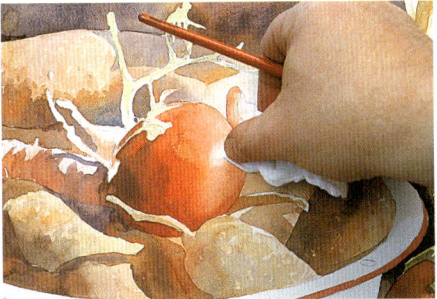

Detail: Lift Color to Create Realistic Highlights

Once the tomatoes have dried completely, soften their highlights. Brush clean water over the highlight area and let this sit for a few seconds. With the brush slightly damp, gently rub the highlight edges to loosen some of the color. Blot the highlight with a tissue. Do not rub the tissue on the paper; this will drag color onto the highlight. Repeat this process a couple of times until the desired softness is achieved.

6 Add More Shadows and Textures

Continue developing the shadow areas on the potatoes. Use the same mix of shadow colors mentioned in step five, adding Cerulean Blue and Quinacridone Red to represent some of the areas of reflected light. The darkest shadow areas are mixes of Ultramarine Blue, Alizarin Crimson and Burnt Sienna. Use short, broken brushstrokes along the edges of the shadows to render the texture of the sweet potatoes. Sprinkle small touches of light value across the potatoes to emulate their rough skin. Deepen the shadow on the pot using a variegated mix of Cobalt Blue, Quinacridone Red and Burnt Sienna.

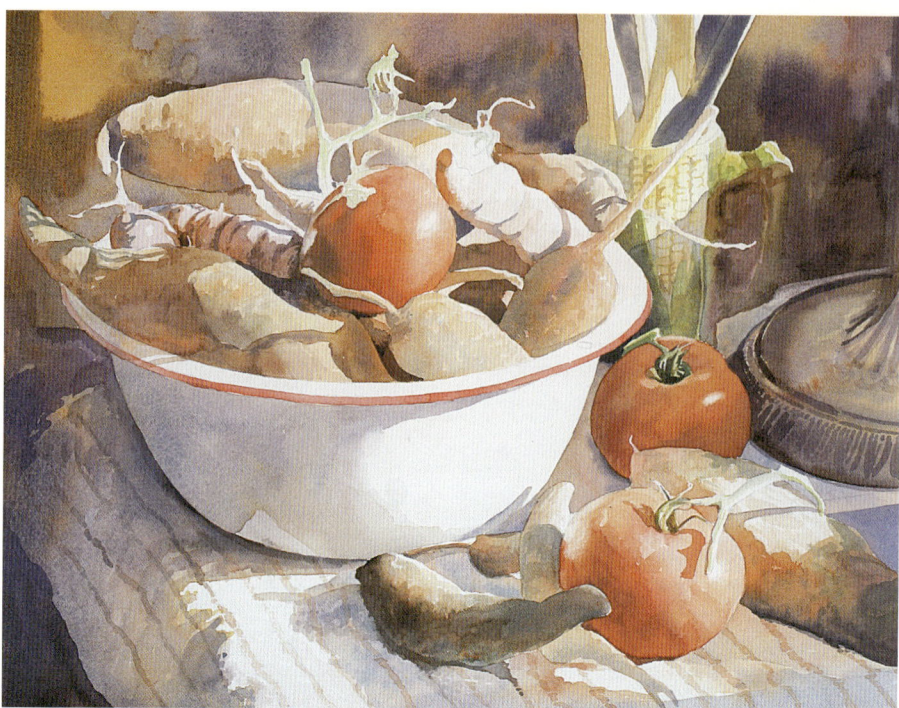

7 Add the Darkest Values

This step really makes the sunlit areas stand out. Mix several puddles of dark, rich shadow color. These are similar to the dark color mixes in step two, but add Phthalo Blue and Burnt Umber to create extra-dark values. Establish the darkest shadow areas around the potatoes, including the dark shape behind the pot and the shadow along its left edge. As the shapes approach the small, threadlike roots, paint negatively around them.

Now the tomato stems need to be developed. Wash in delicate brushstrokes of Green Gold, Aureolin and New Gamboge. Paint the shadows on the stems with Ultramarine Blue, Cobalt Blue and Burnt Sienna. Sharpen the texture of the potatoes with a few more touches of a mixture of Burnt Sienna and Ultramarine Blue.

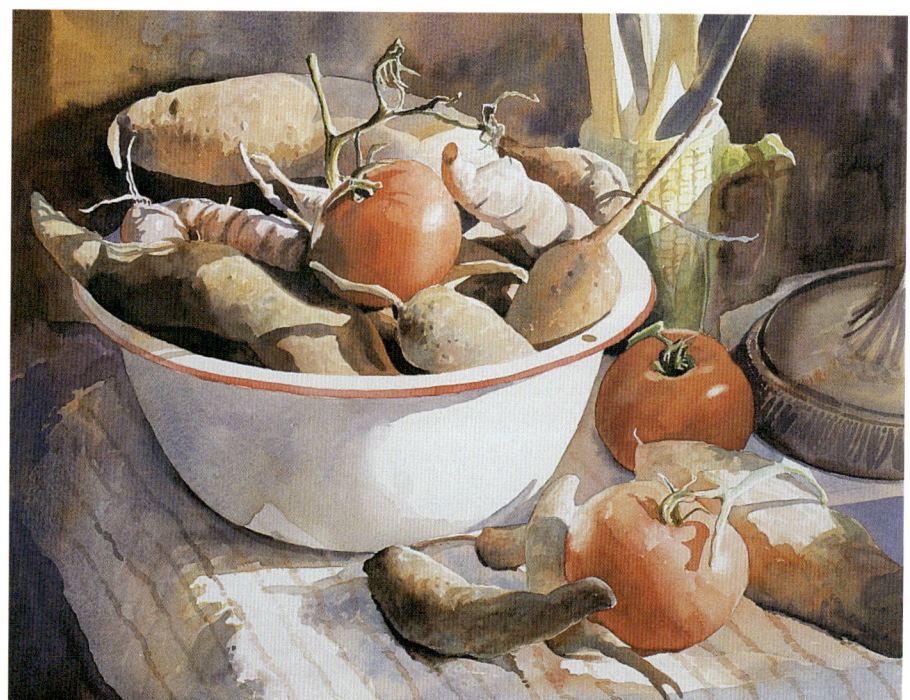

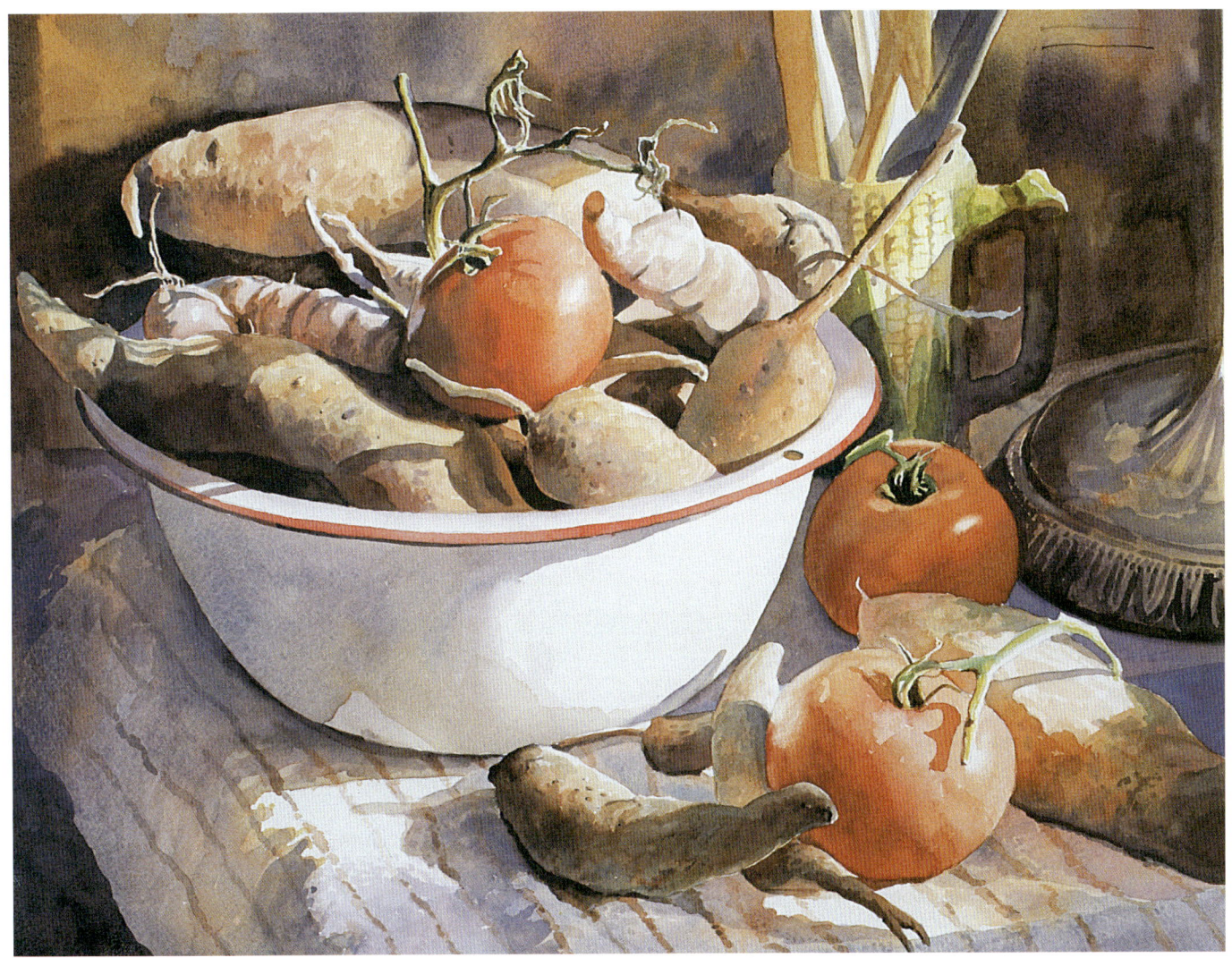

8 Add Final Touches

The last step is to adjust values and soften or harden edges. Add a few small washes of Cobalt Blue, Winsor Violet (Dioxazine) and Burnt Sienna to create darker shadow areas and to add a bit of texture. Deepen the value of and add a few final details to the base of the lamp on the right and the handle of the mug. Using a small, damp brush, soften highlight edges on some of the potatoes. Apply a few light washes of Winsor Red and New Gamboge to the potato roots. Finally, give the shadows on the counter a wash of Cobalt Blue to deepen their value.

Sweet Potatoes and Tomatoes » Watercolor on 140-lb. (300gsm) cold-pressed paper » 15" x 19" (38cm x 48cm)

demonstration » acrylics

A Midday Nap

I photographed my wife, Kathy, as she napped in the living room. The rim lighting on her face and the patterns of the couch and quilt were too much to resist. I used a digital camera and then imported the image into Adobe Photoshop. There, I adjusted the color balance and the contrast. I then cropped the photo and created a grid across the image. I printed the photo with an ink-jet printer and used this for my final drawing. I also got an 8" × 10" (20cm × 25cm) print made without the grid.

Since the composition was set in Adobe Photoshop and since I was going to work so closely from the photo, I didn't create a preliminary drawing. I did, however, do a pencil study of Kathy's face so I could understand the subtle value shifts that I would encounter in the painting.

materials

paper
140-lb. (300gsm) cold-pressed, 20" x 28" (51cm x 71cm)

acrylics
ACRA Crimson • Brilliant Blue • Burnt Sienna • Burnt Umber • Cadmium Orange • Cadmium Yellow Medium • Dioxazine Purple • Hooker's Green Deep • Naphthol Red Light • Permanent Green Light • Phthalo Blue • Titanium White • Ultramarine Blue • Yellow Medium Azo • Yellow Ochre • Yellow Orange Azo

brushes
Nos. 10, 8, 6, 4, 2, 1 and 00 synthetic rounds
½-inch (13mm) synthetic flat

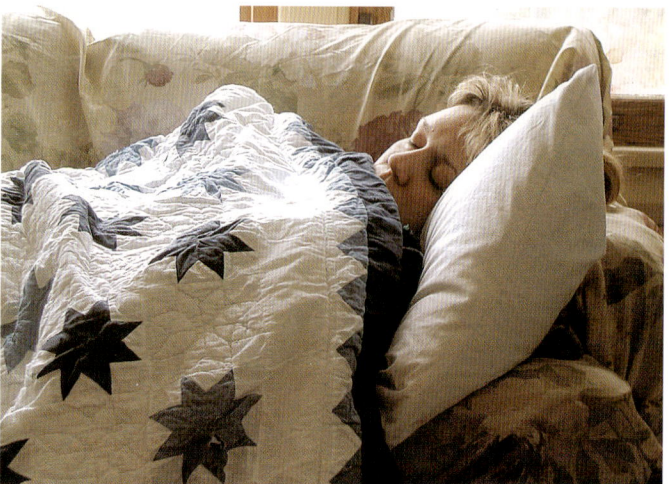

Reference Photo

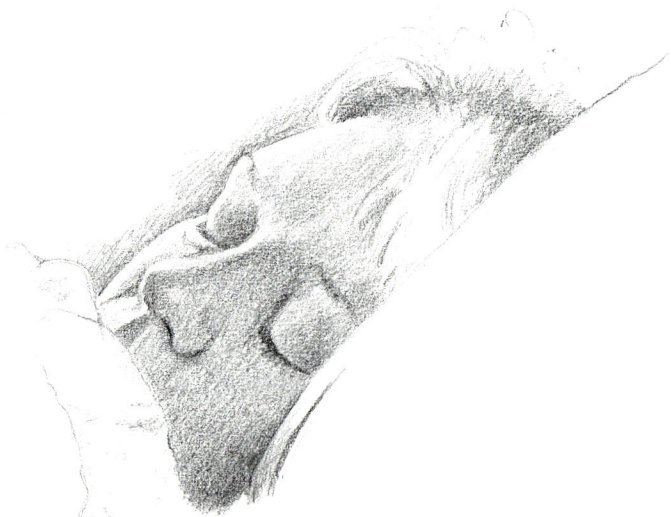

Pencil Study

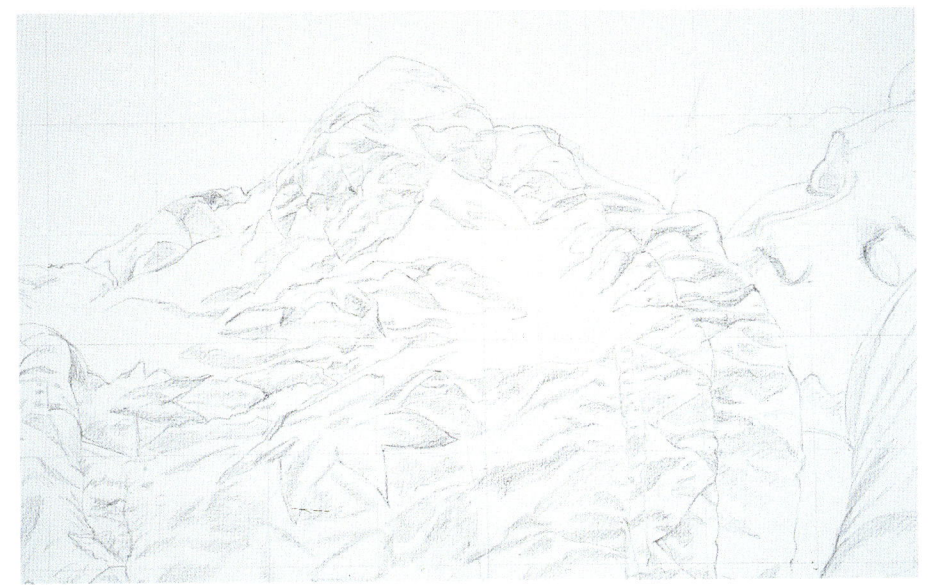

1 Create a Detailed Drawing
After drawing a grid on the paper, establish an extremely detailed drawing, including some value shapes to help define the quilt. Use a sharp no. 2 pencil. Gridding is a great way to accurately transfer an image to a larger format. To be effective, the grid must divide the painting in exactly the same proportions as the source image. Even with the help of the grid, this drawing took over ten hours to complete. (See the drawing in its entirety in the next step.)

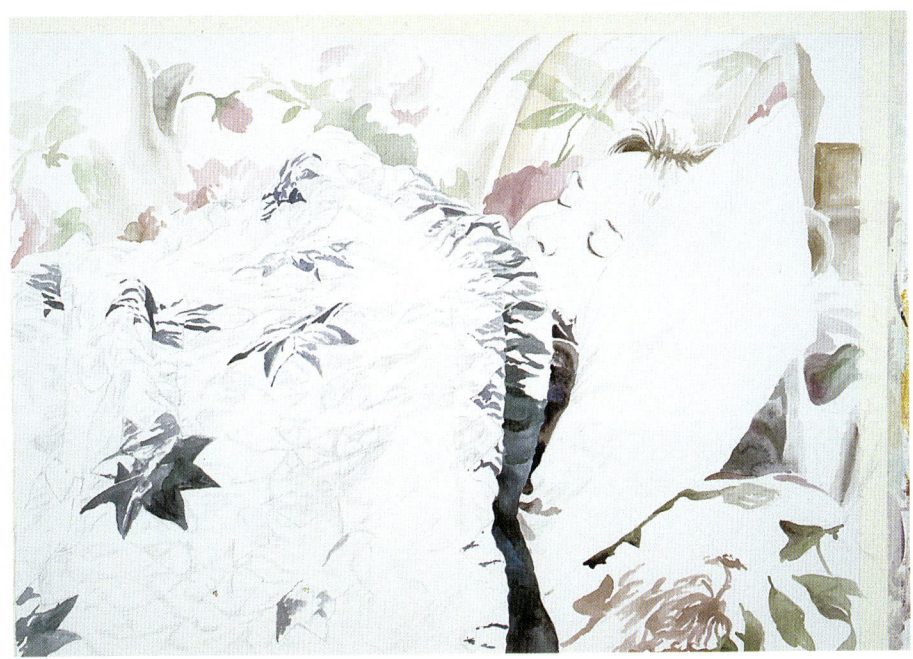

2 Paint the Darkest Values
Establish the dark value pattern first. Using watercolor-like washes, paint the pattern of the quilt as well as the darkest shadow areas. Use a mix of Ultramarine Blue, Brilliant Blue and Burnt Umber. Paint the pattern on the couch with Hooker's Green Deep, Permanent Green Light, Yellow Ochre, ACRA Crimson and Burnt Sienna.

3 Wash on the Local Color
Using the same colors as in the previous step, develop the quilt and couch further. These washes define the light and shadow patterns that create the topography of the fabric. Establish the shadow pattern on the pillow with a wash of Brilliant Blue and Ultramarine Blue. Paint the face with a wash of ACRA Crimson, Cadmium Yellow Medium, Yellow Ochre and a bit of Brilliant Blue.

Establish the local color of the couch with various mixes of Burnt Sienna, Cadmium Orange, Brilliant Blue and a bit of ACRA Crimson. Paint the subtle shadow pattern on the lower half of the quilt and lit side of the pillow with light washes of Ultramarine Blue and ACRA Crimson. Paint the hair with light washes of Yellow Medium Azo and Burnt Sienna.

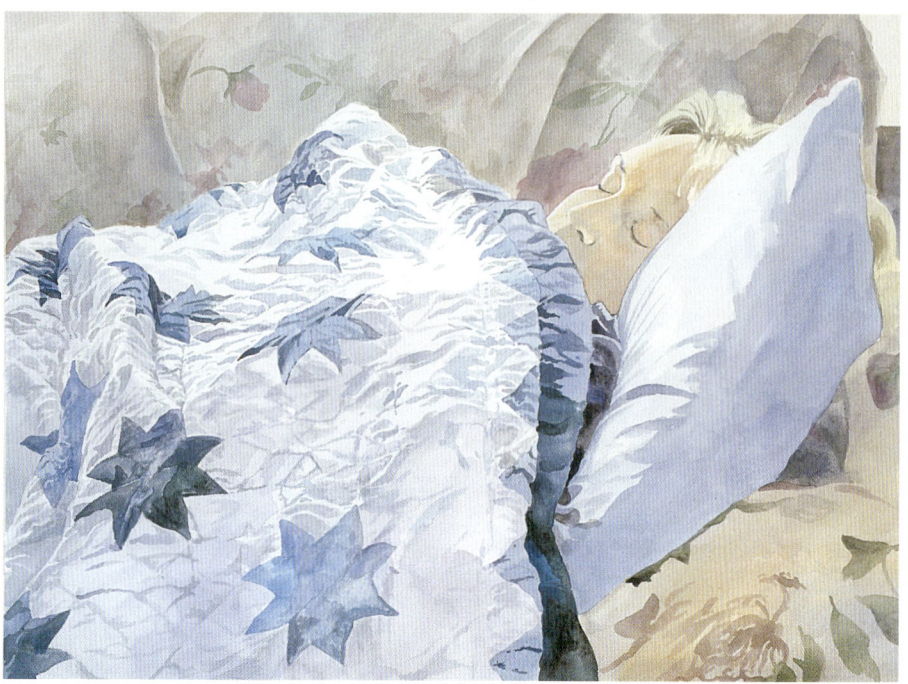

4 Add Another Layer of Washes
Once the previous washes are completely dry, add more thin color washes identical to step three, except do not paint the face. The idea is to build depth and richness to the color and value. The best way to do this is with multiple layers.

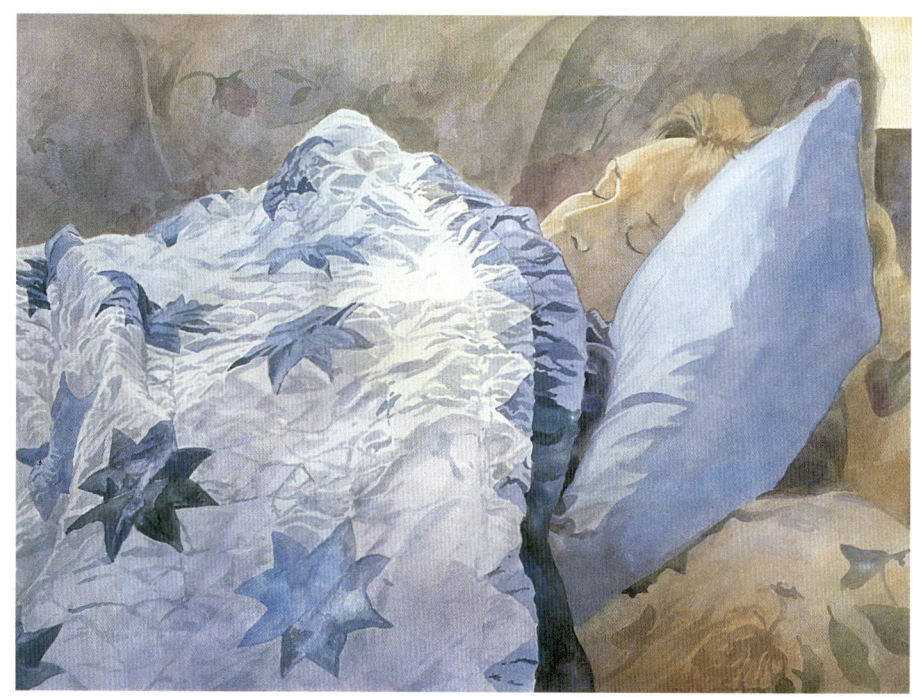

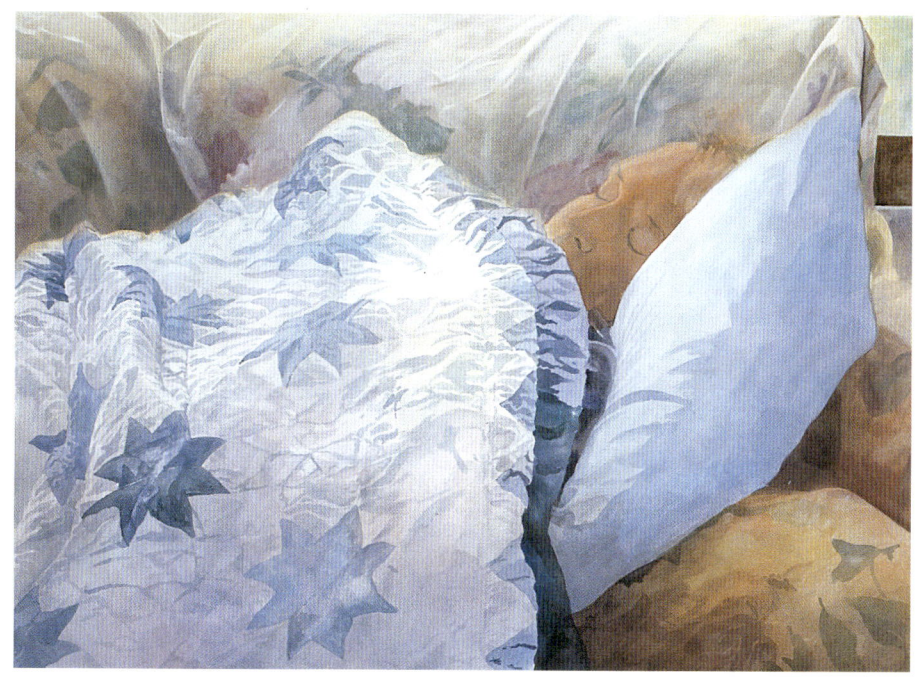

5 Add Layers of White

The top of the couch is bathed in warm light from a large picture window directly behind it. Establish this warmth by painting various mixes of Yellow Medium Azo, Yellow Ochre, Burnt Sienna, Yellow Orange Azo and ACRA Crimson, all of which are mixed with semitransparent Titanium White. Apply several layers to get the correct value and color.

Paint the highlight areas (highest points on the fabric folds) using semiopaque and opaque Titanium White. Finger blend the paint into the surrounding color. Then brush on the brightest highlight areas, but don't finger blend. Glaze with color the areas that seem too white. Cover the quilt and pillow with a semitransparent layer of Titanium White. Deepen the shadows around the pillow and the front of the couch using a semitransparent mix of Ultramarine Blue, Dioxazine Purple and Burnt Umber.

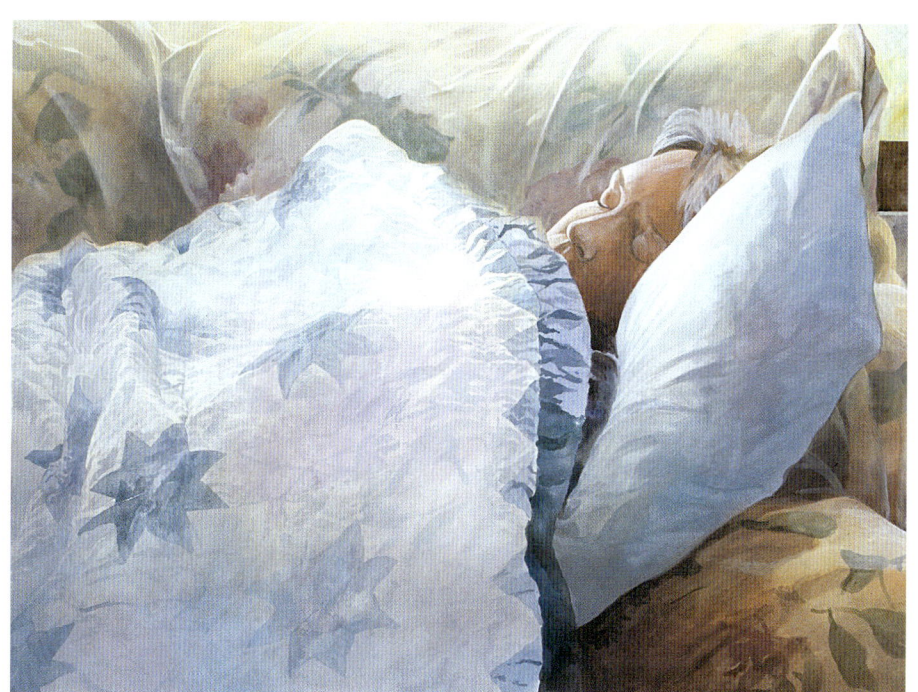

6 Add Another Layer of White

Establish a base of white for later glazes. Cover the pillow and the entire quilt except for the binding with a layer of semiopaque Titanium White. This reduces the contrast of the folds and wrinkles. Use opaque white on some of the highlight folds, finger blending where a soft edge is needed.

Paint around the leaf and flower pattern on the lower-right corner of the couch with opaque and semiopaque Titanium White. Paint a layer of semiopaque white over the hair. Paint several semitransparent washes on the face, using various mixes of ACRA Crimson, Yellow Orange Azo, Cadmium Orange, Burnt Sienna and a bit of Ultramarine Blue. Establish the sunlit side of the face with semiopaque Titanium White.

7 Complete the Face

There is a harsh contrast on the face because of the buildup of color on the shadow side and the Titanium White on the lit side. Let's soften it and render the subtle value shifts that define the form. Scumble a thin, watery mix of ACRA Crimson and Yellow Ochre across the sunlit side. Add a bit of Brilliant Blue and Burnt Sienna for the darker values along the eye and nose. Scumble the same thin colors with a bit of Titanium White across the cheek and down to the deepest shadow areas.

Begin stippling along the nose and cheek with semiopaque and opaque mixes of Titanium White and Yellow Orange Azo, ACRA Crimson and Burnt Sienna. Stipple the darkest values with a mix of Ultramarine Blue, Burnt Umber and Naphthol Red Light. Paint the hair with delicate washes of Yellow Orange Azo and Burnt Sienna. Indicate shadows with Burnt Umber and Ultramarine Blue.

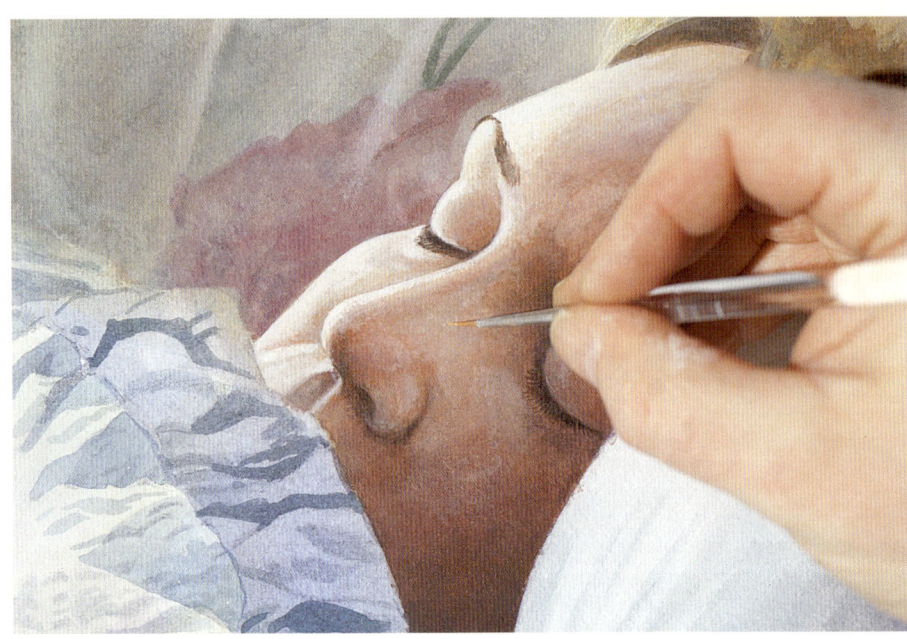

8 Complete the Couch

Add opaque Titanium White highlights to the front of the couch, finger blending where softer edges are needed. Reinforce the leaf and flower pattern: Paint the leaves with a semiopaque mix of Hooker's Green Deep, Yellow Ochre and Burnt Sienna. Add Ultramarine Blue to this mix for the darkest leaves and shadows. Complete the flower with a semiopaque mix of ACRA Crimson, Ultramarine Blue and Burnt Sienna. Add Titanium White for the lighter petals. Finalize the fabric with transparent washes of mixed Burnt Sienna, Cadmium Orange and Ultramarine Blue.

Finish the pillow, painting the highlight folds using opaque and semiopaque Titanium White and finger blending for soft edges. Once this is dry, add the darkest values with transparent washes of Ultramarine Blue, Burnt Umber and Brilliant Blue.

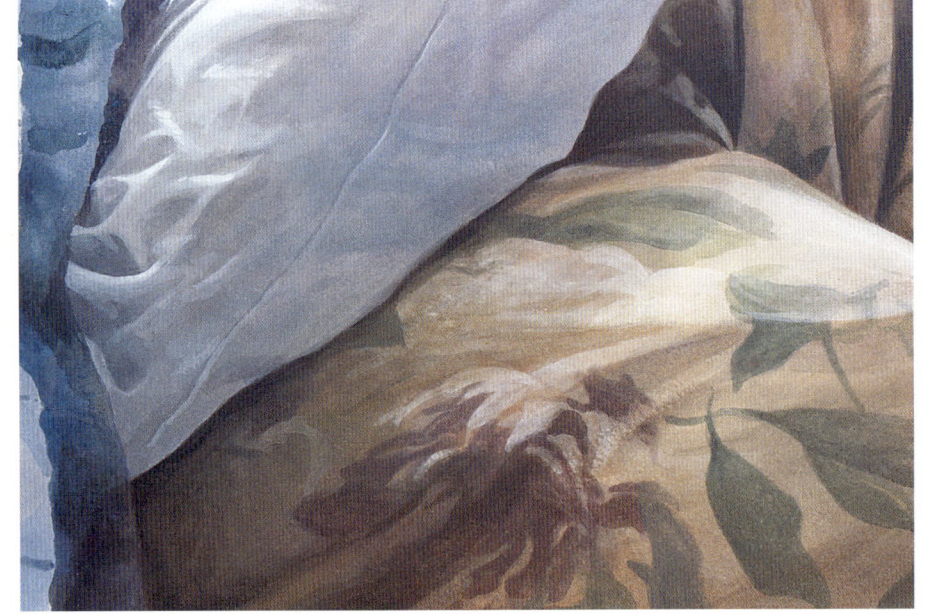

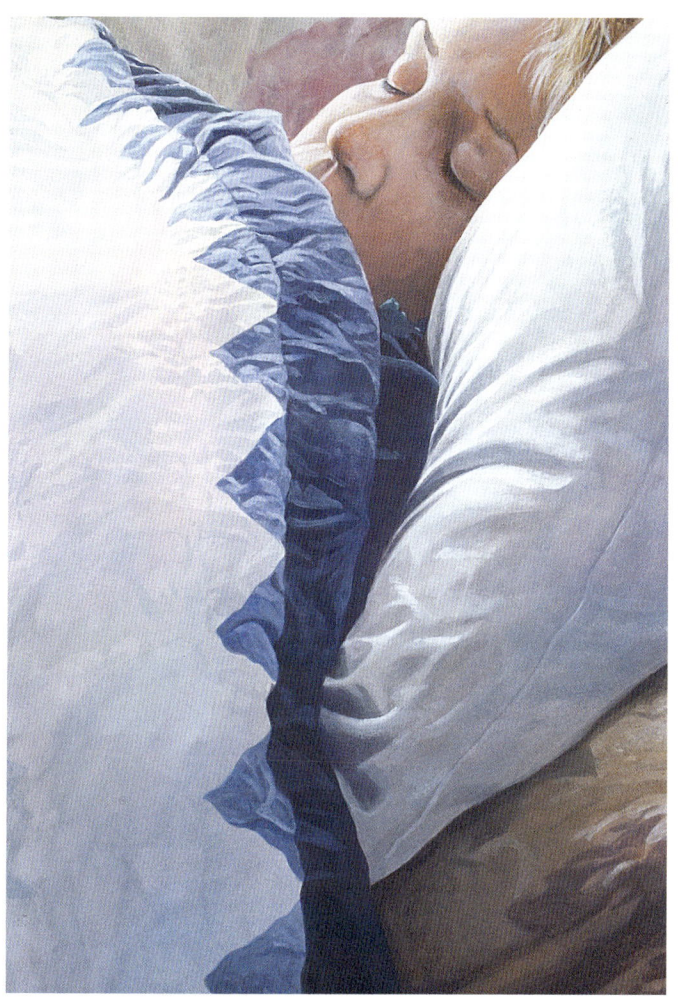

9 Complete the Quilt Binding
To complete the binding along the quilt, first wash a semitransparent layer of Ultramarine Blue over its entire length. Paint the triangles with a semitransparent wash of Brilliant Blue and Ultramarine Blue. Once these are dry, reestablish the shadows using a semiopaque mix of Ultramarine Blue and Burnt Umber. Paint the light blue highlight using opaque and semiopaque mixes of Titanium White, Brilliant Blue and Ultramarine Blue. Just as for the face, take your time to notice all the subtle value shifts.

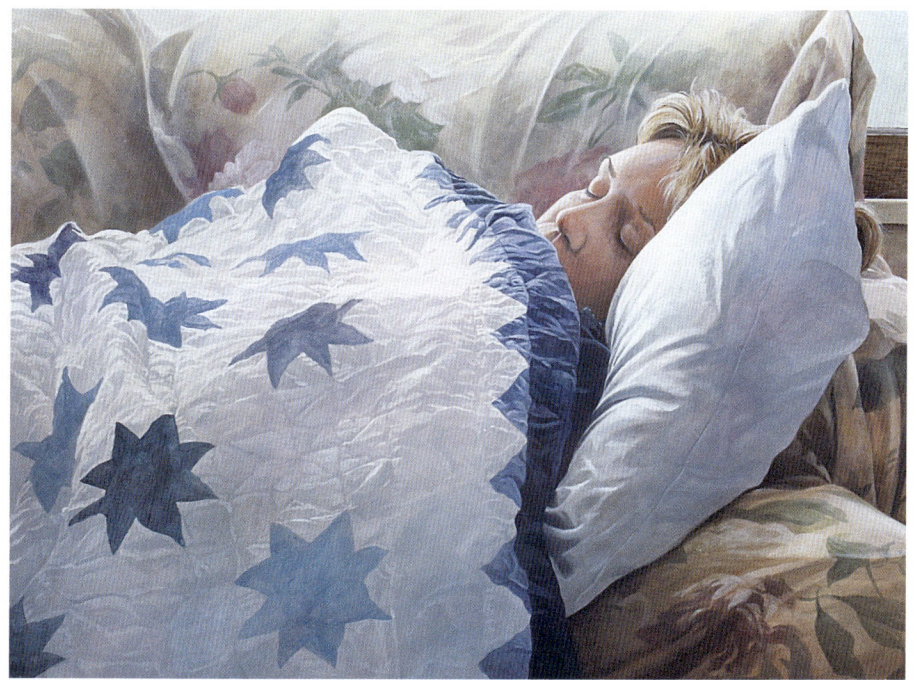

10 Refine the Quilt
The early washes of blue on the quilt have now been covered with several layers of Titanium White. Some have practically disappeared, and others are barely visible. This subtle contrast is what gives the realistic impression of the surface. Reestablish some of the shapes where necessary by painting transparent washes of Ultramarine Blue, Brilliant Blue and a bit of ACRA Crimson. Darken the star pattern with transparent washes of Ultramarine Blue, Phthalo Blue and Brilliant Blue. Add a touch of Burnt Umber to paint the darker blue shapes. Paint the bright sunlight pattern with semiopaque Titanium White.

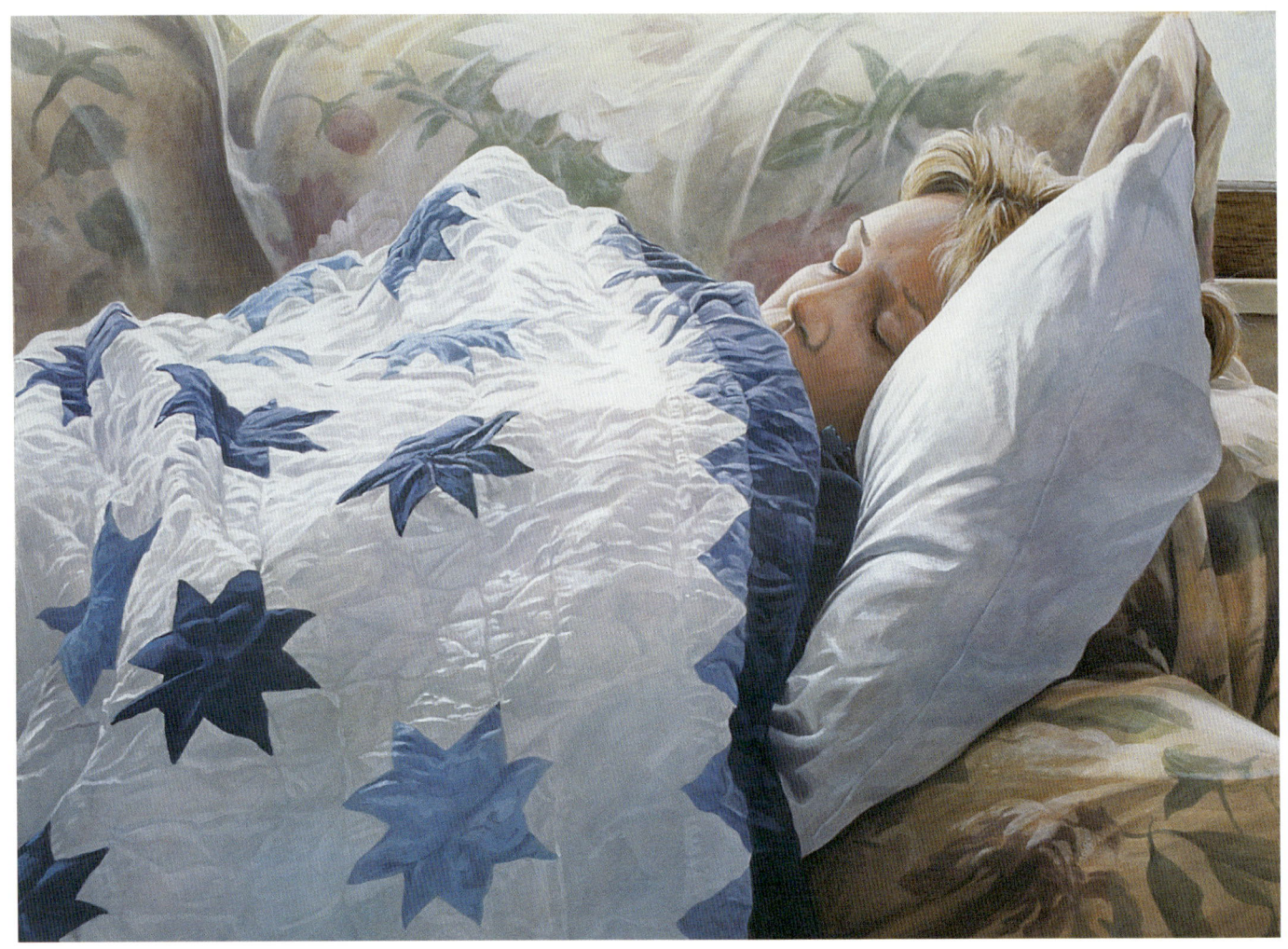

11 Finalize the Painting

Paint the brightest highlights on the quilt with opaque Titanium White. Darken the value on the star pattern where necessary using the same colors as in the previous step. Refine the pattern on the back of the couch using the same colors as before. After this is dry, scumble a semiopaque mix of Cadmium Yellow Medium and Titanium White across the top of the couch. Blend this using your fingers. Wash final glazes of color over the couch where necessary with various transparent mixes of Burnt Sienna, Cadmium Orange, ACRA Crimson and Ultramarine Blue. Finally, refine the face with a few transparent washes of ACRA Crimson, Yellow Ochre and Burnt Sienna.

Afernoon Nap » Acrylic on 140-lb. (300gsm) cold-pressed paper » 20" x 28" (51cm x 71cm)

demonstration » mixed media

Twilight on the Harbor

This painting was inspired by a harbor that I photographed along the coast of Maine. I had many great photos to work from; I used four to create the compositional sketch. Using this sketch as a guide, I scanned the photos into Adobe Photoshop. I pieced together the photos and then copied and pasted the boats until I came up with the final composition.

On a whim, I created a look of fog hanging over the harbor. I liked this effect and decided to make it part of my painting. In Photoshop, I added a grid to the image and then printed it on an ink-jet printer. I also had an 8" × 10" (20cm × 25cm) made without the grid.

materials

paper
300-lb. (640gsm) cold-pressed, 14" x 29" (36cm x 74cm)

acrylics
ACRA Crimson • Brilliant Blue • Burnt Umber • Cadmium Orange • Dioxazine Purple • Naphthol Red Light • Phthalo Blue • Phthalo Green • Titanium White • Ultramarine Blue • Vivid Lime Green • Yellow Medium Azo • Yellow Orange Azo

gouache
Burnt Sienna • Cadmium Orange • Cadmium Yellow • Cobalt Blue • Ivory Black • Phthalo Blue • Quinacridone Red • Titanium White • Ultramarine Blue

colored pencils
Blue Slate • Parma Violet • White

brushes
Nos. 10, 4, 2 and 1 synthetic rounds (for applying acrylics) • 2-inch (51mm), 1-inch (25mm) and ¼-inch (6mm) synthetic flats (for applying acrylics) • Nos. 6, 4, 2, 1 and 00 synthetic rounds (for applying gouache) • ½-inch (12mm) and ¼-inch (6mm) synthetic flats (for applying gouache)

other
Acrylic gesso

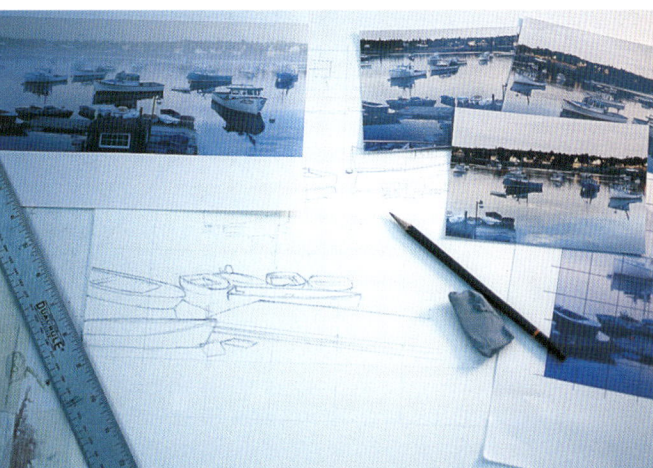

Reference Materials

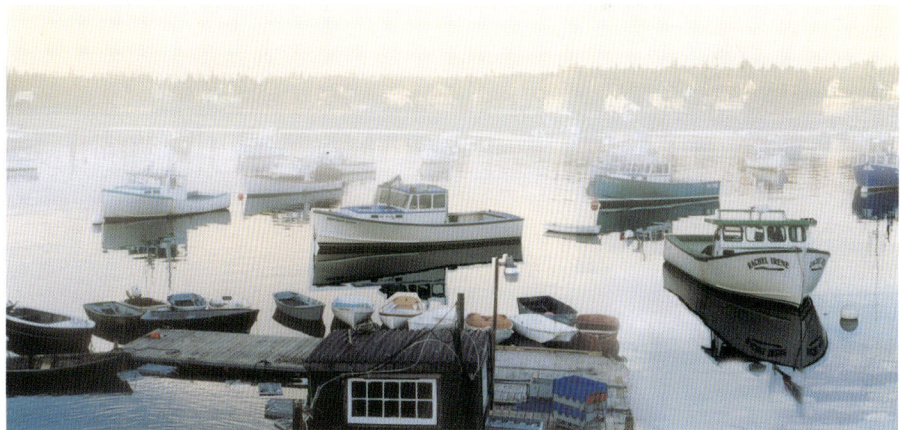

Computer-Altered Final Reference Photo

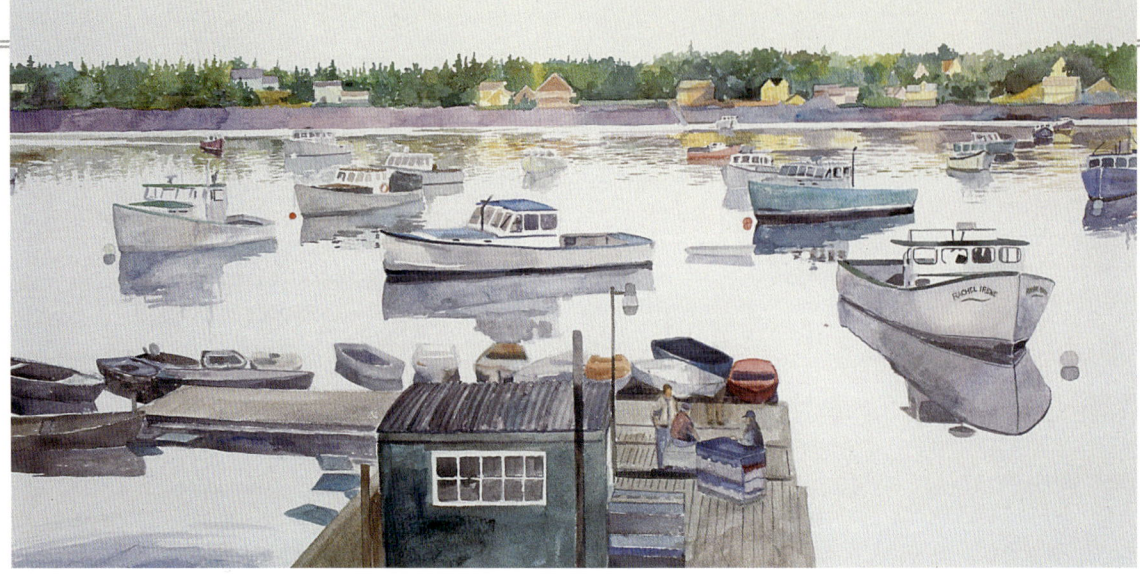

1 Establish Local Color and Value
After gridding the paper, create a very detailed drawing using a no. 2 pencil. Using your full acrylic palette, paint everything except the sky and water. Indicate the local color of each object with watercolor-like washes. The actual color is not that important at this stage. Since many layers will be added to these objects, the idea is to establish their value so they will not be lost in subsequent overpainting. Let this step dry.

I added some figures on the dock; then, just as soon, I painted one out using opaque color. At this stage I wasn't sure about whether to keep the others. Later, you will see that they got painted out of the composition.

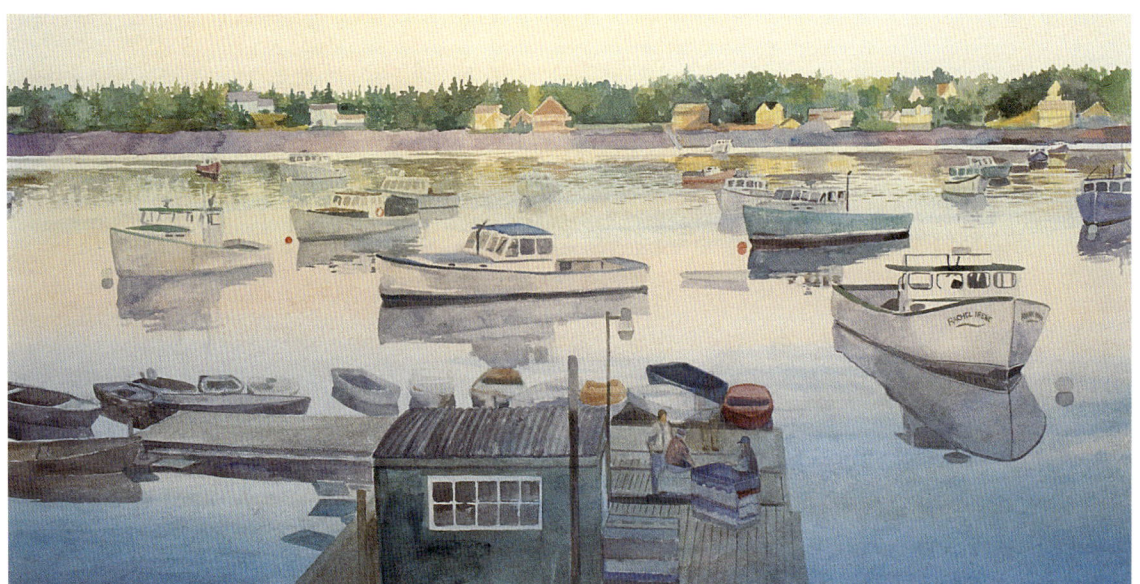

2 Paint the Sky and Water
Wet the entire painting with clean water. With the painting slightly tilted, paint the sky and water with acrylics, starting from the top and working your way down. Use a transparent mixture of Yellow Medium Azo and Cadmium Orange for the sky. Add some ACRA Crimson as you get into the water, and finally finish the water with Brilliant Blue and Phthalo Blue.

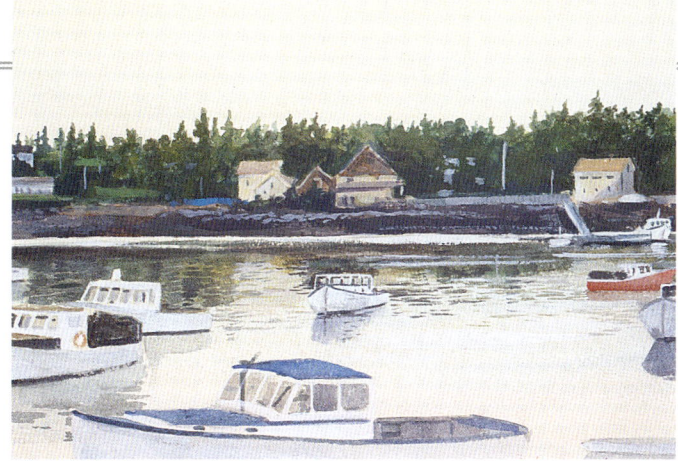

3 Intensify the Shoreline and Reflections

Repaint the opposite shore and its reflections with semitransparent and semiopaque color, using your full acrylic palette.

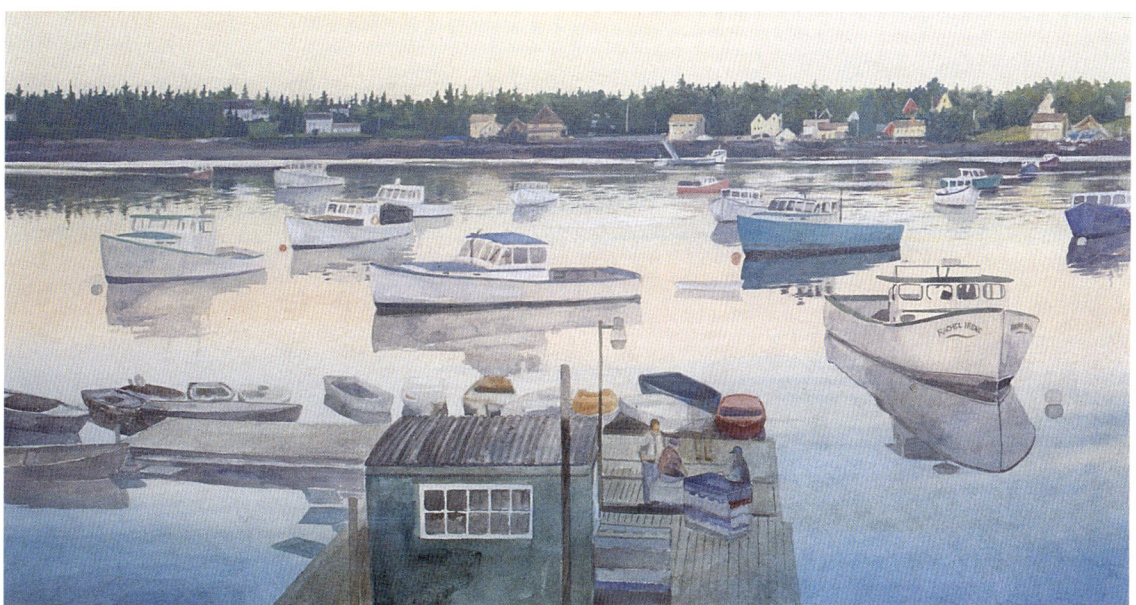

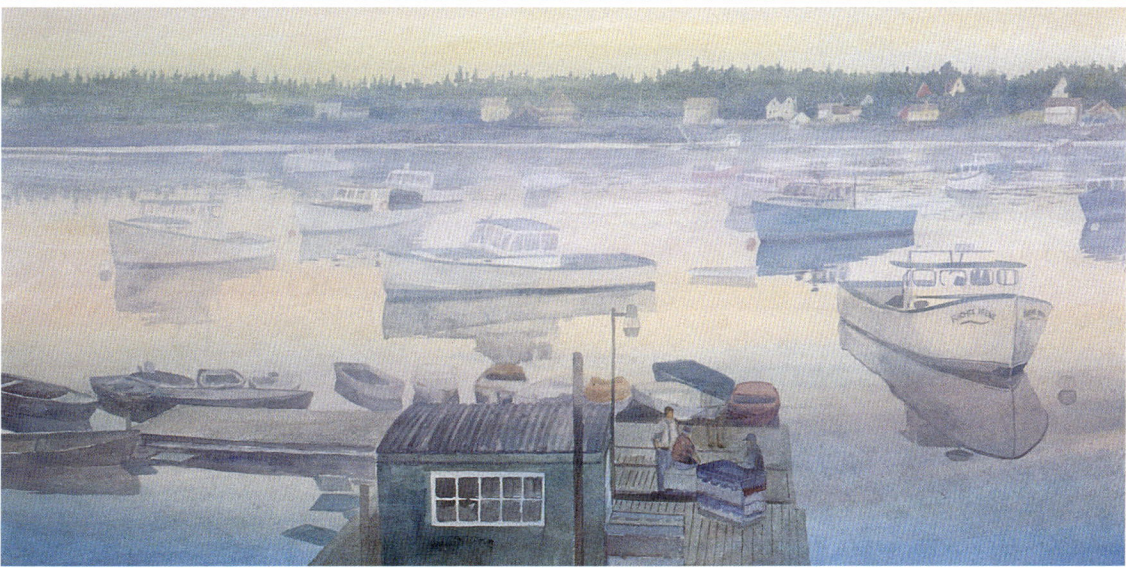

4 Paint the Fog Using Gesso

Wet the top two-thirds of the painting. Brush thinned acrylic gesso across the sky and halfway into the water. Allow this to dry completely. Repeat this step a couple times to intensify the fog effect.

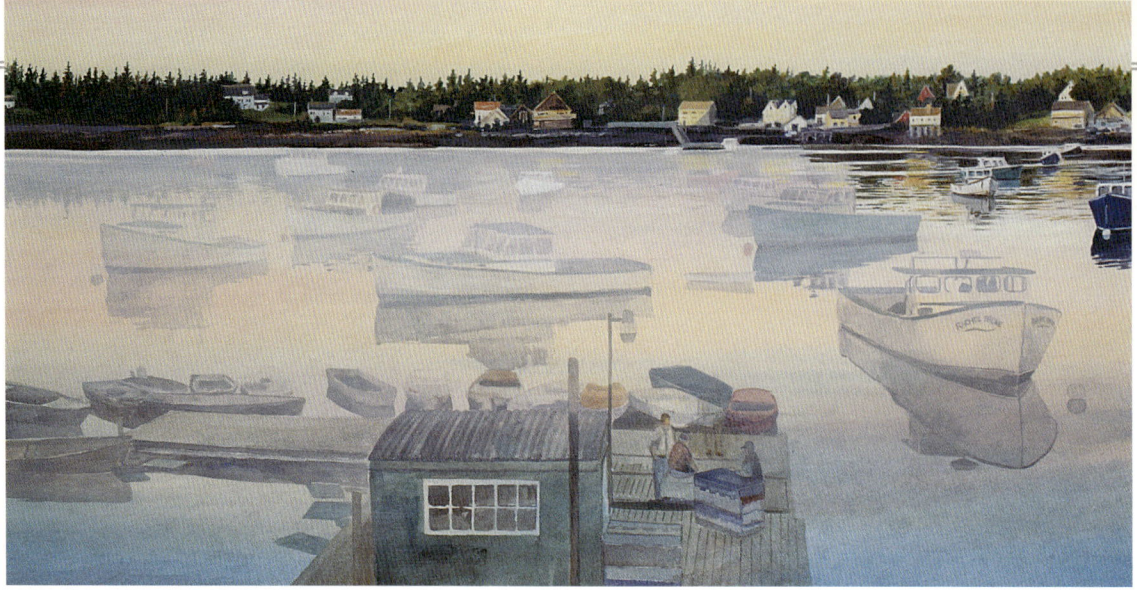

5 Reestablish the Shoreline (Again!)

At this point the painting was too fogged in. I wasn't pleased with the uneven density of the gesso and the amount of shore detail that it obscured. Here I considered that the fog might not be a good idea.

Repaint the shore. Use your full acrylic palette; however, try for cooler color mixes to create a sense of distance. Use Phthalo Blue in your tree colors and Dioxazine Purple, Brilliant Blue and ACRA Crimson in the earth tone mixes.

6 Define the Boats

Paint the boats using thin acrylic mixes. Paint the white hulls of the boats with a mix of Titanium White, Brilliant Blue and a touch of Cadmium Orange. Remember, adding a complement to a color grays it. Some of the boats are aqua or trimmed with aqua colors. Use Vivid Lime Green, Brilliant Blue and Titanium White to create this color.

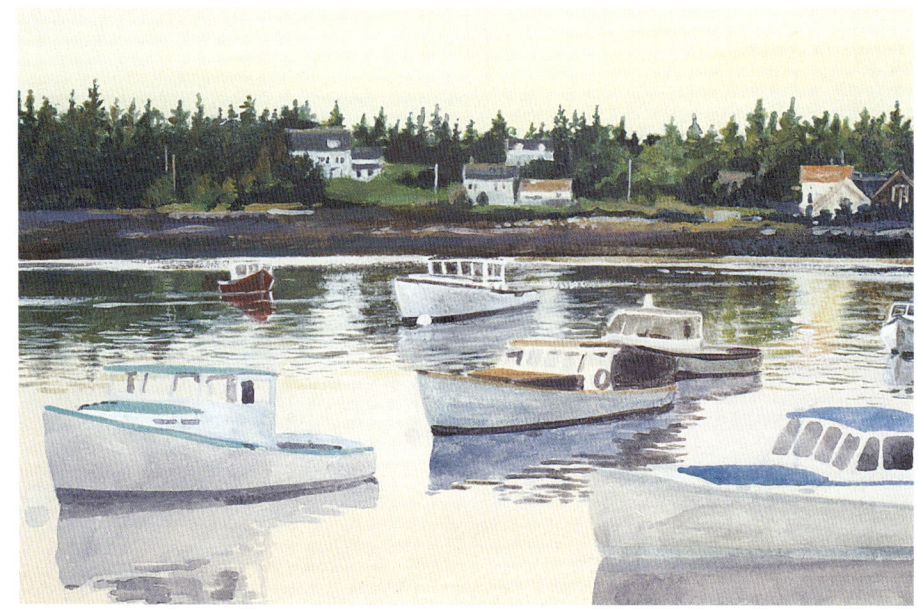

7 Refine the Boats

Use the same colors as in the previous step to add another layer of paint to the boats. This time, however, use a semiopaque application of color. Smooth out the brushstrokes and crisp up the edges.

Reflections are always darker than the objects being reflected. Paint the reflections using a semiopaque mix of Ultramarine Blue, Brilliant Blue, ACRA Crimson and Titanium White. Paint the darkest values with a semiopaque mix of Ultramarine Blue, Burnt Umber and Naphthol Red Light.

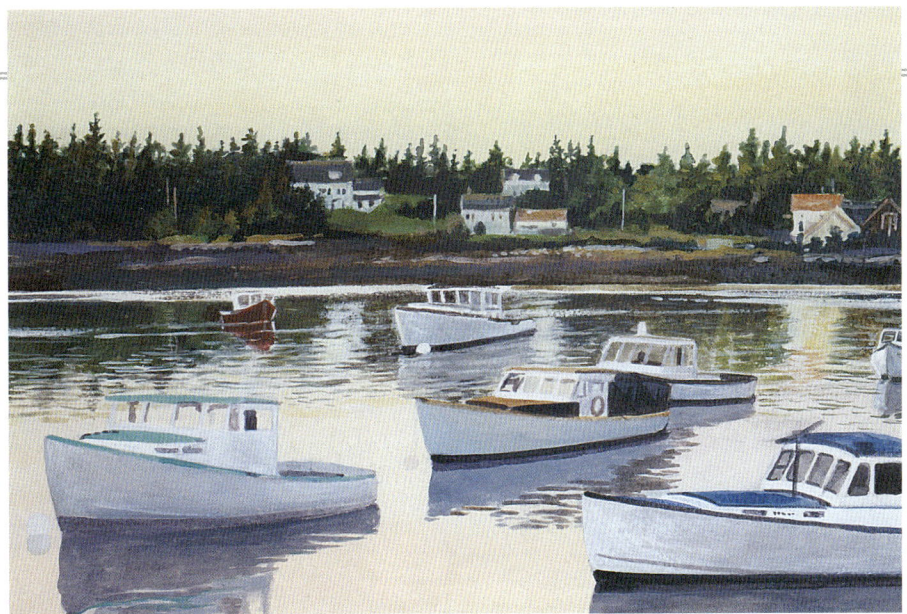

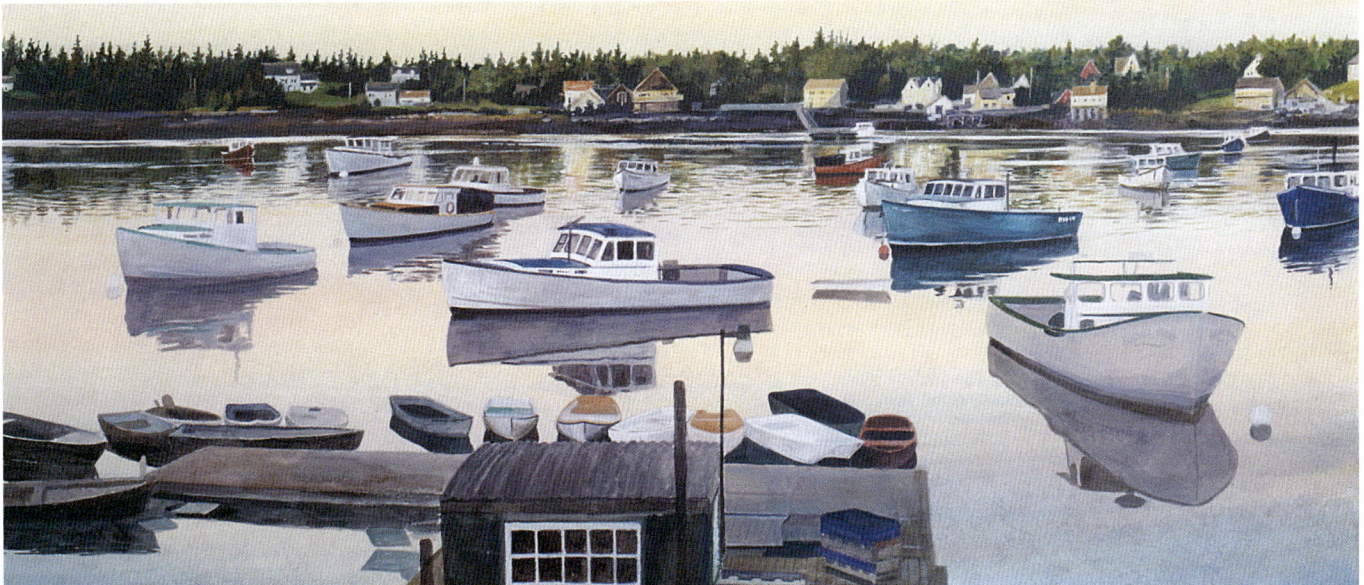

8 Refine the Dock

I decided the figures were unnecessary and painted them out at this stage. Use your full palette of acrylic colors as you refine the dock and small boats that surround it. Use semiopaque and opaque color mixes. Use a mix of Ultramarine Blue, Burnt Umber and Naphthol Red Light for the darkest colors. Paint the building using a mix of Phthalo Green, Burnt Umber and Ultramarine Blue.

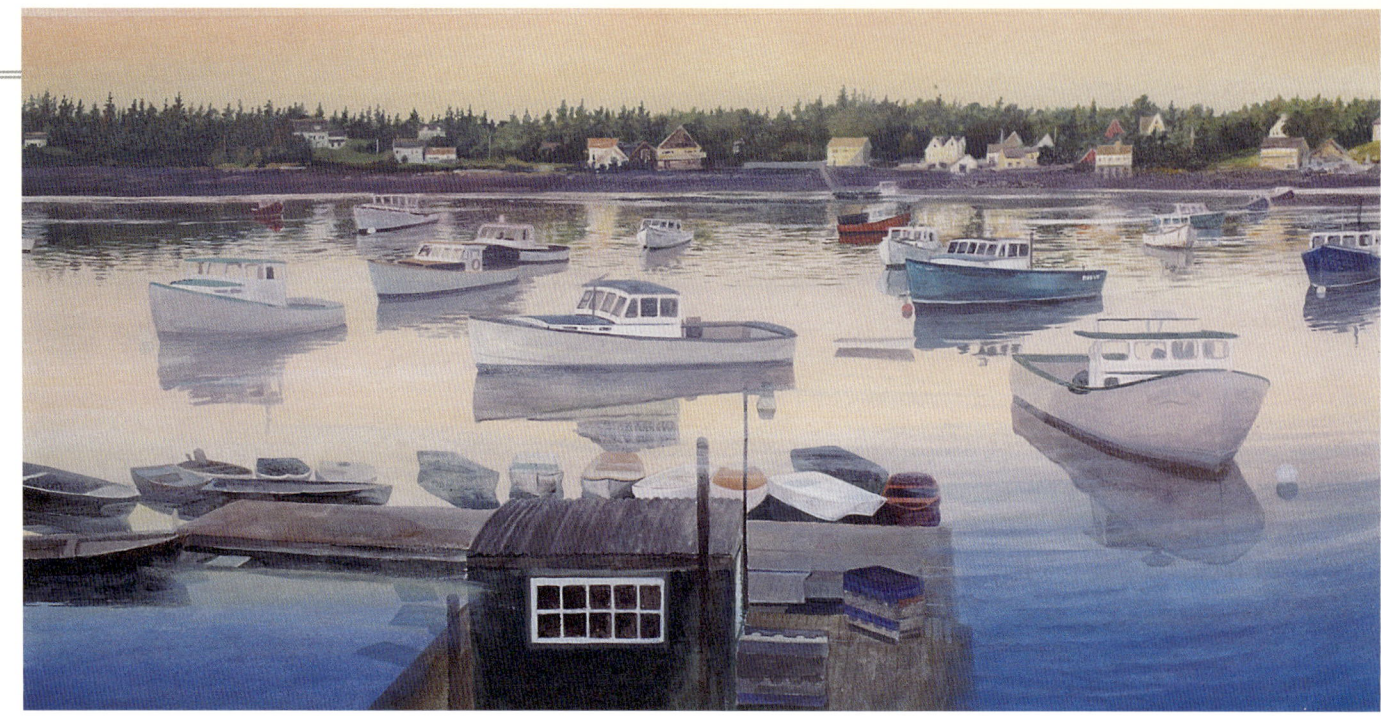

9 Add Fog and Refine the Sky and Water

Perhaps I am a glutton for punishment, but I was determined to try adding a bit of atmosphere to this painting by reconsidering the fog.

Tilt the painting slightly to aid the flow of water and acrylic paint. Then wet the entire painting. Paint a layer of thinned gesso across the sky, shoreline and water. Then paint a thin wash of Yellow Orange Azo and ACRA Crimson across the sky. Paint a rich but thin mix of Phthalo Blue, Brilliant Blue and Titanium White in the foreground water. Mix Ultramarine Blue and a bit of Burnt Umber for the darker areas in the water. Use long, gentle brushstrokes to smooth out the color.

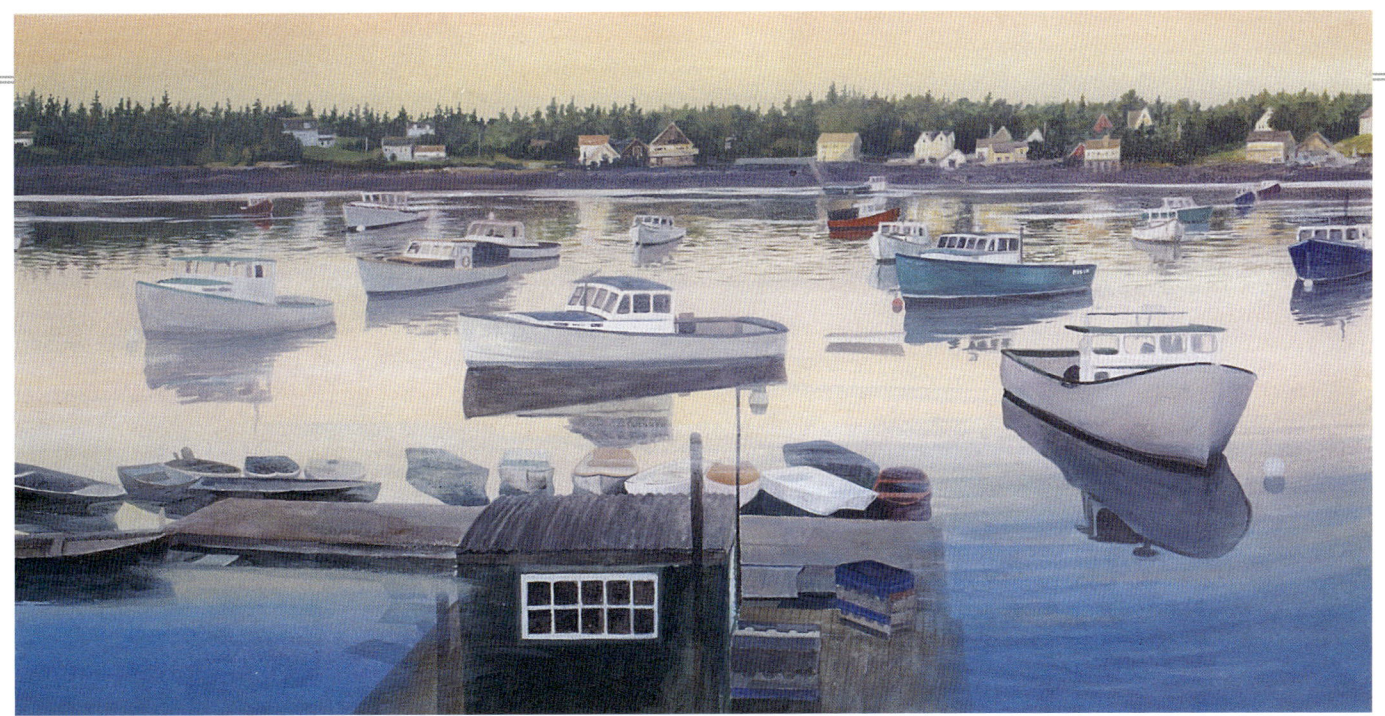

10 **Refine the Sky and Background With Gouache**
Gouache is a good medium for adding final details and accents. The color goes down flat and crisp, and you can control edges and value very easily. Lighten the sky with a mix of Titanium White, Cadmium Yellow and Quinacridone Red. Use Titanium White to add a few subtle cloud shapes.

The last layer of gesso softened the color and value of the distant and middle-ground boats. Complete the boats using your full palette of gouache color. Paint the white boat hulls with a mix of Titanium White, a bit of Cobalt Blue and Cadmium Orange. Add Ultramarine Blue to this mix for the reflections. Add a few ripples to the water using Titanium White.

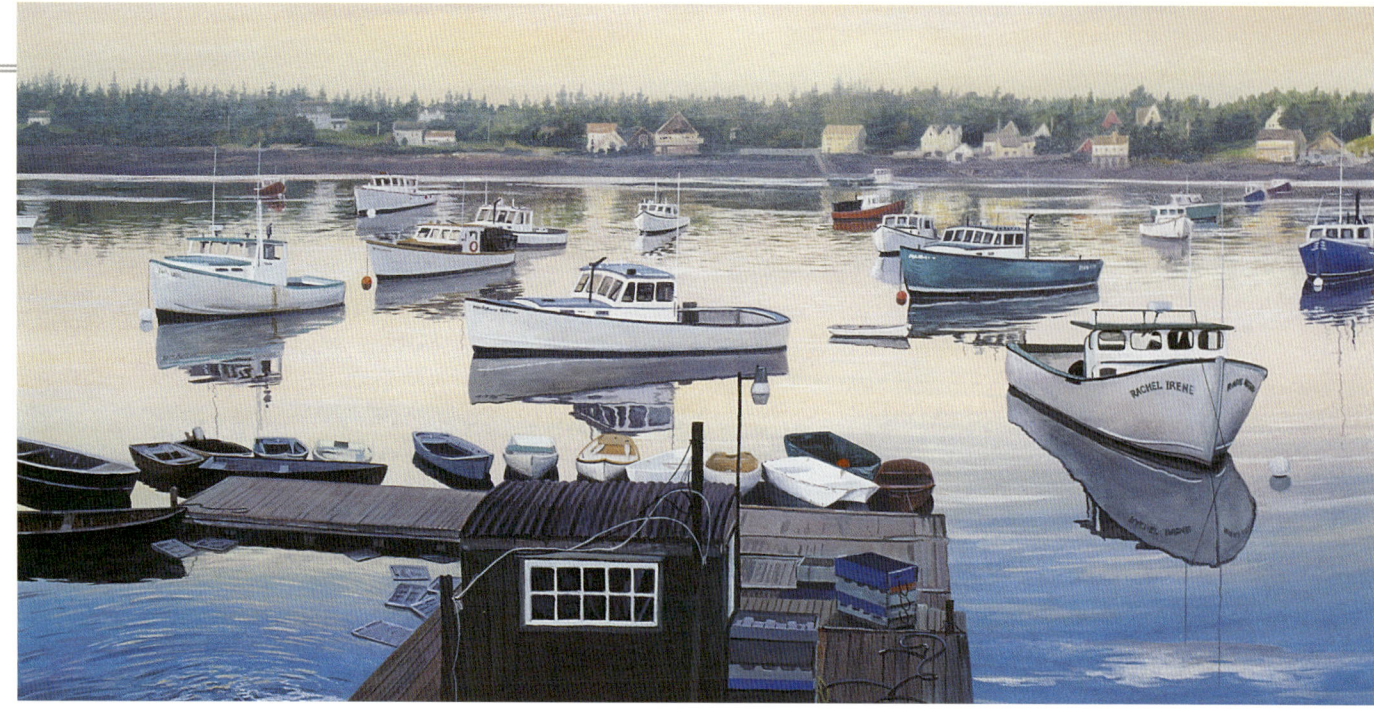

11 Refine the Largest Boats and the Foreground With Gouache

Add the final details to the large boats and the foreground. Mix colors from your full gouache palette. Paint the largest shapes, then convey the fine, linear details. Create a mix of Ivory Black and Phthalo Blue to convey the rich value of the shadows and reflections around the dock. Paint a few reflected clouds using a mix of Titanium White and Cadmium Orange. For the base of the reflected clouds, use small amounts of Quinacridone Red, Ultramarine Blue and Burnt Sienna mixed with Titanium White.

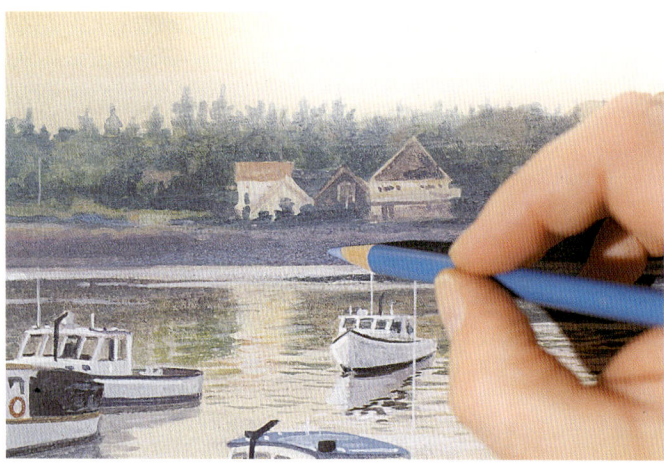

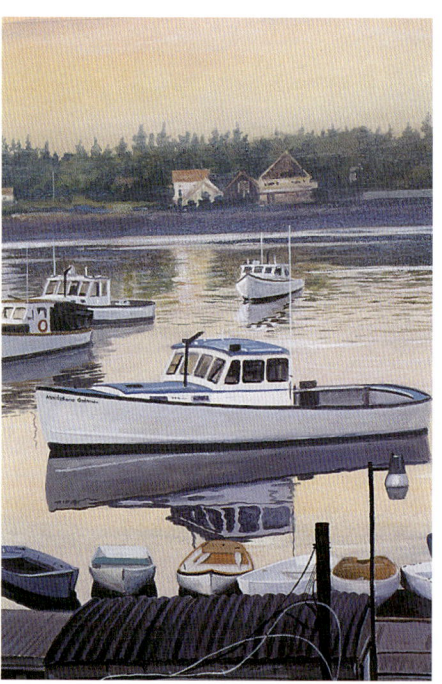

12 Finish the Painting With Colored Pencil Accents

Using Blue Slate and Parma Violet pencils, add a light, even tone across the background shoreline. This adds a bit more atmosphere and increases the sense of aerial perspective. Use a very sharp White pencil to pop out a few highlights and linear details on the boats and dock.

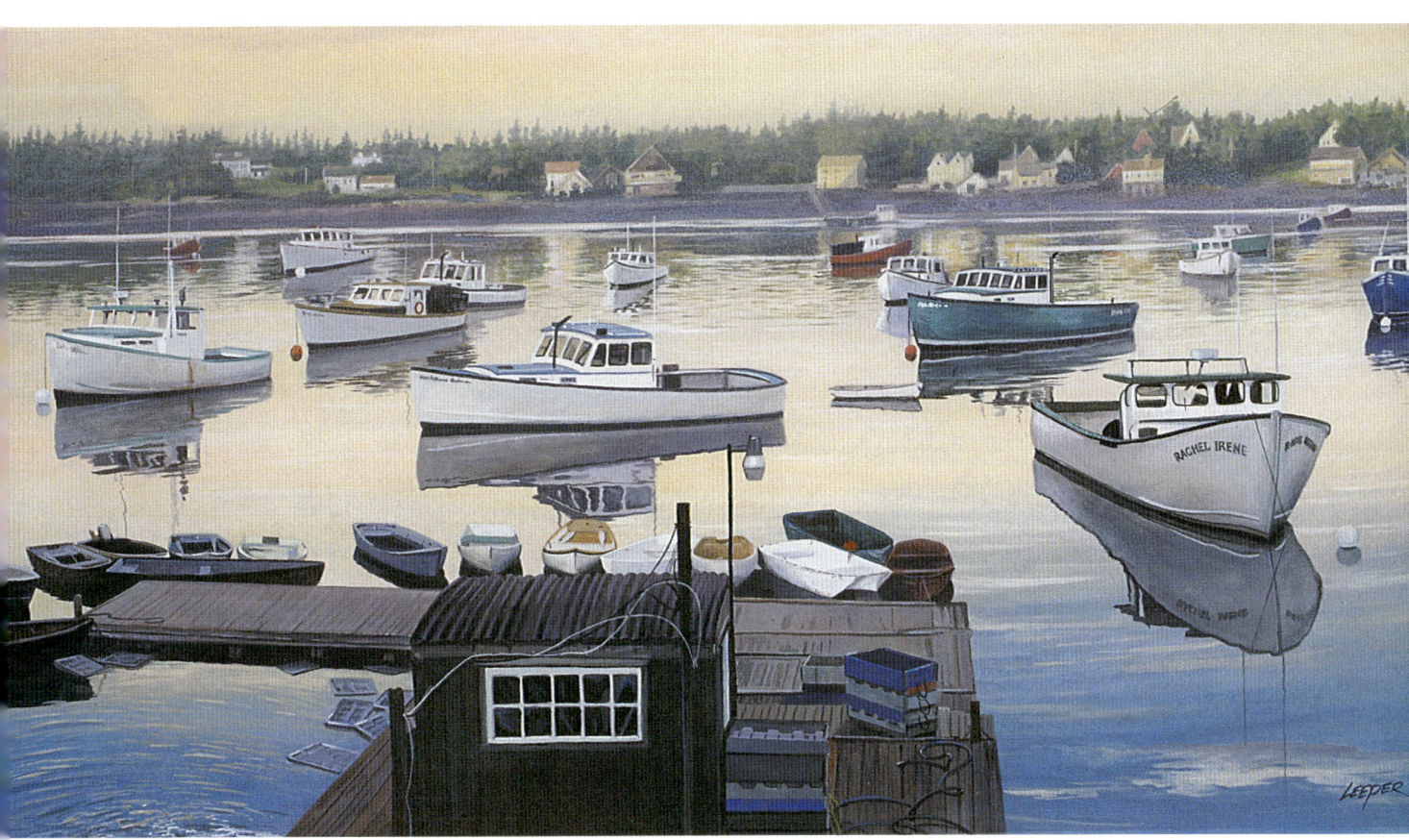

Twilight on Bass Harbor   »   Mixed media on 300-lb. (640gsm) cold-pressed paper   »   14" x 29" (36cm x 74cm)

Index

Accents, adding, 14
   acrylic, 43, 90
   colored pencil, 14, 25, 43, 94, 99, 124
   gouache, 98, 123
   pastel, 14, 43, 94, 99
Acrylics, 13, 36–37, 52, 58, 117–122
   blending, 71–75
   dark values in, 66–67
   finger blending, 71–73, 75, 84–85
   paintings in, examples of, 11, 20, 40–41, 44, 46–47, 49–50, 59, 66, 73, 78, 83, 90–91, 116
   problems and solutions, 25–26
   scumbling in, 73, 75, 84–85, 116
   stippling in, 79, 114
   studies in, 39
Acrylics, layering, 61, 66–68, 71–72, 84–85, 95
   transparent over opaque, 82–85
   over watercolor, 90–91, 97
   wet-into-wet, 73–74
Adobe Photoshop, 51, 56, 66, 110, 117

Backlighting, 83
Boats, 74, 117, 120–121, 123–124
Brushes, 15, 19, 29, 69
Brush techniques, 70

Color
   adjusting, 42–43
   building, 33
   energizing, 42
   lifting, 15, 17, 34–35, 56–57, 107
   local, 26, 32, 67, 71–72, 74, 82, 84, 88, 100, 112, 118
   luminous, 62, 70
   manipulating, 56–58
   opacity of, 13
Colored pencil, 14, 25, 36–37, 40, 43, 58
   and acrylics, combining, 94–96
   and watercolor, combining, 100–101, 117, 124
Color notes, 14, 25, 65
Colors
   choosing, 12–13
   layering, 62, 64
   mixing, 25, 29, 63 (*see also* Watercolor, mixing)
   testing, 69
Color scheme, 53

Color temperature, 12
   cool, 32, 63
   layering, 63, 78, 82, 104
   warm, 26, 32, 34, 53, 55
   warm, laying down, 62–64, 70, 76–77
Compositions
   combining, 55
   creating, with software, 56–59 (*see also* Adobe Photoshop)
   planning, 39
   simplifying, 49
   sketching, 32 (*see also* Drawings; Sketches; Studies; Thumbnail sketches)
   and values, 22–27
Computer. *See* Software, photo-editing
Crosshatching, 78, 80

Deer, 24
Drama, creating
   in acrylics, 84–85
   in watercolor, 69–70
Drawings, 18, 69, 105, 111
   See also Sketches; Studies; Thumbnail sketches
Drybrush, 70, 79–81

Earth tones, 12, 120
Edges, 32–33
   establishing, 101
   hard, 71
   mixing, 87
   softening, 88, 109, 113–114

Finger blending, 71–73, 95, 113–114
Flowers, 62, 64–65, 90, 99
Fog, 34, 117, 119–120, 122
Foliage, 62, 82–83
Food, 86
Form, 79, 88–89, 106–107
Format, 22

Gesso, 17, 34, 73–74, 119–120, 122–123
Glass, 67
Gouache, 12, 52, 117, 125
   accenting with, 98, 123
   painting in, example of a, 79
   stippling in, 79–81
   and watercolor, combining, 80–81, 100–101

Grass, 15, 25, 78, 98
Grid, using a, 110–111, 117–118

Harbor scene, 117–125
Hatching, 78–79
Highlights
   blending, 75
   dry media, 94–95
   gouache, 98
   softening, 107
   stippled, 79
Horses, 100–101

Images, projected, 47
Ink, India, 19

Leaves, 65, 70
Life, painting from, 31–43
   See also Plein air, painting
Lighting, rim, 98
Lowlights, dry media, 94, 96

Materials, 11–19
   See also specific material
Media, dry, 13
   colored pencils, 14, 25, 94–96
   pastels, 14, 94–97
Media, mixed, 14, 97, 99–101
   paintings in, examples of, 24, 52, 54, 58, 93, 98–99, 125
   paintings in, planning, 99
   techniques for, 93–101
   See also specific medium
Media, water. *See* Acrylics; Gouache; Watercolor

Nupastels, 14, 95

Onions, 88–89
Oranges, 57
Outdoors, working. *See* Plein air, painting

Palettes, 15, 18, 70
Paper, 16–17
   gesso-coated, 17, 34 (*see also* Gesso)
Pastels, 14, 94–97
   paper for, 94
   using, over acrylics, 97
   using, over watercolor, 97

Pencils, 18, 22, 36
Pens, sketching, 18, 23
Photos, reference, 23–24, 28, 39, 41, 45–59, 64, 67, 69, 71, 73, 76, 84, 88, 100, 104, 117
    collecting, 48, 51
    combining, 51–52, 57–58, 73, 117
    composing, 48
    cropping, 50, 53, 110
    distortion in, 46–47
    editing, 48–51
    elements in, changing, 50
    projecting, 47
    still-life, 48
    using, pros and cons of, 46
    See also Software, photo-editing
Plein air, painting, 19, 31–43
Pond scene, 32–33
Potatoes, sweet, 104–109

Reference material, using, 41, 117
    See also Photos, reference
Reflections, 28–29, 37, 68, 74, 119, 121, 124
Rocks, 23, 35, 54, 63, 76

Scumbling, 15, 73, 75, 84–85, 95, 116
Setup
    outdoor, 19, 40
    studio, 18
Shadows
    cast, 79, 88–89
    and form, 107–108
    shapes of, 66
Sketches, 32
    pen, 18, 23, 34
    pencil, 18, 22, 36, 41, 50–51
    plein-air, 38–40
    thumbnail, 22, 39
    value, 22–24, 27–28, 49, 69, 104
    See also Drawings; Studies
Skin tones, 71–72
Software, photo-editing, 51, 56–59, 66
    See also Adobe Photoshop
Squirrels, 51–52
Stippling, 79–81, 114
Strathmore paper, 16, 57
Studies
    combining, 55
    limited-palette, 27–29
    nature, 38
    pencil, 40, 110
    plein-air, 38–40
    value, 39, 54
    watercolor, 38–41, 49
    See also Drawings; Sketches; Thumbnail sketches
Studio setup. See Setup, studio
Subjects
    photographing, 48 (see also Photos, reference)
    seeing, 41, 86
    simplifying, 46
Surfaces, painting, 16

Texture, 14, 22–23, 32, 35–37, 80–81
    adjusting, 42–43
    colored pencil, 101
    computer-generated, 57
    crosshatched, 78
    dry media, 94–96
    gouache, 98
    hatched, 78
    mixed media, 76, 80–81
    paper, 16, 70
    scumbled, 75
    tree, 52
    watercolor, 86
Thumbnail sketches, 22, 39
Tomatoes, 79, 104–109
Trees, 15, 25, 35–37, 51–52, 54, 63, 70, 82, 85, 98

Value
    building, 33, 78, 80, 86, 101
    composing with, 21–29
    manipulating, 56–58
    problems and solutions, 25–26
Value contrast, 25–26, 33, 65
Value plan, 27
Value pattern, 23, 46
    changing, 54
    establishing, 65
    seeing, 23, 66
    of shapes, 23, 104
Value range, 22, 24, 65–66, 79, 88
Value relationships, 24–26
Values
    adjusting, 42–43, 84, 109
    checking, 24, 87
    dark, in watercolor, 29, 106–108
    hierarchy of, 25
Value shifts, 24, 66, 91, 114
Value sketches, 22–23, 27–28, 49, 69, 104
Value structure, 53, 69, 100
Value studies, 39
Viewfinder, using a, 53

Washes, acrylic, wet-into-wet, 36–37
Washes, watercolor
    limiting, 29
    variegated, 33–35, 62–65, 80, 88, 100, 105
    wet-on-dry, 88–89
Washes, watercolor, wet-into-wet, 86–89
    drying, 18
    layering, 87
Watercolor, 12, 52
    accents on, acrylic, 90
    acrylics over, layering, 90–91, 97
    dark values in, 29, 106–108
    drama in, creating, 69–70
    drybrush technique, 70, 80–81
    enlivening, with acrylics, 42–43
    and gouache, combining, 80–81, 100–101
    layering, wet and dry, 87
    limited-palette study, 27–29
    mixing, 70, 87
    paintings in, examples of, 23, 30, 32–33, 34–35, 52–56, 62–63, 86–87, 90–91, 109
    problems and solutions, 25–26
    stippling in, 79
    studies in, 38–41 (see also Sketches, watercolor)
    tips, 69
    warm colors in, 62
    See also Washes, watercolor
Water, depicting, 23–24, 29, 34, 54, 74, 76–77, 82, 118–119, 122
Watermedia, techniques for, 61–91
    acrylics, 66–68, 71–75
    acrylics, layering, 82–85
    crosshatching, 78
    hatching, 78–79
    layering, broken-color, 76–77, 80–81
    stippling, 79–81
    watercolor, 62–65, 69–70

The best in watercolor instruction comes from North Light Books!

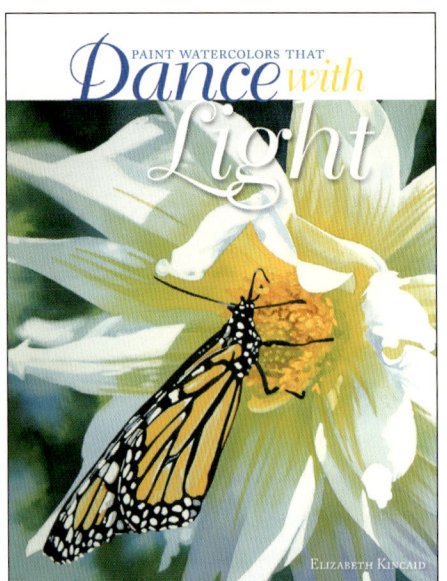

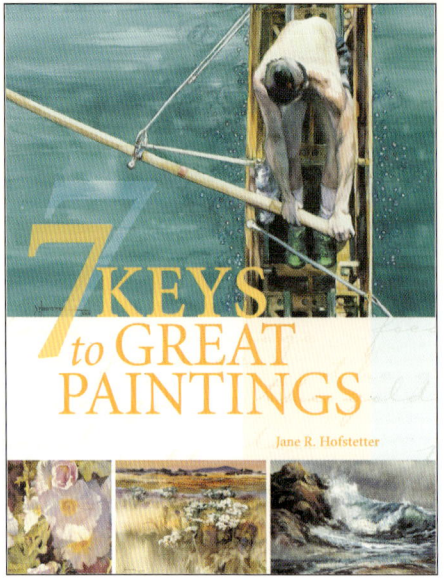

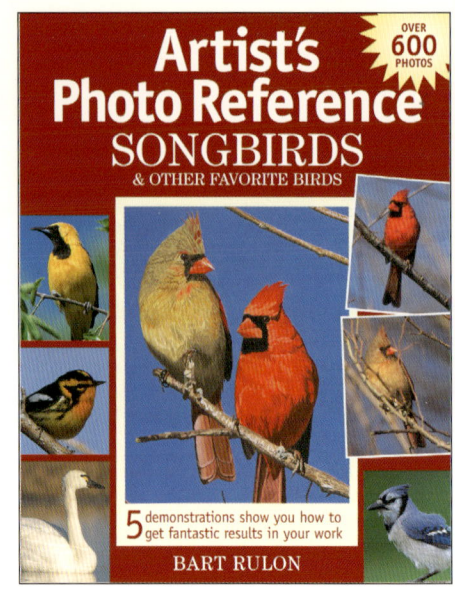

Elizabeth Kincaid takes the mystery out of composition, color, light and shadow with her proven techniques that will have you painting dazzling scenes drenched in color. You'll be visualizing your painting before your brush touches the canvas, perceiving abstract form, value, line and color like never before. Water-colorists at all levels will enjoy using Kincaid's tips to create vivid paintings infused with light.

ISBN 1-58180-468-7, hardcover, 128 pages, #32731-K

Here are the seven strategies every watercolor artist should know to produce great paintings with meaning and substance. With step-by-step instruction, Jane R. Hofstetter shows how any artist, from beginner to experienced painter, can paint a piece that is personal and evokes emotion. Her steps to great paintings include patterns of shape values, focal areas, color, design and emotional depth. By utilizing these and her other keys, the artist can paint from within and create paintings that will be appreciated.

ISBN 1-58180-479-2, hardcover, 128 pages, #32746-K

Artists know how difficult it is to find quality photographs of birds to reference for their work. In this follow-up to his successful *Artist's Photo Reference: Birds*, Bart Rulon comes to artists' aid with more than 600 sharp, high-quality photographs of the birds artists have requested. In this book are popular songbirds such as sparrows, finches, wrens and robins, as well as artist favorites like eagles, hummingbirds and swans. Five painting demos illustrate how successful artists use reference photos to add realism to their work. As a bonus, the introduction offers tips on how to take your own photos and expand your reference collection even more.

ISBN 1-58180-467-9, hardcover, 144 pages, #32730-K

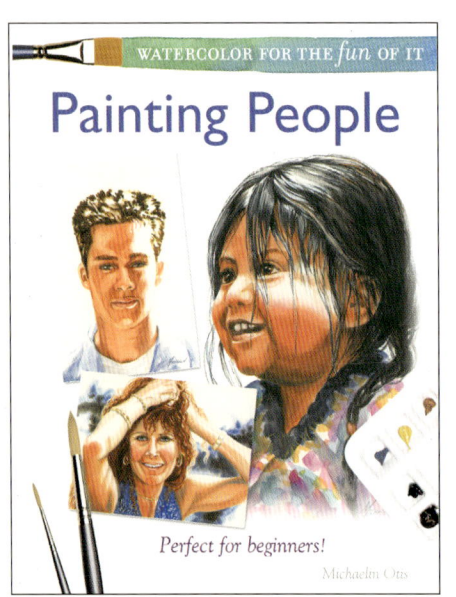

Twelve step-by-step demonstrations that show various poses, like head and shoulders, seated, standing and profile, will have any watercolor artist adding realistic people to their paintings. It's a style that anyone can emulate and the instruction covers drawing, composition, lighting and techniques for producing reliable results. A Quick-Start Guide provides an essential overview of the best materials to use, basic tips and a glossary.

ISBN 1-58180-560-8, paperback, 96 pages, #33016-K

These books and other fine North Light titles are available from your local art & craft retailer, bookstore, online supplier or by calling 1-800-448-0915.